Clinical Psychology and the Philosophy of Science

ABOUT THE AUTHOR

Colly Aleksander, was born in 1986 in Novi Sad, Republic of Serbia. He graduated Psychology from faculty of Philosophy in Novi Sad and Started his Ph.D. Studies. He worked at Children's Hospital where his main tasts were psychological evaluation in order to identify psychosomatic diseases, Psychological support from parents, and child and adolescent psychotherapy.He has many scientific articles written and published in academic journals. He is focused, deligent, fair, ambitious, able to make decisions and determine priorties, focused on achieving results, competitive spirit, intersted in the individual and teamwork, dedicated and reliable.

ABOUT THE BOOK

Clinical psychology is the branch of psychology concerned with the assessment and treatment of mental illness, abnormal behaviour and psychiatric problems. This field integrates the science of psychology with the treatment of complex human problems, making it an exciting career choice for people who are looking for a challenging and rewarding field. Clinical psychology is an integration of science, theory and clinical knowledge for the purpose of understanding, preventing, and relieving psychologically-based distress or dysfunction and to promote subjective well-being and personal development. Central to its practice are psychological assessment and psychotherapy, although clinical psychologists also engage in research, teaching, consultation, forensic testimony, and programme development and administration. In many countries, clinical psychology is a regulated mental health profession. Clinical psychology is an integration of science, theory and clinical knowledge for the purpose of understanding, preventing, and relieving psychologically based distress or dysfunction and to promote subjective well-being and personal development. Central to its practice are psychological assessment and psychotherapy, although clinical psychologists also engage in research, teaching, consultation, forensic testimony, and programme development and administration. In many countries, clinical psychology is a regulated mental health profession. This book explains what clinical psychology is, what clinical psychologists do, their professional ethics, training responsibilities, future of clinical psychologist to a non-specialist but informed readership.

Clinical Psychology and the Philosophy of Science

Colly Aleksander

AMIGA PRESS. INC
Delhi -110051

AMIGA PRESS. INC
H.O :- 28-A, Indra Park, Chander Nagar
Delhi :- 110051 (India)
Tel :- 011-22504028, +91-98736-57000
Email :- info@amigapress.co.in
amigapub@gmail.com
Website :- www.amigapress@co.in

This edition is published by Amiga Press.Inc

ISBN : 978-93-87295-21-6

First Published 2019

Printed and bound in India by Replika Press Pvt. Ltd.

Preface

Clinical psychology is the branch of psychology concerned with the assessment and treatment of mental illness, abnormal behaviour and psychiatric problems. This field integrates the science of psychology with the treatment of complex human problems, making it an exciting career choice for people who are looking for a challenging and rewarding field.

American psychologist Lightner Witmer first introduced the term in a 1907 paper. Witmer, a former student of Wilhelm Wundt, defined clinical psychology as "the study of individuals, by observation or experimentation, with the intention of promoting change." Today, clinical psychology is one of the most popular subfields within psychology.

Clinical psychology is an integration of science, theory and clinical knowledge for the purpose of understanding, preventing, and relieving psychologically-based distress or dysfunction and to promote subjective well-being and personal development. Central to its practice are psychological assessment and psychotherapy, although clinical psychologists also engage in research, teaching, consultation, forensic testimony, and programme development and administration. In many countries, clinical psychology is a regulated mental health profession.

The field is often considered to have begun in 1896 with the opening of the first psychological clinic at the University of Pennsylvania by Lightner Witmer. In the first half of the 20th century, clinical psychology was focused on psychological assessment, with little attention given to treatment. This changed after the 1940s when World War II resulted in the need for a large increase in the number of trained clinicians. Since that time, two main educational models have developed— the Ph.D. scientist–practitioner model (requiring a doctoral dissertation and therefore research as well as clinical expertise); and the Psy.D. practitioner–scholar model.

"Clinical psychology is an applied science in which the principles of psychology are utilised to understand and help alleviate human problems." This somewhat terse statement provides a thumbnail sketch of the field. Like all such brief portraits, it does not do justice to its subject. No single statement could adequately account for the field's diversity and complexity. In many respects, this entire volume could be taken as a definition, specifying what clinical psychologists do, how they think, and what the field encompasses. This chapter, like the brief definition above, will set the stage for later material. As a first step, let us analyse the above definition.

Clinical psychology is, first of all, a branch of psychology. The clinical psychologists share much of their training with general (i.e., experimental) psychologists and employ much basic psychological knowledge in their work. Principles of learning, perception, physiology, group process and social interaction, cognition, and child development all play a central role in the clinical psychologist's methods and in the conceptualisation of human problems. Consider a clinical child psychologist working with a youngster who is having academic problems. In evaluating the problems, the psychologist might consider and assess the child's perceptual ability, neurophysiological functioning (can he comprehend the material?), and social-emotional development (do the problems result from psychological difficulties, such as anxiety?). A remediation programme might well be based on operant conditioning procedures (shaping new skills by systematic reinforcement).

Clinical psychologists study a generalist programme in psychology plus postgraduate training and/or clinical placement and supervision. The length of training differs across the world, ranging from four years plus post-Bachelors supervised practice to a doctorate of three to six years which combines clinical placement. In the USA, about half of all clinical psychology graduate students are being trained in Ph.D. programmes—a model that emphasizes research—with the other half in Psy.D. programmes, which has more focus on practice.

This is a reference book. All the matter is just compiled and edited in nature, taken from the various sources which are in public domain.

This book explains what clinical psychology is, what clinical psychologists do, their professional ethics, training responsibilities, future of clinical psychologist to a non-specialist but informed readership.

—*Editor*

Contents

1

Introduction

Clinical psychologists are now considered experts in providing psychotherapy, psychological testing, and in diagnosing mental illness. They generally train within four primary theoretical orientations—psychodynamic, humanistic, behaviour therapy/cognitive behavioural, and systems or family therapy. Many continue clinical training in post-doctoral programmes in which they might specialize more intensively in disciplines such as psychoanalytic approaches, or child and adolescent treatment modalities.

History

Although modern, scientific psychology is often dated at the 1879 opening of the first psychological laboratory by Wilhelm Wundt, attempts to create methods for assessing and treating mental distress existed long before. The earliest recorded approaches were a combination of religious, magical and/or medical perspectives. Early examples of such physicians included Patañjali, Padmasambhava, Rhazes, Avicenna, and Rumi.

In the early 19th century, one could have his or her head examined, literally, using phrenology, the study of personality by the shape of the skull.

Other popular treatments included physiognomy—the study of the shape of the face—and mesmerism, Mesmer's treatment by the use of magnets. Spiritualism and Phineas Quimby's "mental healing" were also popular.

While the scientific community eventually came to reject all of these methods, academic psychologists also were not concerned with serious forms of mental illness.

That area was already being addressed by the developing fields of psychiatry and neurology within the asylum movement.

It was not until the end of the 19th century, around the time when Sigmund Freud was first developing the recent idea of a "talking cure" in Vienna, that the first scientifically clinical application of psychology began.

WHAT IS CLINICAL PSYCHOLOGY?

"Clinical psychology is an applied science in which the principles of psychology are utilised to understand and help alleviate human problems." This somewhat terse statement provides a thumbnail sketch of the field. Like all such brief portraits, it does not do justice to its subject. No single statement could adequately account for the field's diversity and complexity. In many respects, this entire volume could be taken as a definition, specifying what clinical psychologists do, how they think, and what the field encompasses. This chapter, like the brief definition above, will set the stage for later material. As a first step, let us analyse the above definition.

Clinical psychology is, first of all, a branch of psychology. The clinical psychologists share much of their training with general (i.e., experimental) psychologists and employ much basic psychological knowledge in their work. Principles of learning, perception, physiology, group process and social interaction, cognition, and child development all play a central role in the clinical psychologist's methods and in the conceptualisation of human problems. Consider a clinical child psychologist working with a youngster who is having academic problems. In evaluating the problems, the psychologist might consider and assess the child's perceptual ability, neurophysiological functioning (can he comprehend the material?), and social-emotional development (do the problems result from psychological difficulties, such as anxiety?). A remediation programme might well be based on operant conditioning procedures (shaping new skills by systematic reinforcement).

As the reader is well aware, psychology is a scientific discipline. Clinical psychology, too, has a strong scientific basis. Not only is the clinician's knowledge based on scientific research, but (traditionally) he or she is trained as a scientist. The preeminent model used in training clinical psychologists is the scientist-professional model. This scientific training serves clinical psychologists in three ways: (1) they are prepared to conduct research to add to our basic knowledge about human behaviour, as well as how to assess it and change it in a therapeutic direction; (2) they are trained to evaluate systematically their own (or their colleagues') clinical services; and (3) they are sophisticated consumers of new research, so that skills are continually upgraded along with advances in knowledge. These three advantages are sometimes more apparent in theory than in practice and some clinical psychologists have questioned the wisdom of scientific training. We will consider these arguments, pro and con, in a later section. The types of research conducted by clinical psychologists.

According to our definition, clinical psychology strives to "understand and help alleviate human problems." An applied discipline, it is allied with other human service and mental health professions in an effort to eliminate distress and improve the quality of life for all people.

As scientists, clinical psychologists work to increase our understanding of psychopathology and psychological distress, as well as to develop effective treatment methods, educational programmes, and prevention programmes. As practitioners, they implement these various services and programmes. Besides conducting psychotherapy and psychological assessments, they develop and implement educational and remedial programmes for children, the mentally retarded, and severely disturbed psychiatric patients'. They develop social service programmes for communities and special groups such as the aged, juvenile delinquents, alcoholics, and drug addicts. They also do extensive consultation and teaching.

Clinical psychology has been described (with some fondness) as a "schizophrenic" occupation, with a dual emphasis on science and human service. On the one hand, the clinical psychologist is a scientist, with an unyielding curiosity and a need to know. Inquisitiveness about human behaviour is one of the primary motives of prospective clinical psychology students and helps to shape their activities and approach after graduation. Why do people become anxious? Why does the schizophrenic have hallucinations? What causes depression? Why does this person not get along with anyone? Why is that person so painfully shy? This side of the profession involves an objective, dispassionate, and often skeptical approach to the world.

On the other hand, clinical psychologists are concerned about other people. They see distress and suffering and have a desire to help. They are interested in people and are motivated to listen, to be sympathetic, to do something for others. The vast majority of students who seek to become clinical psychologists do so precisely for this reason. Thus, most clinical psychologists spend much of their time directly serving people. They are humanists and generally politically and socially liberal. They are concerned with injustice, prejudice, poverty, and other aspects of human welfare, as well as with psychological difficulty. This side of the profession is more aligned with the humanities than with science. It involves introspection, philosophy, values, and subjectivity. Clinical psychologists are (and need to be) concerned, sensitive, feeling people.

These two seemingly incompatible orientations, scientist and humanist, have created much controversy in the field. It has been argued that the disparity is basic and will ultimately lead to a split between scientists and practitioners. However, thus far they have been successfully combined to produce a unique, dynamic, and vital profession. The combination of research and clinical skill is a hallmark of clinical psychology, and is probably responsible for the profession's rapid and extensive development. It is also important in the tremendous diversity of roles clinical psychologists fill. If the field is "schizophrenic," it appears to be coping with its difficulties extremely well.

EARLY CLINICAL PSYCHOLOGY

By the second half of the 1800s, the scientific study of psychology was becoming well-established in university laboratories. Although there were a few scattered voices calling for an applied psychology, the general field looked down upon this idea and insisted on "pure" science as the only respectable practice. This changed when Lightner Witmer (1867–1956), a past student of Wundtand head of the psychology department at the University of Pennsylvania, agreed to treat a young boy who had trouble with spelling. His successful treatment was soon to lead to Witmer's opening of the first psychological clinic at Penn in 1896, dedicated to helping children with learning disabilities. Ten years later in 1907, Witmer was to found the first journal of this new field, *The Psychological Clinic,* where he coined the term "clinical psychology," defined as "the study of individuals, by observation or experimentation, with the intention of promoting change." The field was slow to follow Witmer's example, but by 1914, there were 26 similar clinics in the US.

Even as clinical psychology was growing, working with issues of serious mental distress remained the domain of psychiatrists and neurologists. However, clinical psychologists continued to make inroads into this area due to their increasing skill at psychological assessment.

Psychologists' reputation as assessment experts became solidified during World War I with the development of two intelligence tests, *Army Alpha* and *Army Beta* (testing verbal and nonverbal skills, respectively), which could be used with large groups of recruits. Due in large part to the success of these tests, assessment was to become the core discipline of clinical psychology for the next quarter century, when another war would propel the field into treatment.

Early Professional Organizations

The field began to organize under the name "clinical psychology" in 1917 with the founding of the American Association of Clinical Psychology. This only lasted until 1919, after which the American Psychological Association developed a section on Clinical Psychology, which offered certification until 1927. Growth in the field was slow for the next few years when various unconnected psychological organizations came together as the American Association of Applied Psychology in 1930, which would act as the primary forum for psychologists until after World War II when the APA reorganized.

In 1945, the APA created what is now called The Society of Clinical Psychology (Division 12), which remains a leading organization in the field. Psychological societies and associations in other English-speaking countries developed similar divisions, including in Britain, Canada, Australia and New Zealand.

World War II and the Integration of Treatment

When World War II broke out, the military once again called upon clinical psychologists. As soldiers began to return from combat, psychologists started to notice symptoms of psychological trauma labelled "shell shock" (eventually to be termed posttraumatic stress disorder) that were best treated as soon as possible.

Because physicians (including psychiatrists) were over-extended in treating bodily injuries, psychologists were called to help treat this condition. At the same time, female psychologists (who were excluded from the war effort) formed the National Council of Women Psychologists with the purpose of helping communities deal with the stresses of war and giving young mothers advice on child rearing.

After the war, the Veterans Administration in the US made an enormous investment to set up programmes to train doctoral-level clinical psychologists to help treat the thousands of veterans needing care. As a consequence, the US went from having no formal university programmes in clinical psychology in 1946 to over half of all Ph.D.s in psychology in 1950 being awarded in clinical psychology.

WWII helped bring dramatic changes to clinical psychology, not just in America but internationally as well. Graduate education in psychology began adding psychotherapy to the science and research focus based on the 1947 scientist–practitioner model, known today as the *Boulder Model*, for Ph.D. programmes in clinical psychology. Clinical psychology in Britain developed much like in the U.S. after WWII, specifically within the context of the National Health Service with qualifications, standards, and salaries managed by the British Psychological Society.

Development of the Doctor of Psychology Degree

By the 1960s, psychotherapy had become imbedded within clinical psychology, but for many the Ph.D. educational model did not offer the necessary training for those interested in practice rather than research. There was a growing argument that said the field of psychology in the US had developed to a degree warranting explicit training in clinical practice. The concept of a practice-oriented degree was debated in 1965 and narrowly gained approval for a pilot programme at the University of Illinois starting in 1968. Several other similar programmes were instituted soon after, and in

1973, at the Vail Conference on Professional Training in Psychology, the Practitioner–Scholar Model of Clinical Psychology—or *Vail Model*—resulting in the Doctor of Psychology (Psy.D.) degree was recognized. Although training would continue to include research skills and a scientific understanding of psychology, the intent would be to produce highly trained professionals, similar to programmes in medicine, dentistry, and law. The first programme explicitly based on the Psy.D. model was instituted at Rutgers University. Today, about half of all American graduate students in clinical psychology are enrolled in Psy.D. programmes.

A Changing Profession

Since the 1970s, clinical psychology has continued growing into a robust profession and academic field of study. Although the exact number of practicing clinical psychologists is unknown, it is estimated that between 1974 and 1990, the number in the US grew from 20,000 to 63,000. Clinical psychologists continue to be experts in assessment and psychotherapy while expanding their focus to address issues of gerontology, sports, and the criminal justice system to name a few. One important field is health psychology, the fastest-growing employment setting for clinical psychologists in the past decade. Other major changes include the impact of managed care on mental health care; an increasing realization of the importance of knowledge relating to multicultural and diverse populations; and emerging privileges to prescribe psychotropic medication. Approximately 20% of clinical health psychologists identify themselves as counselling psychologists as well.

In the UK psychology is now one of the most popular degree subjects, and over 15,000 people graduate in psychology each year, many with the hope of developing this into a career, although only around 600 places for doctoral training in clinical psychology means there is intense competition for these places. There is also fierce competition to get into US Ph.D. programmes in clinical psychology, with an average acceptance rate of 8%.

CURRENT STATUS OF CLINICAL PSYCHOLOGY

Clinical psychology is an integration of science, theory and clinical knowledge for the purpose of understanding, preventing, and relieving psychologically based distress or dysfunction and to promote subjective well-being and personal development. Central to its practice are psychological assessment and psychotherapy, although clinical psychologists also engage in research, teaching, consultation, forensic testimony, and programme development and administration. In many countries, clinical psychology is a regulated mental health profession.

The field is often considered to have begun in 1896 with the opening of the first psychological clinic at the University of Pennsylvania by Lightner Witmer. In the first half of the 20th century, clinical psychology was focused on psychological assessment, with little attention given to treatment.

This changed after the 1940s when World War II resulted in the need for a large increase in the number of trained clinicians. Since that time, two main educational models have developed—the Ph.D. science-practitioner model and the Psy.D. practitioner-scholar model. Clinical psychologists are now considered experts in providing psychotherapy, and generally train within four primary theoretical orientations—psychodynamic, humanistic, behaviour therapy/cognitive behavioural, and systems or family therapy.

TRAINING AND CERTIFICATION TO PRACTICE

Clinical psychologists study a generalist programme in psychology plus postgraduate training and/or clinical placement and supervision. The length of training differs across the world, ranging from four years plus post-Bachelors supervised practice to a doctorate of three to six years which combines clinical placement.

In the USA, about half of all clinical psychology graduate students are being trained in Ph.D. programmes—a model that emphasizes research—with the other half in Psy.D. programmes, which has more focus on practice.

Both models are accredited by the American Psychological Association and many other English-speaking psychological societies. A smaller number of schools offer accredited programmes in clinical psychology resulting in a Masters degree, which usually take two to three years post-Bachelors.

In the U.K., clinical psychologists undertake a Doctor of Clinical Psychology which is a practitioner doctorate with both clinical and research components. This is a three-year full-time salaried programme sponsored by the National Health Service and based in universities and the NHS. Entry into these programmes is highly competitive, and requires at least a three-year undergraduate degree in psychology plus some form of experience, usually in either the NHS as an Assistant Psychologist or in academia as a Research Assistant. It is not unusual for applicants to apply several times before being accepted onto a training course as only about one-fifth of applicants are accepted each year.

These clinical psychology doctoral degrees are accredited by the British Psychological Society and the Health Professions Council. The HPC is the statutory regulator for practitioner psychologists in the UK. Those who successfully complete clinical psychology doctoral degrees are eligible to apply for registration with the HPC as a clinical psychologist. The practice of clinical psychology requires a license in the United States, Canada, the United Kingdom, and many other countries.

Although each of the U.S. states is somewhat different in terms of requirements and licenses, there are three common elements:

1.Graduation from an accredited school with the appropriate degree

2.Completion of supervised clinical experience or internship

3.Passing a written examination and, in some states, an oral examination

All U.S. state and Canadian province licensing boards are members of the Association of State and Provincial Psychology Boards which created and maintains the Examination for Professional Practice in Psychology. Many states require other examinations in addition to the EPPP, such as a jurisprudence examination and/or an oral examination. Most states also require a certain number of continuing education credits per year in order to renew a license, which can be obtained though various means, such as taking audited classes and attending approved workshops. Clinical psychologists require the Psychologist license to practice, although licenses can be obtained with a masters-level degree, such as Marriage and Family Therapist, Licensed Professional Counselor, and Licensed Psychological Associate.

In the U.K. registration as a clinical psychologist with the Health Professions Council is necessary. The HPC is the statutory regulator for practitioner psychologists in the U.K. In the U.K. the following titles are restricted by law "registered psychologist" and "practitioner psychologist"; in addition the specialist title "clinical psychologist" is also restricted by law.

Assessment

An important area of expertise for many clinical psychologists is psychological assessment, and there are indications that as many as 91% of psychologists engage in this core clinical practice. Such evaluation is usually done in service to gaining insight into and forming hypotheses about psychological or behavioural problems. As such, the results of such assessments are usually used to create generalized impressions in service to informing treatment planning. Methods include formal testing measures, interviews, reviewing past records, clinical observation, and physical examination. There exist literally hundreds of various assessment tools, although only a few have been shown to have both high validity and reliability.

These measures generally fall within one of several categories, including the following:

- *Intelligence and achievement tests*: These tests are designed to measure certain specific kinds of cognitive functioning in comparison to a norming-group. These tests, such as the WISC-IV, attempt to measure such traits as general knowledge, verbal skill, memory, attention span, logical reasoning, and visual/spatial perception. Several tests have been shown to predict accurately certain kinds of performance, especially scholastic.

- *Personality tests*: Tests of personality aim to describe patterns of behaviour, thoughts, and feelings. They generally fall within two categories: objective and projective. Objective measures, such as the MMPI, are based on restricted answers—such as yes/no, true/false, or a rating scale—which allow for computation of scores that can be compared to a normative group. Projective tests, such as the Rorschach inkblot test, allow for open-ended answers, often based on ambiguous stimuli, presumably revealing non-conscious psychological dynamics.
- *Neuropsychological tests*: Neuropsychological tests consist of specifically designed tasks used to measure psychological functions known to be linked to a particular brain structure or pathway. They are typically used to assess impairment after an injury or illness known to affect neurocognitive functioning, or when used in research, to contrast neuropsychological abilities across experimental groups.
- *Clinical observation*: Clinical psychologists are also trained to gather data by observing behaviour. The clinical interview is a vital part of assessment, even when using other formalized tools, which can employ either a structured or unstructured format. Such assessment looks at certain areas, such as general appearance and behaviour, mood and affect, perception, comprehension, orientation, insight, memory, and content of communication. One psychiatric example of a formal interview is the mental status examination, which is often used in psychiatry as a screening tool for treatment or further testing.

Diagnostic Impressions

After assessment, clinical psychologists often provide a diagnostic impression. Many countries use the International Statistical Classification of Diseases and Related Health Problems while the U.S. most often uses the Diagnostic and Statistical Manual of Mental Disorders. Both assume medical concepts and terms, and state that there are categorical disorders that can be diagnosed by set lists of descriptive criteria.

Several new models are being discussed, including a"dimensional model" based on empirically validated models of human differences and a"psychosocial model", which would take changing, intersubjective states into greater account. The proponents of these models claim that they would offer greater diagnostic flexibility and clinical utility without depending on the medical concept of illness.

However, they also admit that these models are not yet robust enough to gain widespread use, and should continue to be developed. Some clinical psychologists do not tend to diagnose, but rather use formulation-an individualized map of the difficulties that the patient or client faces, encompassing predisposing, precipitating and perpetuating factors.

COMPARISON WITH OTHER MENTAL HEALTH PROFESSIONS

Psychiatry

Although clinical psychologists and psychiatrists can be said to share a same fundamental aim—the alleviation of mental distress—their training, outlook, and methodologies are often quite different. Perhaps the most significant difference is that psychiatrists are licensed physicians. As such, psychiatrists often use the medical model to assess psychological problems and rely on psychotropic medications as the chief method of addressing the illness—although many also employ psychotherapy as well. Psychiatrists and medical psychologists are able to conduct physical examinations, order and interpret laboratory tests and EEGs, and may order brain imaging studies such as CT or CAT, MRI, and PET scanning. Clinical psychologists generally do not prescribe medication, although there is a growing movement for psychologists to have prescribing privileges. These medical privileges require additional training and education. To date, medical psychologists may prescribe psychotropic medications in Guam, New Mexico, and Louisiana and military psychologists.

Counseling Psychology

Counseling psychologists study and use many of the same interventions and tools as clinical psychologists, including psychotherapy and assessment. Traditionally, counseling psychologists help people with what might be considered normal or moderate psychological problems—such as the feelings of anxiety or sadness resulting from major life changes or events.

Many counseling psychologists also receive specialized training in career assessment, group therapy, and relationship counseling, although some counseling psychologists also work with the more serious problems that clinical psychologists are trained for, such as dementia or psychosis. There are fewer counseling psychology graduate programmes than those for clinical psychology and they are more often housed in departments of education rather than psychology. The two professions can be found working in all the same settings but counseling psychologists are more frequently employed in university counseling centres compared to hospitals and private practice for clinical psychologists. There is considerable overlap between the two fields and distinctions between them continue to fade.

School Psychology

School psychologists are primarily concerned with the academic, social, and emotional well-being of children and adolescents within a scholastic environment. In the U.K., they are known as "educational psychologists". Like clinical psychologists, school psychologists with doctoral degrees are eligible for licensure as health service psychologists, and many work in private practice. Unlike clinical psychologists, they receive much more training in education, child development and behaviour, and the psychology of learning. Common degrees include the Educational Specialist Degree, Doctor of Philosophy, and Doctor of Education. Traditional job roles for school psychologists employed in school settings have focused mainly on assessment of students to determine their eligibility for special education services in schools, and on consultation with teachers and other school professionals to design and carry out interventions on behalf of students. Other major roles also include offering individual and group therapy with children and their families, designing prevention programmes, evaluating school programmes, and working with teachers and administrators to help maximize teaching efficacy, both in the classroom and systemically.

Clinical Social Work

Social workers provide a variety of services, generally concerned with social problems, their causes, and their solutions.

With specific training, clinical social workers may also provide psychological counseling in addition to more traditional social work. The Masters in Social Work in the U.S. is a two-year, sixty credit programme that includes at least a one year practicum.

Occupational Therapy

Occupational therapy—often abbreviated OT—is the "use of productive or creative activity in the treatment or rehabilitation of physically, cognitively, or emotionally disabled people." Most commonly, occupational therapists work with people with disabilities to enable them to maximize their skills and abilities.

Occupational therapy practitioners are skilled professionals whose education includes the study of human growth and development with specific emphasis on the physical, emotional, psychological, sociocultural, cognitive and environmental components of illness and injury. They commonly work alongside clinical psychologists in settings such as inpatient and outpatient mental health, pain management clinics, eating disorder clinics, and child development services.

OT's use support groups, individual counseling sessions, and activity-based approaches to address psychiatric symptoms and maximize functioning in life activities.

Criticisms and controversies

Clinical psychology is a diverse field and there have been recurring tensions over the degree to which clinical practice should be limited to treatments supported by empirical research. Despite some evidence showing that all the major therapeutic orientations are about of equal effectiveness, there remains much debate about the efficacy of various forms treatment in use in clinical psychology.

It has been reported that clinical psychology has rarely allied itself with client groups and tends to individualize problems to the neglect of wider economic, political and social inequality issues that may not be the responsibility of the client. It has been argued that therapeutic practices are inevitably bound up with power inequalities, which can be used for good and bad. A critical psychology movement has argued that clinical psychology, and other professions making up a "psy complex", often fail to consider or address inequalities and power differences and can play a part in the social and moral control of disadvantage, deviance and unrest.

An October 2009 editorial in the journal Nature suggests that a large number of clinical psychology practitioners in the United States consider scientific evidence to be "less important than their personal – that is, subjective – clinical experience."

APPROACHES TO CLINICAL PSYCHOLOGY

Clinical psychologists who work as psychotherapists often utilize different treatment approaches when working with clients. While some clinicians focus on a very specific treatment outlook, many use what is referred to as an eclectic approach. This involves drawing on different theoretical methods to develop the best treatment plan for each individual client.

Some of the major theoretical perspectives within clinical psychology include:

- Psychodynamic Approach: This perspective grew out of the work of psychoanalyst Sigmund Freud, who believed that the unconscious mind played an important role in our behaviour. Psychologists who utilize this perspective may use techniques such as free association to investigate a client's underlying, unconscious motivations.

- Cognitive Behavioural Perspective: This approach to clinical psychology developed from the behavioural and cognitive schools of thought. Clinical psychologists using this perspective will look at how a client's feelings, behaviours and thoughts interact. Cognitive-behavioural therapy often focus on changing thoughts and behaviours that contribute to psychological distress.
- Humanistic Perspective: This approach to clinical psychology grew out of the work of humanist thinkers such as Abraham Maslow and Carl Rogers. This perspective looks at the client more holistically and is focused on such things as self-actualization and helping people realize their full potential.

Is Clinical Psychology Right for You?

Clinical psychology is one of the most popular areas within psychology, but it is important to evaluate your interests before deciding if this career is right for you. If you enjoy working with people and are able to handle stress and conflict well, clinical psychology may be an excellent choice. Take the psychology career quiz to learn more about the specific careers that are best-suited to your personality and needs.

PSYCHOLOGICAL TESTING

Psychological testing is a field characterized by the use of samples of behaviour in order to assess psychological construct(s), such as cognitive and emotional functioning, about a given individual. The technical term for the science behind psychological testing is psychometrics. By samples of behaviour, one means observations over time of an individual performing tasks that have usually been prescribed beforehand, which often means scores on a test. These responses are often compiled into statistical tables that allow the evaluator to compare the behaviour of the individual being tested to the responses of a norm group.

Psychological assessment is similar to psychological testing but usually involves a more comprehensive assessment of the individual. Psychological assessment is a process that involves the integration of information from multiple sources, such as tests of normal and abnormal personality, tests of ability or intelligence, tests of interests or attitudes, as well as information from personal interviews. Collateral information is also collected about personal, occupational, or medical history, such as from records or from interviews with parents, spouses, teachers, or previous therapists or physicians.

A psychological test is one of the sources of data used within the process of assessment; usually more than one test is used. Many psychologists do some level of assessment when providing services to clients or patients, and may use for example, simple checklists to assess some traits or symptoms, but psychological assessment is a more complex, detailed, in-depth process. Typical types of focus for psychological assessment are to provide a diagnosis for treatment settings; to assess a particular area of functioning or disability often for school settings; to help select type of treatment or to assess treatment outcomes; to help courts decide issues such as child custody or competency to stand trial; or to help assess job applicants or employees and provide career development counseling or training.

A useful psychological measure must be both valid (i.e., there is evidence to support the specified interpretation of the test results) and reliable (i.e., internally consistent or give consistent results over time, across raters, etc.).

Interpreting scores

Psychological tests, like many measurements of human characteristics, can be interpreted in a norm-referenced or criterion-referenced manner. Norms are statistical representations of a population. A norm-referenced score interpretation compares an individual's results on the test with the statistical representation of the population. In practice, rather than testing a population, a representative sample or group is tested. This provides a group norm or set of norms. One representation of norms is the Bell curve (also called"normal curve"). Norms are available for standardized psychological tests, allowing for an understanding of how an individual's scores compare with the group norms. Norm referenced scores are typically reported on the standard score (z) scale or a rescaling of it.

A criterion-referenced interpretation of a test score compares an individual's performance to some criterion other than performance of other individuals. For example, the generic school test typically provides a score in reference to a subject domain; a student might score 80% on a geography test. Criterion-referenced score interpretations are generally more applicable to achievement tests rather than psychological tests. Often, test scores can be interpreted in both ways; a score of 80% on a geography test could place a student at the 84th percentile, or a standard score of 1.0 or even 2.0.

Types of psychological tests

IQ/achievement Tests

IQ tests purport to be measures of intelligence, while achievement tests are measures of the use and level of development of use of the ability. IQ (or cognitive) tests and achievement tests are common norm-referenced tests. In these types of tests, a series of tasks is presented to the person being evaluated, and the person's responses are graded according to carefully prescribed guidelines. After the test is completed, the results can be compiled and compared to the responses of a norm group, usually composed of people at the same age or grade level as the person being evaluated. IQ tests which contain a series of tasks typically divide the tasks into verbal (relying on the use of language) and performance, or non-verbal (relying on eye-hand types of tasks, or use of symbols or objects). Examples of verbal IQ test tasks are vocabulary and information (answering general knowledge questions). Non-verbal examples are timed completion of puzzles (object assembly) and identifying images which fit a pattern (matrix reasoning).

IQ tests and academic achievement tests are designed to be administered to either an individual or to a group of people. The individually-administered tests tend to be more comprehensive, more reliable, more valid and generally to have better psychometric characteristics than group-administered tests. However, individually administered tests are more expensive to administer because of the need for a trained administrator.

Attitude Tests

Attitude test assess an individual's feelings about an event, person, or object. Attitude scales are used in marketing to determine individual preferences for brands, or items. Typically attitude test use either a Thurston Scale, or Likert Scale to measure specific items.

Neuropsychological Tests

These tests consist of specifically designed tasks used to measure a psychological function known to be linked to a particular brain structure or pathway. They are typically used to assess impairment after an injury or illness known to affect neurocognitive functioning, or when used in research, to contrast neuropsychological abilities across experimental groups.

Personality Tests

Psychological measures of personality are often described as either objective tests or projective tests. The terms "objective test" and "projective test" have recently come under criticism in the Journal of Personality Assessment. The more descriptive "rating scale or self-report measures" and "free response measures" are suggested, rather than the terms "objective tests" and "projective tests," respectively.

Objective Tests (Rating Scale or Self-report Measure)

Objective tests have a restricted response format, such as allowing for true or false answers or rating using an ordinal scale. Prominent examples of objective personality tests include the Minnesota Multiphasic Personality

Inventory, Millon Clinical Multiaxial Inventory-III, Child Behaviour Checklist, Symptom Checklist 90 and the Beck Depression Inventory. Objective personality tests can be designed for use in business for potential employees, such as the NEO-PI, the 16PF, and the OPQ (Occupational Personality Questionnaire), all of which are based on the Big Five taxonomy. The Big Five, or Five Factor Model of normal personality, has gained acceptance since the early 1990s when some influential meta-analyses found consistent relationships between the Big Five personality factors and important criterion variables.

Another personality test based upon the Five Factor Model is the Five Factor Personality Inventory – Children (FFPI-C.).

Projective Tests (Free Response Measures)

Projective tests allow for a freer type of response. An example of this would be the Rorschach test, in which a person states what each of ten ink blots might be. Some projective tests are used less often today because they are more time consuming to administer and because the reliability and validity are controversial.

As improved sampling and statistical methods developed, much controversy regarding the utility and validity of projective testing has occurred. The use of clinical judgement rather than norms and statistics to evaluate people's characteristics has convinced many that projectives are deficient and unreliable (results are too dissimilar each time a test is given to the same person). However, many practitioners continue to rely on projective testing, and some testing experts suggest that these measures can be useful in developing therapeutic rapport.

They may also be useful in creating inferences to follow-up with other methods. The most widely used scoring system for the Rorschach is the Exner system of scoring. Another common projective test is the Thematic Apperception Test (TAT), which is often scored with Westen's Social Cognition and Object Relations Scales and Phebe Cramer's Defence Mechanisms Manual. Both"rating scale" and"free response" measures are used in contemporary clinical practice, with a trend towards the former.

Other projective tests include the House-Tree-Person Test, Robert's Apperception Test, and the Attachment Projective.

Sexological Tests

The number of tests specifically meant for the field of sexology is quite limited. The field of sexology provides different psychological evaluation devices in order to examine the various aspects of the discomfort, problem or dysfunction, regardless of whether they are individual or relational ones.

Direct Observation Tests

Although most psychological tests are"rating scale" or"free response" measures, psychological assessment may also involve the observation of people as they complete activities. This type of assessment is usually conducted with families in a laboratory, home or with children in a classroom.

The purpose may be clinical, such as to establish a pre-intervention baseline of a child's hyperactive or aggressive classroom behaviours or to observe the nature of a parent-child interaction in order to understand a relational disorder. Direct observation procedures are also used in research, for example to study the relationship between intrapsychic variables and specific target behaviours, or to explore sequences of behavioural interaction.

The Parent-Child Interaction Assessment-II (PCIA) is an example of a direct observation procedure that is used with school-age children and parents. The parents and children are video recorded playing at a make-believe zoo. The Parent-Child Early Relational Assessment is used to study parents and young children and involves a feeding and a puzzle task. The MacArthur Story Stem Battery (MSSB) is used to elicit narratives from children. The Dyadic Parent-Child Interaction Coding System-II tracks the extent to which children follow the commands of parents and vice versa and is well suited to the study of children with Oppositional Defiant Disorders and their parents.

Test security

Many psychological tests are generally not available to the public, but rather, have restrictions both from publishers of the tests and from psychology licensing boards that prevent the disclosure of the tests themselves and information about the interpretation of the results.

Test publishers consider both copyright and matters of professional ethics to be involved in protecting the secrecy of their tests, and they sell tests only to people who have proved their educational and professional qualifications to the test maker's satisfaction. Purchasers are legally bound from giving test answers or the tests themselves out to the public unless permitted under the test maker's standard conditions for administration of the tests.

CLINICAL THEORIES AND INTERVENTIONS

Psychotherapy involves a formal relationship between professional and client—usually an individual, couple, family, or small group—that employs a set of procedures intended to form a therapeutic alliance, explore the nature of psychological problems, and encourage new ways of thinking, feeling, or behaving. Clinicians have a wide range of individual interventions to draw from, often guided by their training—for example, a cognitive behavioural therapy (CBT) clinician might use worksheets to record distressing cognitions, apsychoanalyst might encourage free association, while a psychologist trained in Gestalt techniques might focus on immediate interactions between client and therapist. Clinical psychologists generally seek to base their work on research evidence and outcome studies as well as on trained clinical judgment.

Although there are literally dozens of recognized therapeutic orientations, their differences can often be categorized on two dimensions: insight vs. action and in-session vs. out-session.

- Insight – emphasis is on gaining greater understanding of the motivations underlying one's thoughts and feelings (e.g. psychodynamic therapy)
- Action – focus is on making changes in how one thinks and acts (e.g. solution-focused therapy, cognitive behavioural therapy)
- In-session – interventions centre on the here-and-now interaction between client and therapist (e.g. humanistic therapy, Gestalt therapy)
- Out-session – a large portion of therapeutic work is intended to happen outside of session (e.g. bibliotherapy, rational emotive behaviour therapy)

The methods used are also different in regards to the population being served as well as the context and nature of the problem. Therapy will look very different between, say, a traumatized child, a depressed but high-functioning adult, a group of people recovering from substance dependence, and a ward of the state suffering from terrifying delusions. Other elements that play a critical role in the process of psychotherapy include the environment, culture, age, cognitive functioning, motivation, and duration (i.e. brief or long-term therapy).

Four Main Schools

The field is dominated in terms of training and practice by essentially four major schools of practice: psychodynamic, humanistic, behavioural/ cognitive behavioural, and systems or family therapy.

Psychodynamic

The psychodynamic perspective developed out of the psychoanalysis of Sigmund Freud. The core object of psychoanalysis is to make the unconscious conscious—to make the client aware of his or her own primal drives (namely those relating to sex and aggression) and the various defences used to keep them in check.

The essential tools of the psychoanalytic process are the use of free association and an examination of the client's transference towards the therapist, defined as the tendency to take unconscious thoughts or emotions about a significant person (e.g. parent) and "transfer" them onto another person. Major variations on Freudian psychoanalysis practiced today include self psychology, ego psychology, and object relations theory. These general orientations now fall under the umbrella term *psychodynamic psychology*, with common themes including examination of transference and defences, an appreciation of the power of the unconscious, and a focus on how early developments in childhood have shaped the client's current psychological state.

Humanistic

Humanistic psychology was developed in the 1950s in reaction to both behaviorism and psychoanalysis, largely due to the person-centred therapy of Carl Rogers (often referred to as Rogerian Therapy) and existential psychology developed by Victor Frankl and Rollo May. Rogers believed that a client needed only three things from a clinician to experience therapeutic improvement: congruence, unconditional positive regard, and empathetic understanding.

By using phenomenology, intersubjectivity and first-person categories, the humanistic approach seeks to get a glimpse of the whole person and not just the fragmented parts of the personality. This aspect of holism links up with another common aim of humanistic practice in clinical psychology, which is to seek an integration of the whole person, also called *self-actualization*.

According to humanistic thinking, each individual person already has inbuilt potentials and resources that might help them to build a stronger personality and self-concept. The mission of the humanistic psychologist is to help the individual employ these resources via the therapeutic relationship.

BEHAVIOURAL AND COGNITIVE BEHAVIOURAL

Cognitive behavioural therapy (CBT) developed from the combination of cognitive therapy and rational emotive behaviour therapy, both of which grew out of cognitive psychology and behaviorism. CBT is based on the theory that how we think (cognition), how we feel (emotion), and how we act (behaviour) are related and interact together in complex ways. In this perspective, certain dysfunctional ways of interpreting and appraising the world (often through *schemas* or *beliefs*) can contribute to emotional distress or result in behavioural problems.

The object of many cognitive behavioural therapies is to discover and identify the biased, dysfunctional ways of relating or reacting and through different methodologies help clients transcend these in ways that will lead to increased well-being. There are many techniques used, such as systematic desensitization, socratic questioning, and keeping a cognition observation log.

Modified approaches that fall into the category of CBT have also developed, including dialectical behaviour therapy and mindfulness-based cognitive therapy.

Behaviour therapy is a rich tradition. It is well-researched with a strong evidence base. Its roots are in behaviorism. In behaviour therapy, environmental events predict the way we think and feel. Our behaviour sets up conditions for the environment to feed back on it. Sometimes the feedback leads the behaviour to increase (reinforcement), and sometimes the behaviour decreases (punishment). Oftentimes behaviour therapists are called applied behaviour analysts.

They have studied many areas from developmental disabilities todepression and anxiety disorders. In the area of mental health and addictions a recent article looked at APA's list for well-established and promising practices and found a considerable number of them based on the principles of operant and respondent conditioning. Multiple assessment techniques have come from this approach including functional analysis (psychology), which has found a strong focus in the school system. In addition, multiple intervention programmes have come from this tradition including community reinforcement and family training for treating addictions, acceptance and commitment therapy, functional analytic psychotherapy, integrative behavioural couples therapy including dialectical behaviour therapy and behavioural activation. In addition, specific techniques such as contingency management and exposure therapy have come from this tradition.

Systems or Family Therapy

Systems or family therapy works with couples and families, and emphasizes family relationships as an important factor in psychological health. The central focus tends to be on interpersonal dynamics, especially in terms of how change in one person will affect the entire system. Therapy is therefore conducted with as many significant members of the "system" as possible. Goals can include improving communication, establishing healthy roles, creating alternative narratives, and addressing problematic behaviours. Contributors include John Gottman, Jay Haley, Sue Johnson, and Virginia Satir.

Other Major Therapeutic Orientations

There exist dozens of recognized schools or orientations of psychotherapy—the list below represents a few influential orientations not given above. Although they all have some typical set of techniques practitioners employ, they are generally better known for providing a framework of theory and philosophy that guides a therapist in his or her working with a client.

- Existential – Existential psychotherapy postulates that people are largely free to choose who we are and how we interpret and interact with the world. It intends to help the client find deeper meaning in life and to accept responsibility for living. As such, it addresses fundamental issues of life, such as death, aloneness, and freedom. The therapist emphasizes the client's ability to be self-aware, freely make choices in the present, establish personal identity and social relationships, create meaning, and cope with the natural anxiety of living. Important writers in existential therapy include Rollo May, Victor Frankl, James Bugental, and Irvin Yalom.

One influential therapy that came out of existential therapy is Gestalt therapy, primarily founded by Fritz Perls in the 1950s. It is well known for techniques designed to increase various kinds of self-awareness—the best-known perhaps being the "empty chair technique"—which are generally intended to explore resistance to "authentic contact," resolve internal conflicts, and help the client complete "unfinished business."

- Postmodern – Postmodern psychology says that the experience of reality is a subjective construction built upon language, social context, and history, with no essential truths. Since "mental illness" and "mental health" are not recognized as objective, definable realities, the postmodern psychologist instead sees the goal of therapy strictly as something constructed by the client and therapist. Forms of postmodern psychotherapy include narrative therapy, solution-focused therapy, and coherence therapy.
- Transpersonal – The transpersonal perspective places a stronger focus on the spiritual facet of human experience. It is not a set of techniques so much as a willingness to help a client explore spirituality and/or transcendent states of consciousness. It also is concerned with helping clients achieve their highest potential. Important writers in this area include Ken Wilber, Abraham Maslow, Stanislav Grof, John Welwood, David Brazier and Roberto Assagioli.

Other Perspectives

- Multiculturalism – Although the theoretical foundations of psychology are rooted in European culture, there is a growing recognition that there exist profound differences between various ethnic and social groups and that systems of psychotherapy need to take those differences into greater consideration. Further, the generations following immigrant migration will have some combination of two or more cultures—with aspects coming from the parents and from the surrounding society—and this process of acculturationcan play a strong role in therapy (and might itself be the presenting problem). Culture influences ideas about change, help-seeking, locus of control, authority, and the importance of the individual versus the group, all of which can potentially clash with certain givens in mainstream psychotherapeutic theory and practice. As such, there is a growing movement to integrate knowledge of various cultural groups in order to inform therapeutic practice in a more culturally sensitive and effective way.

- Feminism – Feminist therapy is an orientation arising from the disparity between the origin of most psychological theories (which have male authors) and the majority of people seeking counselling being female. It focuses on societal, cultural, and political causes and solutions to issues faced in the counselling process. It openly encourages the client to participate in the world in a more social and political way.
- Positive psychology – Positive psychology is the scientific study of human happiness and well-being, which started to gain momentum in 1998 due to the call of Martin Seligman, then president of the APA. The history of psychology shows that the field has been primarily dedicated to addressing mental illness rather than mental wellness. Applied positive psychology's main focus, therefore, is to increase one's positive experience of life and ability to flourish by promoting such things as optimism about the future, a sense of flow in the present, and personal traits like courage, perseverance, and altruism. There is now preliminary empirical evidence to show that by promoting Seligman's three components of happiness—positive emotion (the pleasant life), engagement (the engaged life), and meaning (the meaningful life)—positive therapy can decrease clinical depression.

Integration

In the last couple of decades, there has been a growing movement to integrate the various therapeutic approaches, especially with an increased understanding of cultural, gender, spiritual, and sexual-orientation issues. Clinical psychologists are beginning to look at the various strengths and weaknesses of each orientation while also working with related fields, such as neuroscience, genetics, evolutionary biology, and psychopharmacology. The result is a growing practice of eclecticism, with psychologists learning various systems and the most efficacious methods of therapy with the intent to provide the best solution for any given problem.

Professional Ethics

The field of clinical psychology in most countries is strongly regulated by a code of ethics. In the US, professional ethics are largely defined by the

APA *Code of Conduct,* which is often used by states to define licensing requirements. The APA Code generally sets a higher standard than that which is required by law as it is designed to guide responsible behaviour, the protection of clients, and the improvement of individuals, organizations, and society. The Code is applicable to all psychologists in both research and applied fields. The APA Code is based on five principles: Beneficence and Nonmaleficence, Fidelity and Responsibility, Integrity, Justice, and Respect for People's Rights and Dignity. Detailed elements address how to resolve ethical issues, competence, human relations, privacy and confidentiality, advertising, record keeping, fees, training, research, publication, assessment, and therapy. The BPS *Code of Ethics and Conduct* similarly sets a high standard for psychologist. It is based on four principles: respect, competence, responsibility and integrity.

RESPONSIBILITIES OF CLINICAL PSYCHOLOGIST

There are times when one is faced with a situation or some circumstances when the comforting hugs and conversation with friends and family don't seem to solve the problem. Who does then one go to? This is when a psychologist lends his/her ears to our problems. Clinical psychologist are trained for this kind of work. A clinical psychologist's job description requires him to look into matter objectively and treat the person accordingly.

Clinical Psychologist

The journey to become a clinical psychologist is one which is completed after a lot of hard work and dedication. Before we begin with careers in clinical psychology, we must know that to be a clinical psychologist, one must be a sound person who can think objectively and not be biased. One must be brave enough to guide another person who is going through a difficult phase in his/her life.

A day in a clinical psychologist would consist of meeting clients, having psychotherapy sessions with them, listening to their ills and woes without being judgmental and giving them the right treatment. They also work with institutes like schools and hospitals. They must be skilled to listen well and catch on the undercurrent of the conversation and diagnose the problem. They also have to discuss the available method of treatment with the patient. More on psychologist job description.

Clinical Psychologist Education

Clinical psychologist job description will be easily understood if you take a look at what it takes to be a clinical psychologist. Before one can take the responsibility of another life in one's own hand, a clinical psychologist has to train and sharpen his skills. One has to put in around 5 to 7 years into graduation studies. There are various colleges and universities that provide degrees in psychology.

If one wants to open a private practice, then a doctorate is a must. Ph.D holders usually work with institutes like schools, mental institutions and contribute in teaching and research. Individuals with a masters in psychology work as school councilors and usually work under a Ph.D or psychology doctorate holder.

This requires two years of study time. A bachelor's degree holder works as an assistant with correctional facilities. A year's internship is also a must to be a clinical psychologist. Also to open a private practice, one must be certified or licensed. Also read career information on psychology.

Job Description of a Clinical Psychologist

The duties and responsibilities of a clinical psychologist require him/her to put in minimum of 40 hours of work a week. Clinical psychologist job description also requires him/her to keep abreast with the latest changes in the field of psychology. A psychologist have to talk and listen to patients who are suffering setbacks in their lives due to psychological issues that's troubling them.

These can range from addictions, mental illnesses, stress or even marriage or divorce related issues. He/she must give sound advice and respect professional secrecy while dealing with his/her clients. Clinical psychologists provide individual or group psychotherapy and help mentally or emotionally challenged people settle back into the society amongst their many other duties which are a part of the clinical psychologist job description.

Clinical Psychologist Salary Range

Clinical psychologists earn well and they lead a comfortable lifestyle. A clinical psychologist's salary range from $59,000 to $78,000 annually. Those who are working with health care institutes like hospitals can earn about $63,000 annually and those who are working with correctional facilities earn about $55,000 per annum. A well established clinical psychologist can easily earn more than $75,000 annually.

By reading this clinical psychologist job description, you must have realised that this profession requires serious commitment and a heart that is willing to listen and help without being affected by what is being discussed. For this, emotional detachment from the patient is required in this job. If this is your calling, then follow it with all your passion. Years down the line, you will be a satisfied human being who achieved what he/she had set his/her heart on.

CLINICAL PSYCHOLOGY EDUCATION

In the U.S., clinical psychologists usually have a doctorate in psychology and receive training in clinical settings. The educational requirements to work in clinical psychology are quite rigorous, and most clinical psychologists spend between four to six years in graduate school after earning a bachelor's degree.

There are two different types of degrees available in clinical psychology- a Ph.D. and a Psy.D.Generally speaking, Ph.D. programme are centred on research, while Psy.D. programmes are practice-oriented. Some students may also find graduate programmes that offer a terminal master's degree in clinical psychology.

Before choosing a clinical psychology programme, students should always check to be sure that the programme is accredited by the American Psychological Association. After completing an accredited graduate training programme, prospective clinical psychologists must also complete a period of supervised training and an examination. Specific licensure requirements vary by state, so students should always check with their state's licensing board to learn more.

U.K. students can pursue a doctorate level degree in clinical psychology (D.Clin.Psychol. or Clin.Psy.D.) through programmes sponsored by the National Health Service.

These programmes are generally very competitive and are focused on both research and practice. Students interested in enrolling in one of these programme must have an undergraduate degree in a psychology programme approved by the British Psychological Society in addition to experience requirements.

Clinical Psychology Work Settings and Job Roles

Clinical psychologists often work in medical settings, private practice or in academic positions at universities and colleges. Some clinical psychologists work directly with clients, often those who suffer from severe psychiatric disorders.

Some of the job roles performed by those working in clinical psychology include:

- Assessment and diagnosis of psychological disorders
- Treatment of psychological disorders
- Offering testimony in legal settings
- Teaching
- Conducting research
- Drug and alcohol treatment

- Creating and administering programme to treat and prevent social problems.

Other clinical psychologists may work in private therapeutic settings offering short-term and long-term outpatient services to clients who need help coping with psychological distress. Some clinical psychologists work in other settings, often performing research, teaching university-level courses and offering consultation services.

2

Clinical Psychology and Cognitive Behavioural Therapy

Cognitive behavioural therapy (CBT) is a psychotherapeutic approach that addresses dysfunctional emotions, maladaptive behaviours and cognitive processes and contents through a number of goal-oriented, explicit systematic procedures. The name refers to behaviour therapy, cognitive therapy, and to therapy based upon a combination of basic behavioural and cognitive principles and research.

CBT is thought to be effective for the treatment of a variety of conditions, including mood, anxiety, personality, eating, substance abuse, tic, and psychotic disorders. Many CBT treatment programmes for specific disorders have been evaluated for efficacy; the health-care trend of evidence-based treatment, where specific treatments for symptom-based diagnoses are recommended, has favoured CBT over other approaches such as psychodynamic treatments.

CBT was primarily developed through an integration of behaviour therapy (first popularized by Edward Thorndike) with cognitive psychology research, first by Donald Meichenbaum and several other authors with the label of cognitive-behaviour modification in the late 1970s. This tradition thereafter merged with earlier work of a few clinicians, labelled as Cognitive Therapy (CT), developed by Aaron Beck, and Rational Emotive Therapy (RET) developed by Albert Ellis. While rooted in rather different theories, these two traditions have been characterised by a constant reference to experimental research to test hypotheses, both at clinical and basic level. Common features of CBT procedures are the focus on the "here and now", a directive or guidance role of therapist, a structuring of the psychotherapy sessions and path, and on alleviating both symptoms and patients' vulnerability.

Description

The premise of mainstream cognitive behavioural therapy is that changing maladaptive thinking leads to change in affect and in behaviour but recent variants emphasize changes in one's relationship to maladaptive thinking rather than changes in thinking itself. Therapists or computer-based programmes use CBT techniques to help individuals challenge their patterns and beliefs and replace "errors in thinking such as over generalizing, magnifying negatives, minimizing positives and catastrophizing" with "more realistic and effective thoughts, thus decreasing emotional distress and self-defeating behaviour" or to take a more open, mindful, and aware posture toward them so as to diminish their impact. Mainstream CBT helps individuals replace "maladaptive ... coping skills, cognitions, emotions and behaviours with more adaptive ones", by challenging an individual's way of thinking and the way that he/she reacts to certain habits or behaviours, but there is still controversy about the degree to which these traditional cognitive elements account for the effects seen with CBT over and above the earlier behavioural elements such as exposure and skills training. Modern forms of CBT include a number of diverse but related techniques such as exposure therapy, stress inoculation training, cognitive processing therapy, cognitive therapy, relaxation training, dialectical behaviour therapy, and acceptance and commitment therapy.

According to Gatchel *et al.* (2008), CBT has six phases:

1. Assessment
2. Reconceptualization
3. Skills acquisition
4. Skills consolidation and application training
5. Generalization and maintenance
6. Post-treatment assessment follow-up.

The reconceptualization phase makes up much of the "cognitive" portion of CBT. A summary of modern CBT approaches is given by Hofmann.

There are different protocols for delivering cognitive behavioural therapy, with important similarities among them. Use of the term *CBT*may refer to different interventions, including "self-instructions (e.g. distraction, imagery, motivational self-talk), relaxation and/or biofeedback, development of adaptive coping strategies (e.g. minimizing negative or self-defeating thoughts), changing maladaptive beliefs about pain, and goal setting". Treatment is sometimes manualized, with brief, direct, and time-limited treatments for individual psychological disorders that are specific technique-driven. CBT is used in both individual and group settings, and the techniques are often adapted for self-help applications. Some clinicians and researchers are cognitively oriented (e.g. cognitive restructuring), while others are more behaviorally oriented (e.g. *in vivo* exposure therapy). Interventions such as imaginal exposure therapy combine both approaches.

Cognitive behavioural therapy is most closely allied with the scientist–practitioner model, in which clinical practice and research is informed by a scientific perspective, clear operationalization of the problem, and an emphasis on measurement, including measuring changes in cognition and behaviour and in the attainment of goals.

These are often met through "homework" assignments in which the patient and the therapist work together to craft an assignment to complete before the next session. The completion of these assignments – which can be as simple as a person suffering from depression attending some kind of social event – indicates a dedication to treatment compliance and a desire to change. The therapists can then logically gauge the next step of treatment based on how thoroughly the patient completes the assignment. Effective cognitive behavioural therapy is dependent on a therapeutic alliance between the healthcare practitioner and the person seeking assistance. Unlike many other forms of psychotherapy, the patient is very involved in CBT. For example, an anxious patient may be asked to talk to a stranger as a homework assignment, but if that is too difficult, he or she can work out an easier assignment first. The therapist needs to be flexible and willing to listen to the patient rather than acting as an authority figure.

Specific Applications

CBT has been applied in both clinical and non-clinical environments to treat disorders such as personality conditions and behavioural problems. A systematic review of CBT in depression and anxiety disorders concluded that "CBT delivered in primary care, especially including computer-or Internet-based self-help programmes, is potentially more effective than usual care and could be delivered effectively by primary care therapists."

In adults, CBT has been shown to have a role in the treatment plans for anxiety disorders, depression, eating disorders, chronic low back pain, personality disorders, psychosis, schizophrenia, substance use disorders, in the adjustment, depression, and anxiety associated with fibromyalgia, and with post-spinal cord injuries.

In children or adolescents, CBT is an effective part of treatment plans for anxiety disorders, body dysmorphic disorder, depression and suicidality, eating disorders and obesity, obsessive–compulsive disorder, and posttraumatic stress disorder, as well astic disorders, trichotillomania, and other repetitive behaviour disorders.

Emerging evidence suggests a possible role for CBT in the treatment of attention deficit hyperactivity disorder (ADHD), hypochondriasis, multiple sclerosis, sleep disturbances related to aging, dysmenorrhea, and bipolar disorder, but more study is needed and results should be interpreted with caution. CBT has been studied as an aid in the treatment of anxiety associated with stuttering. Initial studies have shown CBT to be effective in reducing social anxiety in adults who stutter, but not in reducing stuttering frequency.

Cochrane reviews have found no evidence that CBT is effective for tinnitus, although there appears to be an effect on management of associated depression and quality of life in this condition. Other recent Cochrane Reviews found no convincing evidence that CBT training helps foster care providers manage difficult behaviours in the youth under their care, nor was it helpful in treating men whoabuse their intimate partners.

In the case of metastatic breast cancer, a Cochrane Review published in 2008 maintained that the current body of evidence is not sufficient to rule out the possibility that psychological interventions may cause harm to women with this advanced neoplasm.

In the United Kingdom, the National Institute for Health and Clinical Excellence (NICE) recommends CBT in the treatment plans for a number of mental health difficulties, including posttraumatic stress disorder, obsessive–compulsive disorder (OCD), bulimia nervosa, and clinical depression.

Anxiety Disorders

CBT has been shown to be effective in the treatment of all anxiety disorders.

A basic concept in some CBT treatments used in anxiety disorders is *in vivo* exposure, a term describing a technique where the patient is gradually exposed to the actual, feared stimulus. The treatment is based on the theory that the fear response has been classically conditioned, and that avoidance of it negatively reinforces and maintains the fear. This "two-factor" model is often credited to O. Hobart Mowrer. Through exposure to the stimulus, this harmful conditioning can be "unlearned" (referred to as extinction andhabituation).

DEVELOPMENT OF CLINICAL PSYCHOLOGY

Although we could get back to centennial backgrounds of psychology-where Luis Vives (1492-1540) should be highlighted as a precursor of modern psychology-the summary of the history of clinical and health psychology to be shown here starts from the beginning of the proper foundation of psychology and travels through the main institutions which have taken part in its current configuration.

The proper foundation of clinical and health psychology is included in the tradition of modern and experimental psychology, being the official date in 1879 when Wilhelm Wundt's laboratory was founded in the University of Leipzig. In this sense, we could recognize a deep link between clinical and experimental psychology since clinical psychology has a very clear disposition to research as a very important feature of its own nature. This disposition to research is one of the most important contributions of psychologists to the clinical field.

The centennial tradition in the psychology of individual differences should be highlighted also in this summary as a very important part of the clinical and health psychology foundations. Notwithstanding that psychology of individual differences has its official beginning in the first centre dedicated to mental measurement-born in 1885 and established by Francis Galton-and in Alfred Binet's laboratory settled up in 1895, we could not help making here this concise reference to Huarte de San Juan, patron of Spanish psychology and pioneer of differential psychology.

The formal setting-up of the first psychological clinic was dated on March, 1896, at the University of Pennsylvania, and carried out by Lighner Witmer. In the same year, Sigmund Freud used the word "psychoanalysis" for the first time. Hence, 1896 could be proposed as the year of official clinical psychology's setting-up.

Witmer's clinical work (which was a guideline to clinical work in psychology for a time) had the following characteristics: Patients were children (due to founder's particular interests); help advise was preceded by a diagnostic assessment; the centre had a professional team who cooperate in their work; there was a remarkable interest on prevention by means of early diagnosis and treatment, and clinical work was based on scientific psychology.

BEHAVIOUR THERAPY

Behaviour therapy or behaviour therapy is an approach to psychotherapy in thebehaviourism tradition that focuses on a set of methods designed for reinforcing desired and eliminating undesired behaviours without concerning itself with the psychoanalytic state of the subject. In its broadest sense the methods focus on behaviours, not the thoughts and feelings that might be causing them. Behaviour therapy breaks down into two disciplines, a more narrowly defined sense of behaviour therapy and behaviour modification. Within the psychological theories of learning and conditioning, behaviour therapy generally treats psychopathology with Pavlovian or respondent conditioning, while behaviour modification makes use of operant or instrumental conditioning. These distinctions are not absolute with some crossover occurring in practice.

History

Precursors of certain fundamental aspects of behaviour therapy have been identified in various ancient philosophical traditions, particularly Stoicism.

For example, Wolpe and Lazarus wrote, While the modern behaviour therapist deliberately applies principles of learning to this therapeutic operations, empirical behaviour therapy is probably as old as civilization – if we consider civilization as having begun when man first did things to further the well-being of other men. From the time that this became a feature of human life there must have been occasions when a man complained of his ills to another who advised or persuaded him of a course of action. In a broad sense, this could be called behaviour therapy whenever the behaviour itself was conceived as the therapeutic agent. Ancient writings contain innumerable behavioural prescriptions that accord with this broad conception of behaviour therapy.

The first use of the term behaviour modification appears to have been by Edward Thorndike in 1911. His article *Provisional Laws of Acquired Behaviour or Learning* makes frequent use of the term "modifying behaviour". Through early research in the 1940s and the 1950s the term was used by Joseph Wolpe's research group. The experimental tradition in clinical psychology used it to refer to psycho-therapeutic techniques derived from empirical research. It has since come to refer mainly to techniques for increasing adaptive behaviour through reinforcement and decreasing maladaptive behaviour through extinction or punishment (with emphasis on the former). Two related terms are behaviour therapy and applied behaviour analysis. Emphasizing the empirical roots of behaviour modification, some authors consider it to be broader in scope and to subsume the other two categories of behaviour change methods. Since techniques derived from behavioural psychology tend to be the most effective in altering behaviour, most practitioners consider behaviour modification along with behaviour therapy and applied behaviour analysis to be founded in behaviorism. While behaviour modification encompasses applied behaviour analysis and typically uses interventions based on the same behavioural principles, many behaviour modifiers who are not applied behaviour analysts tend to use packages of interventions and do not conduct functional assessments before intervening.

Possibly the first occurrence of the term "behaviour therapy" was in a 1953 research project by B.F. Skinner, Ogden Lindsley, Nathan H. Azrin and Harry C. Solomon. Early pioneers in behaviour therapy include Joseph Wolpe and Hans Eysenck.

In general, behaviour therapy is seen as having three distinct points of origin: South Africa (Wolpe's group), The United States (Skinner), and the United Kingdom (Rachman and Eysenck). Each had its own distinct approach to viewing behaviour problems. Eysenck in particular viewed behaviour problems as an interplay between personality characteristics, environment, and behaviour. Skinner's group in the United States took more of an operant conditioning focus. The operant focus created a functional approach to assessment and interventions focused on contingency management such as the token economy and behavioural activation. Skinner's student Ogden Lindsley is credited with forming a movement called precision teaching, which developed a particular type of graphing programme called the standard celeration chart to monitor the progress of clients. Skinner became interested in the individualising of programmes for improved learning in those with or without disabilities and worked with Fred S. Keller to develop programmed instruction. Programmed instruction had some clinical success in aphasia rehabilitation. Gerald Patterson used programme instruction to develop his parenting text for children with conduct problems. With age, respondent conditioning appears to slow but operant conditioning remains relatively stable.

While many behaviour therapists remain staunchly committed to the basic operant and respondent paradigm, in the second half of the 20th century, many therapists coupled behaviour therapy with the cognitive therapy of Aaron Beck and Albert Ellis, to form cognitive behavioural therapy. In some areas the cognitive component had an additive effect (for example, evidence suggests that cognitive interventions improve the result of social phobia treatment.) but in other areas it did not enhance the treatment, which led to the pursuit of Third Generation Behaviour Therapies. Third generation behaviour therapy uses basic principles of operant and respondent psychology but couples them with functional analysis and a clinical formulation/case conceptualisation of verbal behaviour more inline with view of the behaviour analysts. Some research supports these therapies as being more effective in some cases than cogntive therapy, but overall the question is still in need of answers.

Scientific Basis

Behaviour therapy is based upon the principles of classical conditioning developed by Ivan Pavlov and operant conditioning developed byB.F. Skinner. There has been a good deal of confusion on how these two conditionings differ and whether the various techniques of behaviour therapy have any common scientific base.

Contingency management programmes are a direct product of research from operant conditioning. These programmes have been highly successful with those suffering from panic disorders, anxiety disorders, and phobias.

Systematic desensitisation and exposure and response prevention both evolved from respondent conditioning and have also received considerable research.

Behaviour avoidance test (BAT) is a behavioural procedure in which the therapist measures how long the client can tolerate an anxiety-inducing stimulus. The BAT falls under the exposure-based methods of Behaviour Therapy. Exposure-based methods of behavioural therapy are well suited to the treatment of phobias, which include intense and unreasonable fears (e.g., of spiders, blood, public speaking). The therapist needs some type of behavioural assessment to record the continuing progress of a client undergoing an exposure-based treatment for phobia. The simplest possible assessment approach for this is the BAT. The BAT approach is predicted on the reasonable assumption that the client's fear is the main determinant of behaviour in the testing situation. BAT can be conducted visual, virtually, or physically, depending on the clients' maladaptive behaviour. Its application is not limited to phobias, it is applied to various disorders such as Post-Traumatic Stress Disorder (PTSD) and Obsessive-Compulsive Disorder (OCD).

Social skills training teaches clients skills to access reinforcers and lessen life punishment. Operant conditioning procedures in meta-analysis had the largest effect size for training social skills, followed by modelling, coaching, and social cognitive techniques in that order. Social skills training has some empirical support particularly for schizophrenia. However, with schizophrenia, behavioural programmes have generally lost favour.

APPLIED TO PROBLEM BEHAVIOUR

Behaviour therapy based its core interventions on functional analysis. Just a few of the many problems that behaviour therapy have functionally analysed include intimacy in couples relationships, forgiveness in couples, chronic pain, stress-related behaviour problems of being an adult child of an alcoholic, anorexia, chronic distress, substance abuse, depression, anxiety, and obesity.

Functional analysis has even been applied to problems that therapists commonly encounter like client resistance, partially engaged clients and involuntary clients. Applications to these problems have left clinicans with considerable tools for enhancing therapeutic effectiveness. One way to enhance therapeutic effectiveness is to use positive reinforcement or operant conditioning.

Many have argued that behaviour therapy is at least as effective as drug treatment for depression, ADHD, and OCD. Although, two large studies done by the Faculty of Health Sciences at Simon Fraser University indicates that both behaviour therapy and cognitive-behavioural therapy (CBT) are equally effective for OCD. CBT has been proven to perform slightly better at treating co-occurring depression.

Considerable policy implications have been inspired by behavioural views of various forms of psychopathology. One form of behaviour therapy (habit reversal training) has been found to be highly effective for treating tics.

Third Generation

Of particular interest, in behaviour therapy today are the areas often referred to as Third Generation Behaviour Therapy. This movement has been called clinical behaviour analysis because it represents a movement away from cognitivism and back toward radical behaviourism and other forms of behaviourism, in particular functional analysis and behavioural models of verbal behaviour.

This area includes Acceptance and Commitment Therapy (ACT), Cognitive Behavioural Analysis System of Psychotherapy (CBASP), behavioural activation (BA), Kohlenberg & Tsai's Functional Analytic Psychotherapy, integrative behavioural couples therapy and dialectical behavioural therapy. These approaches are squarely within the applied behaviour analysis tradition of behaviour therapy.

Acceptance and Commitment Therapy is probably the most well-researched of all the third generation behaviour therapy models. It is based on Relational Frame Theory. Other authors object to the term "third generation" or "third wave" and incorporate the many of the "third wave" therapeutic techniques under the general umbrella term of modern cognitive behavioural therapies. Functional Analytic Psychotherapy is based on a functional analysis of the therapeutic relationship. It places a greater emphasis on the therapeutic context and returns to the use of in-session reinforcement. In general, 40 years of research supports the idea that in-session reinforcement of behaviour can lead to behavioural change.

Behavioural activation emerged from a component analysis of cognitive behaviour therapy. This research found no additive effect for the cognitive component. Behavioural activation is based on a matching model of reinforcement. A recent review of the research, supports the notion that the use of behavioural activation is clinically important for the treatment of depression.

Integrative behavioural couples therapy developed from dissatisfaction with traditional behavioural couples therapy. Integrative behavioural couples therapy looks to Skinner (1966) for the difference between contingency-shaped and rule-governed behaviour.

It couples this analysis with a thorough functional assessment of the couple's relationship. Recent efforts have used radical behavioural concepts to interpret a number of clinical phenomena including forgiveness.

Organisations

Many organisations exist for behaviour therapists around the world. The World Association for Behaviour Analysis offers a certification in behaviour therapy . In the United States, the American Psychological Association's Division 25 is the division for behaviour analysis. The Association for Contextual Behaviour Therapy is another professional organisation. ACBS is home to many clinicians with specific interest in third generation behaviour therapy. The Association for Behavioural and Cognitive Therapies (formerly the Association for the Advancement of Behaviour Therapy) is for those with a more cognitive orientation. Internationally, most behaviour therapists find a core intellectual home in the International Association for Behaviour Analysis (ABAI) .

Characteristics

By nature, behavioural therapies are empirical (data-driven), contextual (focused on the environment and context), functional (interested in the effect or consequence a behaviour ultimately has), probabilistic (viewing behaviour as statistically predictable), monistic (rejecting mind–body dualism and treating the person as a unit), and relational (analysing bidirectional interactions).

Behavioural therapy develops, adds and provides behavioural intervention strategies and programmes for clients, and training to people who care to facilitate successful lives in the communities.

GROUP THERAPY

Since people are social animals, it is not surprising that much human activity has always been done in groups. Education, emotional support, help giving, and other therapy like functions are no exception. Religious organisations provide mutual support and guidance to their members. Funeral rituals serve a therapeutic function for bereaved friends and relatives by preventing isolation, aiding the expression of grief, sharing distress, and so on. It can even be argued that political clubs and organisations are therapeutic in that they channel emotion and provide a forum for complaints and new ideals. These strategies for mutual help are the basis of the more systematic forms known as group therapy.

The first true therapy group was formed in 1905, in Boston, by Joseph Hersey Pratt (Shaffer and Galinsky, 1974). Pratt organised groups of tuberculosis patients in order to give them inspiration, encouragement, and information about their disorder. In time, group members interacted more and more, and Pratt increasingly emphasised mutual support among them. While group treatments continued, this approach receive little attention until after World

War II. In the early part of the twentieth century, theory and treatment were mainly psychoanalytic. Freud's intrapsychic, biological model focused on the person since pathology was individual, it was only natural that treatment required the privacy, intensity, and concentration of a one-to-one relationship. Group approaches, it was believed, could only dilute treatment.

Several factors interacted to promote group therapy. First was the development of the neo-Freudian and ego psychology orientations. These approaches placed greater emphasis on interpersonal forces and the person's present life. Hence, group interactions are in some ways more relevant to the person's sources of distress than the unique relationship of individual psychotherapy. In addition, transference was deemphasised even in individual treatment, so that dilution of transference in a group is less important. A second factor was the work done by Gestalt and social psychologists, such as Kurt Lewin, which highlighted the unique attributes and functions of groups. It was suggested that groups are more than just a collection of individuals. Just as, in perception, the whole is greater than the sum of its parts, group interactions involve processes which are not apparent in individual or dyadic behaviour. The third major stimulus was economic. After World War II, there was a great need for therapy a need which intensive individual analysis could never handle. Group treatment offered a fine opportunity for the few trained therapists available to increase their caseloads. A group therapist can see more persons in one day than would be possible in a week of individual therapy.

Group therapy has increased dramatically in the past two decades. One of the main reasons is still the economic advantage. Hence, group approaches may we be the most common form of treatment in institutions and community mental health facilities. Group methods are also commonly used to treat individuals with similar, specialised problems, such as parents of children undergoing treatment, recently divorced or widowed adults, alcoholics, and drug addicts. Group therapies generally predominate in day hospital programmes for chronic psychiatric patients (Hersen and Luber, 1977). Because members share common problems and experiences, these groups are especially useful for providing support and understanding, communicating information, and teaching members how to solve common problems. Group procedures are usually somewhat limited in their goals and range of application. However, there are now many theories for explaining and conducting intensive group therapy, and many clinicians regard group methods as the best treatment for many neurotic patients.

Psychodynamic approaches to group therapy usually fall into two or three categories, differing in the relative emphasis on the individual and the group. The two primary orientations involve treatment of the individual patient *in* the group and treatment of the individual *by* or *through* the group. These orientations are described in the left and right portions. The third approach represents a compromise or integration of these two views.

The approaches which emphasise treatment in the group place little emphasis on the group itself. The group setting is viewed simply as a convenient means of treating several patients simultaneously. The focus of treatment throughout is the individual patient's pathology. This orientation is best represented by classic psychoanalytic group therapy, as developed by Slavson (1950) and Wolf and Schwartz (1962). In this approach the basic psychoanalytic strategy and techniques are translated to the group setting with as little alteration as possible. An attempt is made to individualise the psychoanalysis of each member. Group size is generally held to six to eight members, the preferred size of most group therapies. Obviously it is impossible for all group members to free-associate simultaneously. Wolf and Schwartz (1962) have adapted this technique to the group by members, in which each patient is encouraged to free-associate to the topic discussed. Interruptions, digressions, and reference to fantasies are all encouraged. In addition groups employ a "go around" procedure in which each member, in turn reports his or her associations at that moment.

As in individual psychoanalysis, the therapist's primary role in group therapy is to interpret transference and resistance. Interpretations are usually directed to individual patients or dyads, rather than the group as a whole. The therapist is aided by group members, who can often identify the interfering resistances of other clients (e.g., changing the topic, avoiding or generating conflict between members) as well as the ways they are misperceived an treated inappropriately (due to transference). Naturally, they react negatively to such behaviour and respond accordingly, confronting the resistive client and interpreting inappropriate behaviour. These statements are often very powerful precisely because they come from several peers. Because group members serve a major therapeutic role, the therapist can be relatively passive. He or she organises the group, gets it started, makes occasional interpretations, and sets limits, allowing the clients essentially to act as co-therapists.

Groups therapies which emphasise treatment of the individual by or through the group are characterised by group dynamic approaches, such as those of Foulkes (1965) and Whitaker and Lieberman (1965). These theorists, who are mainly psychoanalytic, view the goal of treatment as individual change. However, they see the group as the mechanism for producing change. As stated above, the group is seen as more than a collection of persons; it has a dynamism of its own. Power struggles between members, rivalries over the attention and affection of the therapist and one another, shifting alliances and subgroups, and mutual resistances all shape the nature and flow of the interaction. These forces, or *dynamics,* can all serve a therapeutic function for individual group members.

The interactive nature of group dynamics is especially clear in Whitaker and Lieberman's (1965) model. Each therapy session is presumed to turn on a *focal conflict* or concern, such as relationships to spouses. The more significant conflicts are periodically repeated as *group themes.* In interactions based on these conflicts and themes, each group member has unique associations to personal conflicts and responds in a characteristic fashion. For example, if the theme is anger, one client could be responding to another as if she were his wife, a second could be responding as he or she does to a parent, and a third could be attempting to defuse the conflict because of an inability to accept angry feelings.

Over time, each group develops a unique *group culture* which establishes rules and sets a pattern for interaction. One function of the culture is to find solutions for the focal conflicts. Early in therapy, these solutions are usually defensive and prevent extensive exploration of underlying motives. For example, the group might agree not to talk about sex. However, as progress is made, these solutions increasingly move the group forward and stimulate exploration. These so-called "enabling" solutions allow the individual members to come to grips with their own particular conflicts. The therapist's task is to help the group reach these facilitating or enabling solutions. Interpretations are directed much more toward the group and what the group is doing than toward individual clients. Therapist responses to individual clients are designed to steer the person in a direction the group should pursue. For example, the therapist might reflect on a patient's anger when he or she believes the group should be confronting anger as a general issue. Eventually all the major conflicts experienced by individual members will be covered, and the group process will facilitate resolution of each of these conflicts.

FAMILY THERAPY

Family therapy is a general term encompassing variety of approaches that focus on the family unit. It can entail group sessions for all family members living under one roof, the nuclear family (mother, father, child), the parents alone, or even one family member (cf. Bowen, 1966). Family therapy can also consist of alternating sessions with different subsets of family members. Regardless of who is actually present in the sessions, the various family approaches all see the family as the focus of treatment. Any change in individual members, including any identified patient (I.P.) for whom treatment was initially requested is presumed to insult from change in the family interaction pattern.

Family therapy became a major treatment strategy in the 1950s and 1960s. It grew out of several interrelated sources. First, the 1930s and 1940s saw a dramatic increase in therapeutic services for children the so-called "child guidance movement." The primary treatment for children was *play therapy.* In this form of psychoanalysis, play is substituted for free association. In keeping with the psychoanalytic orientation, classic play therapy focuses on the child's fantasies and unconscious, and essentially ignores current life experiences. The analyst periodically meets with the parents to keep them informed of their child's progress, but they are not involved in treatment. However, with the increased emphasis on ego psychology and social psychology, as well as observation of the course of treatment, it became apparent that the parents play in central role in the child's current behaviour, not just a historical role in its development. Parents could dramatically improve or worsen their child's behaviour outside of therapy.

This same observation was made by clinicians working with adult schizophrenics. Their parents, too, seemed to have a tremendous ongoing influence on their behaviour and adjustment. Improvement gradually and tediously achieved in the hospital might be undone by a weekend at home. Thus, it became clear that both parents and siblings should be involved in the treatment. Individual treatment of each family member would, of course, be too costly. However, the development of group therapy showed the feasibility of multiple treatment. This possibility was seized upon, and the family therapy movement began.

As with individual and group therapy, numerous theories to explain family interaction patterns and systems for family therapy have been developed. Also, in a parallel manner, the differences are much greater in theory than in practice. All the therapies consider the family interaction pattern to be at the core of the pathology of any one member. Families develop a variety of rules governing their interactions, many of which are covert.

These rules cover such things as the expression of emotion, roles and responsibilities of family members, and communication patterns. All these aspects of family interaction reach a homeostatic level or style, which governs the functioning of all family members. In disturbed families, this homeostasis is pathological and prevents the healthy growth and adaptation of individual members. For example, some families exist by having a "sick child." Parents rationalise or ignore their poor relationship by identifying the child as the source of all family distress. The child, on the other hand, can avoid certain unacceptable feelings or responsibilities by being a "problem." Siblings can discount their own failings by blaming their rotten (or sick) brother or sister. Thus, the disturbed child plays a necessary role in the family's adjustment precisely by being disturbed.

Fox (1976) has identified three broad goals of family therapy, each of which is emphasised differently by various theorists: (1) strengthening the family system, (2) increasing separation—individuation, and (3) strengthening the marriage.

In strengthening the family system, the primary strategy is to improve communication between members and change pathological interaction patterns (e.g., maintaining the sick child). For example, the Palo Alto group of family therapists (Gregory Bateson, Don Jackson, Jay Haley) has emphasised the role of *double bind* communications in disturbed families. Family members (especially the mother) send complex messages to one another in which the overt and covert elements contradict one another. Compliance with one part of the message required noncompliance with another part. The recipient of the message is punished for noncompliance *in either case,* and is thus in a "double bind." For example, the mother might ask a child to provide a affection, yet turn away when the child reaches out and then complain if no further affection is offered. The goal of therapy would be to clarify this process and teach family members to respond consistently in verbal and non-verbal ways and on both overt and covert levels.

Increased separation-individuation refers to the growth and development of individual family members. While the immediate focus of treatment is improved family functioning, this ultimately requires (and facilitates) the individuality and independence of each member. Murray Bowen (1966) views the lack of individuation as a primary factor in disturbed family adjustments. He tries to facilitate personal growth and improve the family system by reducing each member's dependence on the family, and especially, its pathological homeostasis.

The third goal, strengthening the marriage, comes from the observation (and assumption) that a disturbed marital relationship is often the basis of broader family pathology. The classic example here is the couple that remains married "for the children's sake." This naturally produces hidden conflict and distorted interaction patterns. Children's symptoms (e.g., depression, phobias, aggression) often disappear once the parental relationship is improved. Couples therapy is a common variant of family therapy in which the children are not included. Sexual problems, as well as more general family matters and communication patterns, are often part of couples therapy.

Family therapists, as a group, are much more active and demonstrative than most dynamic individual or group therapists. This is partially because the family comes to treatment with an established interaction pattern which the therapist must interfere. Also, there is a greater emphasis on changing ongoing interaction patterns. Awareness, insight, and understanding are generally viewed as less important than directly changing the family's behaviour. Therefore, there is less need for the therapist to sit back and allow the family members to cognitively appraise their situation and free-associate. In fact, such a tactic would simply encourage the ingrained pathological interactions.

Beels and Ferber (1969) see family therapists as *conductors* and *reactors.* Conductors, such as Ackerman, Satir, and Bowen, actively direct and structure therapy. All communication flows through them as they challenge, confront and manipulate family members. Reactors exert control as well, but in more subtle, often covert fashion. Zuk (1967) has coined the term "go-between" to describe this role. The therapist serves as a mediator or negotiator between family members, often stimulating conflict or temporarily taking sides in an effort to modify the interaction pattern. Beels and Ferber divide reactors in two groups: *analysts* and *system purists.* The analysts, including Wynne and Whitaker, are the most traditionally psychoanalytic family therapists. They often work in male-female co-therapy teams so as to facilitate transference reactions and avoid becoming too enmeshed in the family. They place more emphasis on insight and individual anxieties and defences than do other family therapists. System purists, such as the Palo Alto group, place primary emphasis on current relationships and communication patterns. As stated above, insight is seen as unnecessary; changing interaction patterns is viewed as the sole concern.

The actual process of family therapy includes various techniques. Family members role-play each other or different roles. In order to change communication patterns, they are directed to remain silent, sit on the side, or even observe the interaction from an adjoining room. Dyadic or triadic interactions may occur, or the therapist may talk to or challenge a single family member. Homework assignments, such as to spend time together without talking, are common. With their open, active, and "anything goes" style, family therapists are often called "happy exhibitionists" (Lecker, 1976). perhaps more than with any other group of practitioners, their work is more an expression of their individual style than of any systematic theoretical perspective.

EMPIRICAL EVALUATION

We have described clinical psychology as an applied science and identified psychotherapy as the major area of applied work. Thus, one would expect psychotherapeutic practices to be based on a long history of carefully controlled research. Unfortunately, that is not the case. Despite three decades of research efforts, we still know very little about how therapy works, or for whom, or even if it works. The material presented earlier in this chapter represents the experience and wisdom of many astute clinicians. However, very little of it is based on research or supported by empirical analysis. Instead, the various techniques and theories are based mainly on inference, intuition, and agreement among practitioners.

The reasons for this range from the economic security provided by traditional practices to the need to provide immediate help to troubled persons. The greatest limitation is the complexity of the subject matter and the tremendous difficulty of conducting valid research. This final section of the chapter will focus or research on the outcome of psychotherapy: Does it work? Reflecting the state of the art, we will emphasise the problems rather than answer the question.

At first glance, an outcome study appears to present no problem at all: recruit some persons, test them, give half of them treatment, test them again, and see if those who received treatment fared better than those who did not. In fact, that is the basic outcome design. However, major questions involve the types of persons to recruit, the types of tests (i.e., dependent measures) to administer, the therapists to employ, the form of therapy to use, the types of control groups required, and interpretation of results.

Subjects

Clinicians beginning with Freud have realised that not everyone responds well to psychotherapy. Some persons do not profit from the experience, even after many attempts with various therapists. Others actually seem to be harmed by psychotherapy, leaving with greater distress than when they began (Bergin, 1971). Still others simply dislike therapy and terminate before it has a chance to work. In fact, some data suggest that the majority of patients simply fail to return after five to eight sessions (Garfield, 1971). However, little is known about what kinds of persons benefit most from treatment. Much research has focused on the characteristics of successful and unsuccessful persons. There appears to be general support for the YAVIS pattern first identified by Schofield (1964). Successful patients tend to be young, attractive, verbal, intelligent, and successful. Psychotherapy appears to work better with middle—and upper-class persons than for those in the lower class. Persons beginning treatment with high motivation and high expectation for change do better than those who do not. Psychotherapy in general is not effective with schizophrenics (Bergin and Suinn, 1975). Finally, persons who are not extremely disturbed yet are experiencing severe anxiety or depression seem to do better than those who are highly disturbed or are not experiencing acute distress.

There are many possible explanations for this pattern. Psychotherapy is a tedious, painful process requiring time, money, verbal skill, and the ability to introspect and integrate information. Thus, to be successful persons may require enough distress to justify the pain of self-exploration, enough "ego strength" to withstand it, and the time, money, and verbal skills to participate. In addition, they must understand what the process involves (Frank, 1978). Those (including many lower socio-economic persons) who expect the "doctor" to do all the work often drop out or do very poorly. On the other hand, he attributes of the successful client might be required more by the therapist than by the nature of psychotherapy. That is, verbal middle—and upper-class therapists might like to work with persons who are like them, who are pleasant and easy to work with, and who are cooperative and motivated to change. Positive outcomes for such patients may simply reflect more effective therapist efforts and/or a halo effect in therapist judgments (e.g., therapists see improved persons as more verbal, attractive, and motivated). Further research is needed to identify patient characteristics which predict success with specific types of procedures.

Dependent Measures

The measures to be used in assessing therapeutic change have been a major source of controversy. Kazdin and Wilson (1978a) identify three problems: the manner of assessment, the source of data, and the generality or specificity of the assessment. The *manner* of assessment refers to the type of procedure employed, such as projective tests, interviews, or observation of overt behaviour. A major source of disagreement stems from theoretical differences about the nature of pathology and the goals of therapy. Classic psychoanalysts tend to regard changes in overt behaviour and self-reports as superficial; hence, assessment must tap psychodynamics. Conversely, many family therapists and ego psychologists target overt behaviour and changes (and assessment) at that level are more relevant.

Data about the effects of therapy can come from three sources: the individual, the therapist, and outside observers (e.g., family members, independent judges). The individual is the best judge of his or her own subjective feeling state. But such judgments about improvement are often biased, and self-reports often do not relate to independent judgments of behaviour. Because of his or her close involvement with the client, the therapist should be an excellent judge of change, especially at the intrapsychic level. However, therapists are generally as biased as their clients, and therapist ratings have also been shown to differ widely from independent judgments. While independent ratings thus would seem to be ideal, it has been argued that only the client and therapist know what the critical issues are and whether they have been resolved. Thus, although independent ratings may be objective, they fail to assess the relevant factors (Luborsky, 1971). For example, a wife might think her husband's primary difficulty is alcoholism, yet the husband

and therapist might believe that a more basic issue is the feeling of inadequacy which stimulates drinking—something of which the wife is unaware.

The question of generality versus specificity of ratings involves many similar issues. Specific ratings (e.g., work performance, test scores, episodes of drunkenness) can be objective and represent particular aspects of functioning, but they cannot present a broad picture of the client's adjustment and sense of well-being. General measures often take the form "Much improved," "Slightly improved," "Not improved." Such measures can represent feeling states and the overall balance of various aspects of the client's adjustment, but they are highly susceptible to bias and distortion (e.g., halo effects) Garfield et al., 1971).

These controversies about assessment strategies are critical because they severely confound the interpretation of research results. A particularly study can be viewed as supportive, unsupportive, or irrelevant depending on the dependent measures included and the changes in these measures. For example, Paul (1966) found that a behaviour therapy group was most effective on the basis of physiological and behavioural measures of change, but that behaviour therapy, psychotherapy, and control groups all improved equally on self-report measures. Does this mean that all persons showed meaningful decreases in subjective distress, or that the self-report measures were biased and invalid? Numerous recommendations have been made about how the effects of psychotherapy should be assessed. However, the only point of agreement is that a battery of measures is required, covering various aspects of client functioning and sources of information.

Therapists

Psychotherapy is an intense interpersonal activity whose course cannot be planned by a simple, step-by-step blueprint. The moment-to-moment flow of communication depends largely on the particular client and therapist. Obviously, the therapist plays a critical role in the outcome of therapy. Summarising the literature, Luborsky et al. (1971) conclude that more experienced therapists generally produce better results than less experienced ones, and that therapists judged (by colleagues) to be skilful generally have greater success than those judged less skilful.

Unfortunately, therapists simply do not vary from good to excellent; they range from harmful to helpful. Bergin (1971) found that up to 10 per cent of persons in psychotherapy actually deteriorated during treatment. Some were getting worse before they entered treatment and may have been untreatable. However, Bergin concludes that some were deteriorating but could have been helped if their therapists were not "inept," while others were actually made worse by an inept therapist who disturbed a neurotic equilibrium. These findings have major implications for society given the confidence placed in mental health professionals. They also have more specific implications in regard to out discussion of outcome research. Some critics argue that the effects of therapy should be judged on the basis of the average patient and the average therapist (i.e., what can the average person expect?). Others believe that a fair evaluation requires only good therapists working with appropriate patients (cf. Luborsky, Singer, and Luborsky, 1975) (what is the best that can be achieved?). This disagreement is another factor which confounds interpretation of outcome research. In addition, experienced, highly skilled therapists are often unavailable for participation in research studies. Most outcome research has been conducted with graduate students or relatively inexperienced professionals as therapists.

Type of Therapy

Earlier in this chapter we described many variations of individual therapy, group therapy, and family therapy. Outcome research generally suggests that these variations are roughly equal in effectiveness. However, the literature is flawed by many methodological inadequacies. No series of well-controlled studies has evaluated any particular type of therapy, let alone systematically compared diverse approaches. In addition, it seems likely, on an intuitive basis, that different types of persons would profit from different types of treatment. Specific client-therapist-therapy matches have not yet been adequately identified or tested.

Nonspecific Factors in Therapy

Any treatment procedure, psychological or otherwise, must be evaluated on a relative basis. It makes little sense to say that a certain percentage of persons receiving some treatment improve when we do not know how many would improve with no treatment of with some alternative. Thus, the question becomes, how effective is psychotherapy compared to other treatments or no treatments? This issue is highlighted by the classic papers of Hans J. Eysenck (1952; 1965). Reviewing the outcome literature, he concluded that psychotherapy had an average success rate of 67 per cent. However, Eysenck also attempted to ascertain the amount of recovery which could be expected without treatment *spontaneous remission.*

One of the most notable critics is Bergin (1971), who argues that spontaneous remission rates are really between 30 and 50 per cent. "He also indicates that 10 per cent of persons deteriorate, reducing the average" change rate for all treated subjects. Thus, about 80 per cent improve with treatment while only 30 to 50 per cent improve without it. Bergin also questions the term "spontaneous remission," with its implication that improvement simply occurs with no rhyme or reason. Rather, he suggests, many distressed individuals who are not in therapy receive informal treatment elsewhere.

Religious counselling, as well as help from family physicians, friends, and relatives, are all potential sources of therapeutic aid. These sources are also used by persons in the waiting list control groups included in most outcome studies. By implication, subjects in such groups cannot be assumed to be "untreated."

A related issue is the role of specific and nonspecific factors in therapy. It is widely agreed that a significant part of psychotherapy is a group of so-called "nonspecific factors" which relate more to the general nature of the interaction than to anything the therapist does. These include: the act of admitting a problem and seeking help, expectation of change, being understood and accepted, talking about one's problems, and having someone warmly listen.

Many of these factors are often called a *placebo* effect. In contrast to the stereotype of the placebo as a useless "sugar pill." Jerome Frank (1978), among others, regards placebo effects as crucial in the effectiveness of psychotherapy.

The presence of these factors in all forms of therapy may well explain why their effectiveness is about equal (cf. Luborsky et al., 1975). The placebo effect may also explain why posttreatment differences between treated and untreated subjects seem to disappear over time.

Untreated therapy simply provides a more concentrated lose of the placebo factors than does the environment, rather than providing something unique. If so, therapy may simply speed up change rather than produce more change or a different type of change than would otherwise occur.

COGNITIVE BEHAVIOURAL THERAPY WITH OLDER ADULTS

CBT is used to help people of all ages, but the therapy should be adjusted based on the age of the patient with which the therapist is dealing. Older individuals in particular have certain characteristics that need to be acknowledged and the therapy altered to account for these differences thanks to age. Some of the challenges to CBT because of age include the following:

The Cohort Effect

The times that each generation lives through partially shape their thought processes as well as values, so a 70 year-old may react very differently to the therapy than a 30 year-old, because of the different culture they were brought up in. A tie-in to this effect is that each generation has to interact with one another, and the differing values clashing with one another may make the therapy more difficult.

Established Role

By the time one reaches old age, the person has a definitive idea of their role in life and is invested in that role. This social role can dominate who the person thinks they are and may make it difficult to adapt to the changes required in CBT therapy.

Mentality toward Aging

If the older individual sees aging itself as a negative, this can exacerbate whatever malady the therapy is trying to help (depression and anxiety for example).

Processing Speed Decreases

As we age, we take longer to learn new information, and as a result may take more time to learn and retain the cognitive therapy. Therefore, therapists should slow down the pacing of the therapy and use any tools both written and verbal that will improve the retention of the cognitive behavioural therapy.

Later Age Hardships

Problems that are found more in later life versus dealing with younger individuals, such as chronic illness, disability, and grief from loss of loved ones, can also affect the patient's mentality and greatly influence the work and efficacy of any CBT therapy.

Computer-based therapy

Computerized Cognitive Behavioural Therapy (CCBT) has been described by NICE as a "generic term for delivering CBT via an interactive computer interface delivered by a personal computer, internet, or interactive voice response system", instead of face-to-face with a human therapist. While it cannot replace face-to-face therapy, this can provide an option for patients, especially in light of prohibitive costs and lack of availability associated with retaining a human therapist. A relatively new avenue of research is the combination of artificial intelligence and CCBT. It has been proposed to use modern technology to create CCBT that simulates face-to-face therapy. This might be achieved in cognitive behaviour therapy for a specific disorders using the comprehensive domain knowledge of CBT.One area where this has been attempted, is the specific domain area of social anxiety in those who stutter.

Randomized controlled trials have, however, proven the effectiveness of CCBT in treating depression and anxiety disorders, and in February 2006 NICE recommended that CCBT be made available for use within the NHS across England and Wales for patients presenting with mild-to-moderate depression, rather than immediately opting for antidepressant medication. The 2009 NICE guideline recognized that there are likely to be a number of computerized CBT products that are useful to patients. They have, however, removed their endorsement of any specific product.

HISTORY

Behaviour therapy roots

Precursors of certain fundamental aspects of CBT have been identified in various ancient philosophical traditions, particularly Stoicism. For example, Aaron T. Beck's original treatment manual for depression states, "The philosophical origins of cognitive therapy can be traced back to the Stoic philosophers". The modern roots of CBT can be traced to the development of behaviour therapy in the early 20th century, the development of cognitive therapy in the 1960s, and the subsequent merging of the two. Behaviorally-centred therapeutic approaches appeared as early as 1924 with Mary Cover Jones' work on the unlearning of fears in children. In 1937, American psychiatrist Abraham Low developed cognitive training techniques for patient aftercare following psychiatric hospitalization.

It was during the period 1950 to 1970 that behavioural therapy became widely utilized by researchers in the United States, the United Kingdom, and South Africa, who were inspired by the behaviourist learning theory of Ivan Pavlov, John B. Watson, and Clark L. Hull. In Britain, this work was mostly focused on the neurotic disorders through the work of Joseph Wolpe, who applied the findings of animal experiments to his method of systematic desensitization, the precursor to today's fear reduction techniques. British psychologist Hans Eysenck, inspired by the writings of Karl Popper, criticized psychoanalysis in arguing that "if you get rid of the symptoms, you get rid of the neurosis", and presented behaviour therapy as a constructive alternative. In the United States, psychologists were applying the radical behaviorism of B. F. Skinner to clinical use. Much of this work was concentrated on severe chronic psychiatric disorders, such as psychotic behaviour and autism.

Other Roots

Although the early behavioural approaches were successful in many of the neurotic disorders, they had little success in treating depression. Behaviorism was also losing in popularity due to the so-called "cognitive revolution". The therapeutic approaches of Albert Ellis and Aaron T. Beck gained popularity among behaviour therapists, despite the earlier behaviourist rejection of "mentalistic" concepts like thoughts and cognitions. Both of these systems included behavioural elements and interventions and primarily concentrated on problems in the present. Albert Ellis' system, originated in the early 1950s, was first called rational therapy, and can (arguably) be called one of the first forms of cognitive behavioural therapy. It was partly founded as a reaction against popular psychotherapeutic theories at the time (mainly psychoanalysis). Beck, inspired by Ellis, developed cognitive therapy in the 1960s. Beck describes his therapeutic approach as originating in a realization he made while conducting free association with patients in the context of classical psychoanalysis. He noted that patients had not been reporting certain thoughts at the fringe of consciousness-thoughts which often preceded intense emotional reactions. This realization led Beck to begin viewing emotional reactions as resulting from *cognitions,* rather than understanding emotion within the abstract psychoanalytic framework. He named these cognitions "automatic thoughts" because he believed that people were not necessarily aware that the cognitions existed, but that they could identify these types of thoughts when questioned closely. Beck believed that pushing his clients to identify these automatic thoughts was integral to overcoming a particular difficulty.

In initial studies, cognitive therapy was often contrasted with behavioural treatments to see which was most effective. During the 1980s and 1990s, cognitive and behavioural techniques were merged into cognitive behavioural therapy. Pivotal to this merging was the successful development of treatments for panic disorder by David M. Clark in the UK and David H. Barlow in the US.

Starting in the late 1950s and continuing through the 1970s, concurrently with the contributions of Ellis and Beck, Arnold A. Lazarus developed what was arguably the first form of "broad-spectrum" cognitive behavioural therapy. He later broadened the focus of behavioural treatment to incorporate cognitive aspects. Lazarus, seeking to optimize the efficacy of therapy and effect durable treatment using cognitive and behavioural methods, developed a new form of therapy called multimodal therapy, based on CBT, but also including interpersonal relationships, biological factors, physical sensations (as distinct from emotional states), and visual images (as distinct from language-based thinking).

Samuel Yochelson and Stanton Samenow pioneered the idea that cognitive behavioural approaches can be used successfully with a population of criminal offenders.

SCHIZOPHRENIA, PSYCHOSIS AND MOOD DISORDERS

Cognitive behavioural therapy has been shown as an effective treatment for clinical depression. The American Psychiatric Association Practice Guidelines (April 2000) indicated that, among psychotherapeutic approaches, cognitive behavioural therapy and interpersonal psychotherapy had the best-documented efficacy for treatment of major depressive disorder. One etiological theory of depression isAaron T. Beck's cognitive theory of depression. His theory states that depressed people think the way they do because their thinking is biased towards negative interpretations. According to this theory, depressed people acquire a negative schema of the world in childhood and adolescence as an effect of stressful life events, and the negative schema is activated later in life when the person encounters similar situations.

Beck also described a negative cognitive triad, made up of the negative schemata and cognitive biases of the person, theorizing that depressed individuals make negative evaluations of themselves, the world, and the future. Depressed people, according to this theory, have views such as, "I never do a good job", "It is impossible to have a good day", and "things will never get better." A negative schema helps give rise to the cognitive bias, and the cognitive bias helps fuel the negative schema. This is the negative triad. Beck further proposed that depressed people often have the following cognitive biases: arbitrary inference, selective abstraction, over-generalization, magnification, and minimization. These cognitive biases are quick to make negative, generalized, and personal inferences of the self, thus fuelling the negative schema.

In long-term psychoses, CBT is used to complement medication and is adapted to meet individual needs. Interventions particularly related to these conditions include exploring reality testing, changing delusions and hallucinations, examining factors which precipitate relapse, and managing relapses. Several meta-analyses have shown CBT to be effective in schizophrenia, and the American Psychiatric Association includes CBT in its schizophrenia guideline as an evidence-based treatment. There is also some (limited) evidence of effectiveness for CBT in bipolar disorder and severe depression.

A 2010 meta-analysis found that no trial employing both blinding and psychological placebo has shown CBT to be effective in either schizophrenia or bipolar disorder, and that the effect size of CBT was small in major depressive disorder. They also found a lack of evidence to conclude that CBT was effective in preventing relapses in bipolar disorder. Evidence that severe depression is mitigated by CBT is also lacking, with anti-depressant medications still viewed as significantly more effective than CBT, although success with CBT for depression was observed beginning in the 1990s.

Chronic Fatigue Syndrome

CBT has been shown to be moderately effective for treating chronic fatigue syndrome.

VARIATIONS OF VERBAL PSYCHOTHERAPY

Psychotherapy, in one form or another, has probably been practiced since human languages developed. Sympathetic listening, suggestion, exhortation, and confession have all been used throughout history to reduce depression, fear, anxiety, and ambivalence.

However, systematic verbal psychotherapy as we now know it can be traced back to she creative genius of Sigmund Freud in the late nineteenth century. Freud began work with Charcot and then Breur, employing hypnotism to alleviate hysterical symptoms. He soon discovered that hypnotism had two major failings. First, many potential patients could not be hypnotised; second, hypnotic "cures" did not prevent the occurrence of new symptoms. In his search for an alternative, Freud discovered that the illness could also be treated by having patients talk freely and extensively about themselves, their feelings, their lives, and anything else that came to mind. This procedure developed into the "talking cure": psychoanalysis.

With psychoanalysis as a model and stimulus, many different forms of psychotherapy have been developed over the years. Like psychoanalysis, most of them have evolved from theories of personality. Most personality theories have different conceptions of human nature, of psychological health, and of psychopathology and its development.

These conceptions typically dictate specific goals for treatment, as well as the therapeutic process by which change can be achieved and the goals reached. Thus. Freud viewed early childhood experiences as crucial to further development, and psychoanalysis focuses on uncovering repressed memories of those experiences. Alfred Adler considered feelings of inferiority to be a critical factor in neuroses; his therapy, therefore, aims at rectifying those feelings and altering the life style which evolved to compensate for them. These various theories of personality and therapy are usually referred to as "schools," under the name of its creator—e.g., Rogerian, Adlerian, Sullivanian, Freudian.

Unfortunately, these diverse positions are often viewed as religious, each being seen as the only and final answer to all problems. If one attempted to compare these models based on the writing of their most zealous adherents (who are often the most prolific as well), they would each appear to be quite different in many critical ways. However, the differences are more apparent in terminology than in actual therapeutic practice (Weiner. 1976). Furthermore, the adherents of the various schools do not all practice the same way. Wolberg (1967) has suggested that the variations *within* schools are often greater than those *between* schools. Consequently, these self-applied labels do not reflects real differences between approaches.

Psychoanalysis

Classic psychoanalysis is the model for most current psychotherapies. This approach was developed over many years by Freud as he sought to understand and modify human behaviour. The ideas and procedures of psychoanalysis have remained relatively unchanged since his death in 1939. Despite the incursions and modifications made by the neo-Freudian and psychodynamic therapies, classic psychoanalysis retains much influence, prestige, and something of a mystique.

According to Freud, the seeds of neurosis are planted in childhood, when the child fails to pass successfully through the oral, anal, or phallic stages of development. As a result of conflict, trauma, overindulgence, or underindulgence, the child becomes fixated at some level. Unacceptable impulses are repressed, and various defence mechanisms are employed to keep them under control.

The defensive network gradually expands and solidifies, and it becomes more and more difficult to deal with new life experiences and normal day-to-day environmental stresses. By the time a full-blown neurosis develops, a substantial part of life experience has been repressed, and the individual is still plagued by anxiety, guilt, and the like. The task of psychoanalysis is to make the person aware of the repressed material, recognise that it is a harmless residue of childhood fears and confusion, and thus accept the feelings and end the defensive process. As a result, the person would then be more open to experience and better able to function, while the major symptoms and distress would be eliminated.

Free Association. The primary tool of psychoanalysis is *free association;* the person is told to talk about whatever comes to mind. He or she can follow any train of thought, discuss any experience, person, or feeling. The stream of association moves from one topic to another, sometimes dealing with important issues, other times not. Periodically the person touches on a focal issue which is close to the defensive structure or the depressed material. Early in therapy, these critical associations are infrequent. Also, they produce great distress and can be considered only briefly. However, over time the person becomes more and more capable of considering such highly sensitive material, and the association stream moves closer and closer to deeply repressed issues.

Interpretation. Of course, if the process were limited to free association, the patient could do this therapy alone. The therapist serves two critical functions, without which the treatment could not work. First, he or she helps the associative process along by making periodic *interpretations.* These are statements which relate various aspects of the person's behaviour, explain something, provide new information which helps to clarify the association, or point out something of which the person was unaware. Interpretations can range from simple declarative statements such as, "You're angry about that!" to questions such as, "Is that what you really want to do?" to mini speeches. Regardless of their specific form, they are designed to move the patient in the direction of unconscious material.

The proper use of interpretation is the therapist's greatest and most difficult responsibility. First of all, the interpretation must be *accurate.* The therapist must have tremendous insight into the person's thoughts and feelings, as well as considerable knowledge about behaviour and psychopathology, to know what a particular response means.

Second, the interpretation must be *timed* properly. Unless the person is ready to hear and consider the material, it can break a train of thought and temporarily disrupt the whole course of therapy. Finally, the interpretation must be of the right level or *depth.* That is, it must present something that is just slightly beyond the person's current level of understanding. If it deals with material which is still too threatening, it will be ignored or perhaps arouse too much distress and interfere with progress. Conversely, it must do more than repeat what the person already knows. The effective interpretation leads but does not push.

The goal of both free association and interpretation is to promote *insight:* understanding and acceptance of unconscious material. The terms "insight" and "interpretation" are deceptively simple. Many nonprofessionals assume that the therapist sits back "analysing" the patient, and then suddenly makes one brilliant interpretation which gets right to the heart of the problem, such as "Aha, you really hated it when your mother bathed you, and that is why you have a phobia for water!" The patient then has a sudden burst of insight after which all troubles vanish; the so-called "aha" experience makes everything clear. In reality, the process of therapy is exceedingly slow and irregular. It involves many small steps, including frequent dead ends and periods of backsliding, when progress is reversed. A complete analysis can require three to five years of treatment, with five sessions per week.

The session-by-session progress in therapy involves a process known as *working through* (Hartley and Strupp, 1980). The therapist's interpretations are often repeated, rephrased, and directed to different situations, experiences, and associations which have some common element. The person sometimes rejects the interpretation and sometimes accepts part of it; rarely is it totally understood and accepted at any one time. Gradually the person begins to understand, and then to accept what is understood. Even at that point, the process is not complete. At its ultimate, insight involves the ability to generalise and to apply understanding to various new experiences, as well as to be aware of the childhood sources of distress. Thus, by the end of treatment, the person can provide his or her own interpretations, explaining feelings and behaviour and identifying the sources of new distress.

Transference. The therapist, we have said, serves two critical functions, the first being interpretation. The second involves facilitating and helping the person work through a *transference neurosis.* The neurotic person employs various defences to control anxiety, guilt, and id impulses. These defences result in some distortion of reality. This distortion occurs with the analyst in therapy, in the same manner as with other people in other situations. For example, a person who uses projection might see the analyst—rather than the self—as angry. This process is known as *transference.* Transference is not simply recognised by the analyst but is deliberately fostered. The person lies on a couch while the analyst is seated behind, out of sight. (This position is designed to facilitate the associative process.) The analyst remains almost anonymous, avoiding many of the usual social amenities before and after sessions and remaining relatively silent during sessions. Interpretations are made infrequently. The therapist is relatively passive, providing a blank screen for the person to play against. Faced with this relative vacuum, the person is free to create a picture of what the analyst is like. This picture is distorted by the defensive processes. Furthermore, because the person is steeped in associations to unconscious and emotionally charged material, the analyst becomes involved in these matters. Eventually the entire neurosis is re-created with the analyst as focus: the transference neurosis. For example, the person might begin to see the analyst as a rejecting parent, critical of his or her achievements. Or the analyst might become the focus of sexual urges and a fantasied sexual object. It would be difficult for the analyst to get the person to see how he or she is distorting experience outside of sessions; after all, the analyst is not there and does not know the person's family, friends, and other important objects. However, the transference reaction can be interpreted more easily precisely because the person knows that the analyst it not a parent or lover, and is not critical, seductive, angry, and so on. Thus, the person gains insight into the distortion and its motivation by working through the transference neurosis. This insight is then generalised to behaviour and people outside of the analyst's office. This process is the core of psychoanalysis (Wolberg, 1967).

Countertransference. Just as the person brings his or her conflicts, anxieties, and defences to therapy, so too does the therapist come to the office with family problems, financial concerns, and psychological difficulties. While ideally the therapist's personality and problems should remain apart from the therapy, this is not always the case. In a manner analogous to transference, the therapist sometimes distorts the person's behaviour and feelings and responds to things other than the material itself. This process can be a mild interference with misinterpretation of certain communications, such as failure to perceive anger or inability to recognise certain types of conflicts. Or, at the other extreme, the therapist can develop strong emotional reactions to the patient, including hostility and sexual arousal. In either case, this process is called *Countertransference* and interferes with treatment. The major strategy for dealing with countertransference is for the therapist to have his or her own psychoanalysis. In fact, a personal analysis is a requirement and one of the major training vehicles for prospective analysts. In this way, the therapist eliminates most of his or her own conflicts and defensive blind spots, and is thus more open to the diverse materials presented. In addition, the therapist can examine his or her own emotional reactions to the person and use them as clues to the effect on others.

Resistance. Psychotherapy, of any form, is a necessarily painful and threatening process. The person must continually deal with highly stressful issues: feelings of inadequacy and guilt, terrifying anxiety unacceptable urges, and emotional reactions. In addition, change itself is a terrifying prospect. Even though the person's current adjustment is painful and unsatisfactory, it is nevertheless an adjustment. Things might be worse. And so, persons approach each therapy session with ambivalence and trepidation.

Sometimes they overcome these feelings and come to grips with the difficult issues, but at other times they avoid them. This avoidance, which is largely an unconscious process, is called *resistance.* Resistance can take many forms. The person might miss a session or come late when therapy is focusing on an especially painful issue. Free association can be stymied as the person reports that nothing comes to mind. Conversely, irrelevant material or issues might be raised, including complaints about the therapist. The therapist's bills may go unpaid, or the accuracy of interpretations may be denied. As with transference, resistance is a potential form of interference which can be turned into a valuable therapeutic tool. The therapist carefully monitors resistive behaviour, identifies its source or motivation, and eventually interprets them to the person. Ultimately, the interpretation of resistance and the associated unconscious processes is one of the most important activities of psychoanalysis (Fine, 1973).

Neo-Freudian and Ego Psychology Approaches

Almost from the beginning of the analytic movement, many of Freud's followers began to question his theory and therapeutic strategy. These questions have ranged from rather esoteric points to basic issues, and have led to corresponding changes in theory and technique. In this section, we will consider some of the more important changes which have been adopted by various analytic therapies. Weiner (1976) has distinguished between therapeutic strategies and tactics. *Strategies* are the guiding principles which determine the direction of therapy: its goals and the plans for reaching them (e.g., stimulating a transference neurosis). *Tactics* are the procedures and techniques used to implement the strategy (e.g., making interpretations, asking questions). We will first consider modifications in strategy and then innovations in tactics.

Therapeutic Strategies. Human behaviour, according to Freud, is rooted in biological factors, especially instinctual (id) drives. The most important of these is Eros: sexuality. The major "psychological" factor in behaviour is the ego, which is more a servant of the id than an independent force. The environment, like the ego is of secondary importance. Its primary influence is negative or repressive and is exerted during childhood. Neurosis is considered to be largely a result of society's inhibition of the expression of sexuality. Thus, the primary therapeutic strategies are designed to uncover and free the instinctual drives. Little attention is paid to the person's current environment or to any nondefensive aspects of the ego. Freud's emphasis on sexuality (and biological factors in general), and his relative neglect of the ego and environmental influences on behaviour, have been the subject of considerable criticism from within the analytic camp (as well as from other orientations).

Two of Freud's earliest critics were Jung and Adler, both of whom felt that he placed far too much emphasis on sexuality. Jung hypothesised that human beings had a *collective or inherited unconscious* in addition to the personal unconscious emphasised by Freud. One of the major goals of Jungian analysis is to foster insight into both types of unconscious forces and facilitate an accommodation between both of them and the environment (Weiner, 1976). Adler argued that all people are born with feelings of *inferiority* and *helplessness*. In an attempt to compensate for these anxiety-provoking feelings, they strive for superiority and develop unique life styles to deal with environmental demands and pressures. Adlerian therapy emphasises the person's current life situation and the way that situation affects and is affected by the life style. Interpretations focus on the ongoing interaction between inferiority feelings, life style, and daily events: accomplishments, failures, relationships with others, and so on.

Among those who criticised Freud for his comparative disregard of social and environmental influences on behaviour, Harry Stack Sullivan, Karen Homey, and Erich Fromm are the most representative. While their particular theories and emphases varied, all three highlighted the central role of *social* factors in shaping adult as well as early childhood behaviour. For example. Homey described how the neurotic adapts a defensive posture characterised by moving toward people away from people, or against people in an effort to curtail and avoid anxiety. Thus, an analysis based on one of these models would emphasise current interpersonal functioning. Interpretations would focus on conflicts between the person, the environment, and defensive interpersonal style, rather than on intrapsychic conflicts and drives.

Probably the most significant modification of Freudian theory has come from the *ego psychologists,* including Erikson, Hartmann, Kris, and Loewenstein. According to these theorists, the ego is independent of the id rather than its servant. The ego has its own energy and functions, including thinking, remembering, perceiving, and conscious awareness. All behaviour is not motivated by drive reduction; instead, the ego has its own sources of gratification and motivation, such as love, creativity, and achievement.

The healthy adult is not bound by unconscious instinctual forces but has a good deal of conscious control over behaviour and strives to grow and improve. The personality is not solidified by puberty; instead, growth and development continue throughout life. The neurotic individual is characterised by poor ego development. Like children, neurotics are much more under the control of instincts and the environment. Thus, they are less capable of determining the course of their lives and fulfilling their potential.

Treatment based on an ego psychology model strives to strengthen the ego and increase the degree of conscious and adaptive control over behaviour. In keeping with the analogy between the neurotic and the child, Hartley and Strupp (1980) have referred to therapy as "reparenting"; the therapist, like the parent, helps the person to become more independent and capable of functioning effectively. Little attention is paid to historical and instinctual influences on development. The emphasis is on current conflicts and anxieties, and the inadequacy of current coping strategies (Weiner, 1976). The ego analysts, like most other neo-Freudians, stress the transference neurosis less than the classic analysts. Transference is either viewed as an impediment to therapy and quickly resolved or it is interpreted as a reflection of current interpersonal style. In neither case is it facilitated by the therapist or viewed as a critical element of therapy.

Therapy Techniques. The theoretical conceptions of the post-Freudian analysts lead to different ways of thinking about behaviour and of understanding patient reports. As a result, their therapeutic strategies differ greatly. Their techniques, however, are quite similar (Weiner, 1976). As stated previously, there is greater variation between individual therapists than between schools.

One reason for this peculiar pattern is that research has failed to identify a set of specific techniques to be applied in a particular way at a particular time with a particular client. Therapists are left to their own experience and "best guess" as to what to do. Thus it would be quite unusual for two therapists to provide the same interpretation at any point. This fact is dramatised at case conferences and supervision sessions, when recordings of therapy sessions are reviewed. While there is often agreement as to very poor and highly effective interpretations, the middle ground is the area where each listener responds differently.

In reviewing the various psychodynamic techniques, it is difficult to even identify their source, let alone tie them to any particular school. The most notable changes from Freudian procedures probably involve the activity and behaviour of the therapist. Without the need to develop a transference neurosis, the therapist became free of the classic need for passivity and anonymity. Therapist and client now sit face-to-face in armchairs. Some therapists like to sit behind a desk while others prefer a more casual arrangement such as around a coffee table. Style of dress also varies with the person, although coat and tie (for men) and dress or skirt and blouse (for women) predominate. The general tone of the therapist-client relationship is often more relaxed and pleasant. While the use of the title "Dr." is most common, some therapists and clients are on a first name basis. While the therapist's personal life is still usually kept out of the relationship, there is less rigidity about this as well. Pre—and post-session conversation takes on a more social atmosphere, with occasional references to vacation plans, family activities, and attitudes about public events. References to personal experiences (e.g., "You know, I felt that way once") are also sometimes used therapeutically by some therapists. A positive relationship is often attempted, and is used to facilitate therapeutic progress.

Therapy sessions are also marked by greater therapist responsiveness. In addition to interpretations typical responses include questions, clarifications, reflections. exclamations and confrontations (Weiner, 1976). Open-ended and indirect questions are most often employed. Clarifications are responses which move the patient in a certain direction while providing no new information. For example, "That seems to be an important issue; I think we should focus on it some more." Clarifications are similar in effect to indirect questions. Reflections summarise and integrate client responses. They usually involve some feelings the patient has directly or indirectly expressed. Examples include. "You seem to be angry," and "I have the feeling you are afraid of what you might learn." Weiner (1976) defines exclamations as noncommittal response facilitators, including "Mm-hmm," "Uh-huh," and "I see." They convey the therapist's interest and reinforce the topic of conversation. Confrontations give the client new information about his or her behaviour. They typically involve direct, objective statements about specific responses or issues, rather than the non-definitive hypotheses offered in interpretations. For example, "You've been late for the last three sessions, and we need to talk about that," or "You say that it's not important, but I find that hard to believe."

Confrontations are used sparingly because of their potentially threatening or conflict producing nature. They are usually reserved for roadblocks or issues left unresolved by more indirect means.

It is clear that free association is no longer the main form of interaction. The process is much more of a two-way conversation, in contrast to the semimonologue format of classic psychoanalysis. The dialogue moves back and forth between the two participants, although the client still does most of the talking. The topics covered deal much more with current experiences and interpersonal relationships, and with ego-relevant issues (e.g., feelings of competence, the direction of one's life, sources of pleasure). Some therapists (notably Adlerian) give clients homework assignments—for example, to initiate interpersonal activity (Mosak and Dreikurs, 1973).

The nature of a therapeutic interaction can best be portrayed by an example. The following transcript segments are from Wolberg (1967), a prominent therapist and training analyst. The comments in parentheses indicate the nature and purpose of certain therapist responses. The first segment illustrates transference and its interpretation.

Th. It sounds as if you would like to let loose with me, but you are afraid of what my response would be. *(summarising and restating)*

Pt. I get so excited by what is happening here. I feel I'm being held back by needing to be nice. I'd like to blast loose sometimes, but I don't dare.

Th. Because you fear my reaction?

Pt. The worst thing would be that you wouldn't like me. You wouldn't speak to me friendly; you wouldn't smile, you'd feel you can't treat me and discharge me from treatment. But I know this isn't so, I know it.

Th. Where do you think these attitudes come from?

Pt. When I was nine years old, I read a lot about great men in history. I'd quote them and be dramatic. I'd want a sword at my side; I'd dress like an Indian. Mother would scold me. Don't frown, don't talk so much. Sit on your hands, over and over again. I did all kinds of things. I was a naughty child. She told me I'd be hurt. Then at fourteen I fell off a horse and broke my back. I had to be in bed. Mother then told me on the day I went riding not to, that I'd get hurt because the ground was frozen. I was a stubborn, self-willed child. Then I went against her will and suffered an accident that changed my life, a fractured back. Her attitude was, "I told you so." I was put in a cast and kept in bed for months.

Th. You were punished, so to speak, by this accident.

Pt. But I gained attention and love from mother for the first time. I felt so good. I'm ashamed to tell you this. Before I healed I opened the cast and tried to walk to make myself sick again so I could stay in bed longer.

Th. How does that connect up with your impulse to be sick now and stay in bed so much? *(The patient has these tendencies, of which she is ashamed).*

Pt. Oh...*(pause)*

Th. What do you think?

Pt. Oh, my God, how infantile, how ungrown up. *(pause)* It must be so, I want people to love me and be sorry for me. Oh, my God. How completely childish. It is, *is* that. My mother must have ignored me when I was little, and I wanted so to be loved. *(This sounds like insight.)*

Th. So that it may have been threatening to go back to being self-willed and unloved after you got out of the cast. *(interpretation)*

Pt. It did. My life changed. I became meek and controlled. I couldn't get angry or stubborn afterward.

Th. Perhaps if you go back to being stubborn with *me,* you would be returning to how you were before, that is, active stubborn but unloved.

Pt. *(excitedly)* And, therefore, losing your love. I need you, but after all you aren't going to reject me. The pattern is so established now that the threat of the loss of love is too overwhelming with everybody, and I've got to keep myself from acting selfish or angry. (Wolberg, 1967, p. 662)

The patient in the next segment is a woman who began to experience a variety of symptoms after becoming pregnant and quitting her job.

Pt. And on Wednesday I began thinking *(laughs)* The funniest thing happened. I was working in the kitchen and suddenly I got that awful feeling. It came on me like a squirmy wave,. I got scared and tense and the muscles back here *(strokes the muscles in the back of her neck)* got tight and my head filled up as if I had a tight bandage around, and queasy feelings in the pit of my stomach.

Th. Mm hmm.

Pt. And there was something else that happened. I knew something was bothering me and I just didn't know what.

Th. Mm hmm.

Pt. Something bothering. It's like something I had to do supposed to do. It was such a frustrating feeling. *(pause)*

Th. A frustrating feeling, as if you just couldn't grasp what was going on?

Pt. Yes, just like that. So out of desperation, I guess, I turned on the radio. The first thing was one of those breakfast Mr. and Mrs. programmes. They were bantering back and forth, and I detected a snide attitude toward the woman. This made me boil. And all of a sudden the thing flashed in mind. It came to me that I promised my husband that I'd buy him several pairs of socks a week ago. I've been putting if off, and putting it off, and not thinking of it. When I'd go out, it wouldn't occur to me to get the socks until I'd remember when I got home. *(laughs)*

Th. *(smiles)* You suspected something was going on inside of you?

Pt. I knew it. As I was listening to the programme, it came to me. I suddenly got mad, furious and said, "Darn him, why doesn't he buy socks for himself? Why should I do his dirty work?" *(laughs)*

Th. You resented his making this demand on you?

Pt. *(laughs)* No question about that. My next thought *(laughs)*...it was, Damn him, why doesn't he buy socks for *himself.* Why do I have to do *all* the dirty work around here. He wants and expects me to be a slave, just tidy up the place and get nowheres. I thought of him in his nice comfortable office. Then I thought of how wonderful I felt when I was working. At least I felt appreciated and didn't get the constant criticism I get now.

Th. This must really burn you up.

Pt. I suppose marriage is a sacrifice. I do love the children, I don't know what they'd do if I went back to work. But it's the noise, noise, the howling of the kids and the criticism of my husband.

Th. When you were working, you felt you were doing something significant that gave you status.

Pt. You know, doctor, I sometimes feel as if I was absolutely crazy to give up my job. I don't know what I imagined marriage was going to be like.

Th. And it turned out to be something where you have to take care of howling kids and buy socks for your husband.

Pt. You know, as soon as I had these thoughts I got very mad. I screamed out loud, "Why doesn't he buy the socks himself." I had a picture of him *(laughs)* this is silly...slipping on, *(laughs)* slipping on a banana peel and turning a half somersault in the air, I started laughing. Doctor, do I want him to break his neck? When this all happened I noticed that I felt better. My headache went away and the stiffness in the neck. *(Apparently, realisation and acknowledgment of her hostility removed the necessity for its repression and its conversion into symptoms.)*

Before concluding this overview of new-Freudian technique, one further contrast with classic psychoanalysis must be mentioned. As indicated above, classic analysis typically requires five (fifty-minute) sessions per week for several years. This type of intervention obviously is extremely costly in terms of money as well as in a patient and therapist time. Many neu-Freudians have argued that such deep, extensive analysis is of intellectual value rather than a necessity for effective treatment. Many of the modified approaches attempt to speed up the process. Sessions are still often fifty minutes, but longer sessions are not uncommon. Sessions typically are held once or (at most) twice a week, and treatment usually lasts from six months to one to two years. It is presumed that the focus on more current issues and greater therapist activity can produce meaningful change with less intensive and extensive treatment.

A related change involves the timing and nature of termination. Classic analysis continues until all major unconscious conflicts are resolved and the client has relatively complete insight into his or her experience. The briefer neo-Freudian approaches often conclude with less than total personality reorganisation. Given the emphasis on current experience, good adjustment with sufficient ego strength to withstand future stress and to grow after treatment are more typical expectations. In any case, termination is always a painful process, much like the adolescent's leaving home for the first time. The client is eager to try to live independently, yet questions his or her ability to function without the therapist. For this reason, termination is usually a gradual weaning process, requiring several sessions and marked by ambivalence and a sense of loss.

3

Health and Clinical Psychology

New clinic centres were established all over the world. The University of Pennsylvania offered formal courses on clinical psychology in 1904-1905, promoted by Witmer. The first specialized journal, The Psychological Clinical, was founded by Witmer in 1907. This fast growing number of clinical psychologists was one of the most important causes to make the American Psychological Association (APA) split and create the American Association of Clinical Psychologists. However this new association went back to APA as a clinical section in 1919. So, Clinical Psychology creates its own institutions (journals, associations) into the frame of the academic and scientific psychology, mainly represented by University and APA.

World War I impelled the making and application of tests, and promoted clinical psychologists role. On one hand, clinical psychologists developed research and theories on several topics, such as the nature of personality, the origin of intelligence (i.e.: the influence of heritage and environment), the causes of behaviour disorders, the uses of hypnosis, and the link between learning principles and abnormal behaviour. On the other hand, clinical psychologists became more interested in the functions of treatment following diagnosis, re-educational training and research, than in educational problems. In this sense, we must remark that, in the beginning, the therapeutic function was focused on children's disorders, keeping together assessment and treatment tasks. The prestige reached by the use of personality tests such as Rorschach and TAT (Thematic Apperception Test), which made possible a common language between the psychologist (as the clinician assessing) and the psychiatrist (the clinician treating), grately contributed to psychologist's commitment to treatment.

As the number of clinical psychologists increased and their functions were extended, they and other applied psychologists became unsatisfied with the support given by APA colleagues (academicians and scientists most of them) and decided to create a separated organization in 1937: the American

Association of Applied Psychology. Eight years later the new organization was back into APA.

In the late thirties, the field of modern clinical psychology was organized in six main activities: assessment, treatment, research, teaching, counselling and management. At that moment, clinical psychologists have extended their activities further on the first clinics to hospitals, prisons, and other places, aimed to work with children as much as to adults.

In World War II, 40.000 people received attention in the neuropsychiatric hospitals of USA Veteran Administration (VA), a fact which ment a new impulse to consolidate Clinical Psychology. As there were not enough clinical psychologists at that time, the Veteran Administration had to get involved with developing accreditation criteria to become a clinical psychologist, and so it went ahead of APA and University Departments.

Precisely, a VA document made in 1946 defined clinical psychology as "a profession which implies doing diagnosis, treatment and research related to adult disorders". According to this document, clinical psychologists should have a doctor degree to exert their profession (Ph.D.).

This VA's activity (and anothers in USA's public health departments) in developing accreditation criteria prompted to APA and Universities to meet a Committee in order to define programmes of training in clinical psychology and to establish the rules to be followed. The task of this Committee (David Shakow's Committee on Training in Clinical Psychology) was to recommend the programme contents, to establish training criteria, to be followed by Universities, and internship training services, in order to evaluate and report on the current programmes.

Three main recommendations of Shakow's report to clinical training were:

1. First of all, a clinical psychologist would be trained as a psychologist-hence, as a scientist-with practical skills and knowledge.
2. Clinical training should be as strict as in other non-clinical fields of psychology. It should involve the setting up of standards for post-graduate training.
3. The content of clinical training would be focused on assessment, treatment and research.

This proposal of clinical psychologist training, which is called Boulder model on behalf of the place where a Conference was held in 1949 and where this proposal was assumed, is used as a pattern since then. The Boulder model is followed the most, but this does not mean that the former point of view is the only proposal and that there are no others concerned with the scientific contents and thr research role in training programmes. In any case, this development and setting up of clinical psychology as a profession had its legal acknowledgment as well as its own ethical code.

CLINICAL PSYCHOLOGY

Clinical psychology is an integration of science, theory and clinical knowledge for the purpose of understanding, preventing, and relieving psychologically based distress or dysfunction and to promote subjective well-being and personal development. Central to its practice are psychological assessment and psychotherapy, although clinical psychologists also engage in research, teaching, consultation, forensic testimony, and programme development and administration. In many countries, clinical psychology is a regulated mental health profession.

The field is often considered to have begun in 1896 with the opening of the first psychological clinic at the University of Pennsylvania by Lightner Witmer. In the first half of the 20th century, clinical psychology was focused on psychological assessment, with little attention given to treatment. This changed after the 1940s when World War II resulted in the need for a large increase in the number of trained clinicians. Since that time, two main educational models have developed—the Ph.D. scientist-practitioner model (focusing on research) and the Psy.D. practitioner-scholar model (focusing on clinical practice). Clinical psychologists are now considered experts in providing psychotherapy, and generally train within four primary theoretical orientations—psychodynamic, humanistic, behaviour therapy/cognitive behavioural, and systems or family therapy.

History

Although modern, scientific psychology is often dated at the 1879 opening of the first psychological laboratory by Wilhelm Wundt, attempts to create methods for assessing and treating mental distress existed long before. The earliest recorded approaches were a combination of religious, magical and/or medical perspectives. Early examples of such physicians included Patañjali, Padmasambhava, Rhazes, Avicenna, and Rumi. In the early 19th century, one could have his or her head examined, literally, using phrenology, the study of personality by the shape of the skull. Other popular treatments included physiognomy—the study of the shape of the face—and mesmerism, Mesmer's treatment by the use of magnets. Spiritualism and Phineas Quimby's "mental healing" were also popular. While the scientific community eventually came to reject all of these methods, academic psychologists also were not concerned with serious forms of mental illness. That area was already being addressed by the developing fields of psychiatry and neurology within the asylum movement. It was not until the end of the 19th century, around the time when

Sigmund Freud was first developing his "talking cure" in Vienna, that the first scientifically clinical application of psychology began.

CHRONIC DISEASE MANAGEMENT

The burden of chronic illness will increase in Scotland as the population ages. Psychological interventions have an important role to play, both in preventing the onset of such conditions and supporting people with their symptoms. The main burden of care will fall on primary care services and CHPs. At the moment there are only a small number of psychologists working in this area, mostly in acute settings.

The following points emerged from the workshop discussions

- There are many positive examples of the contribution psychology can make to improving chronic disease management
- The priorities for CHPs will be reducing waiting times, avoidance of hospitalisation, wherever possible, and the promotion of self care. Is psychology aligned to these priorities?
- Psychology is seen to be largely a mental health service and not so relevant to present or future primary care needs. Where it is seen as valuable, it is often unattainable
- There is a need for psychology to begin a dialogue with primary care based around service need
- The profession needs to be more proactive in communicating what it does to develop services in a realistic way
- Psychology needs to shift away from being seen as an add-on to psychiatry. One potential way forward is to target areas of CHP interest such as CHD or diabetes
- Training other professionals is important in extending the reach of psychology. This will need ongoing supervision to maintain skill levels.
- Support could be sought from the Scottish Executive and NES for a pilot to develop systems for training other health-care professionals.

There is a need for more preventative psychology in older people's services to keep people functioning better for longer. Psychologists should be spending less time on resource intensive face to face work and more on broad prevention and health improvement approaches. Other staff could be trained to do one-to-one work. Psychologists should become more involved in providing advice, training and consultancy to psychiatrists, nurses, users and carers.

Health Psychology

Health psychology is concerned with understanding how biology, behaviour, and social context influence health and illness. Health psychologists work alongside other medical professionals in clinical settings, work on behaviour change in public health promotion, teach at universities, and conduct research. Although its early beginnings can be traced to the kindred field of clinical psychology, four different divisions within health psychology and one allied field have developed over time. The four divisions include clinical health psychology, public health psychology, community health psychology, and critical health psychology. The allied field is occupational health psychology. Organizations closely associated with the field of health psychology include Division 38 of the American Psychological Association and the Division of Health Psychology of the British Psychological Society.

Overview

Recent advances in psychological, medical, and physiological research have led to a new way of thinking about health and illness. This conceptualization, which has been labelled the bio-psychosocial model, views health and illness as the product of a combination of factors including biological characteristics (e.g., genetic predisposition), behavioural factors (e.g., lifestyle, stress, health beliefs), and social conditions (e.g., cultural influences, family relationships, social support). Psychologists who strive to understand how biological, behavioural, and social factors influence health and illness are called health psychologists. The term "health psychology" is often used synonymously with the terms "behavioural medicine" and "medical psychology". Health psychologists work with many different health care professionals (e.g., physicians, dentists, nurses, physician's assistants, dietitians, social workers, pharmacists, physical and occupational therapists, and chaplains) to conduct research and provide clinical assessments and treatment services. Many health psychologists focus on prevention research and interventions designed to promote health and reduce the risk of disease. While more than half of health psychologists provide clinical services as part of their duties, many health psychologists function in non-clinical roles, primarily involving teaching and research. Leading journals include *Health Psychology*, the *Journal of Health Psychology*, the *British Journal of Health Psychology*, and *Applied Psychology: Health and Well-Being*.

- Clinical health psychology (ClHP) is a term for a division of health psychology that reflects the fact that the field was originally a branch of clinical psychology. ClHP is also a major contributor to the field of behavioural medicine within psychiatry. Clinical practice includes education, the techniques of behaviour change, and psychotherapy. In some countries, a clinical health psychologist, with additional training, can become a medical psychologist and, thereby, obtain prescription privileges.

- Public health psychology (PHP) is population oriented. A major aim of PHP is to investigate potential causal links between psychosocial factors and health at the population level. Public health psychologists present research results to educators, policy makers, and health care providers in order to promote better public health. PHP is allied to other public health disciplines including epidemiology, nutrition, genetics and biostatistics. Some PHP interventions are targeted toward at-risk population groups (e.g., under-educated, single pregnant women who smoke) and not the population as a whole (e.g., all pregnant women).
- Community health psychology (CoHP) investigates community factors that contribute to the health and well-being of individuals who live in communities. CoHP also develops community-level interventions that are designed to combat disease and promote physical and mental health. The community often serves as the level of analysis, and is frequently sought as a partner in health-related interventions.
- Critical health psychology (CrHP) is concerned with the distribution of power and the impact of power differentials on health experience and behaviour, health care systems, and health policy. CrHP prioritizes social justice and the universal right to health for people of all races, genders, ages, and socioeconomic positions. A major concern is health inequalities. The critical health psychologist is an agent of change, not simply an analyst or cataloger. A leading organization in this area is the International Society of Critical Health Psychology.

Health psychology is both a theoretical and applied field. Health psychologists employ diverse research methods. These methods include controlled randomized experiments, quasi-experiments, longitudinal studies, time-series designs, cross-sectional studies, and case-control studies as well as action research.

Health psychologists study a broad range of variables including genotype, cardiovascular disease, smoking habits, religious beliefs, alcohol use, social support, living conditions, emotional state, social class, and much more.

Some health psychologists treat individuals with sleep problems, headaches, alcohol problems, etc. Other health psychologists work to empower community members by helping community members gain control over their health and improve quality of life of entire communities.

Relationship to Occupational Health Psychology

A separate but related discipline, occupational health psychology (OHP) is a relatively new field that emerged out of the confluence of health psychology, industrial/organizational psychology, and occupational health.

The field is concerned with identifying psychosocial characteristics of workplaces that affect the health and well-being of people who work. OHP is also concerned with developing strategies to effect change at workplaces in order to improve the health of people who work.

UNDERSTANDING BEHAVIOURAL AND CONTEXTUAL FACTORS

Health psychologists conduct research to identify behaviours and experiences that promote health, give rise to illness, and influence the effectiveness of health care. They also recommend ways to improve health care and health-care policy. Health psychologists have worked on developing ways to reduce smoking and improve daily nutrition in order to promote health and prevent illness.

They have also studied the association between illness and individual characteristics. For example, health psychology has found a relation between the personality characteristics thrill seeking, impulsiveness, hostility/anger, emotional instability, and depression, on one hand, and high-risk driving, on the other.

Health psychology is also concerned with contextual factors, including economic, cultural, community, social, and lifestyle factors that influence health. The bio-psychosocial model can help in understanding the relation between contextual factors and biology in affecting health.

Physical addiction plays an important role in smoking cessation. However, seductive advertising also contributes to psychological dependency on tobacco. Research in occupational health psychology indicates that people in jobs that combine little decision latitude with a high psychological workload are at increased risk for cardiovascular disease. Other OHP research reveals a relation between unemployment and elevations in blood pressure.

OHP research also documents a relation between social class and cardiovascular disease. Health psychologists also aim to change health behaviours for the dual purpose of helping people stay healthy and helping patients adhere to disease treatment regimens. Health psychologists employ cognitive behaviour therapy and applied behaviour analysis for that purpose.

Preventing Illness

Health psychologists work towards promoting health through behavioural change; however, they attempt to prevent illness in other ways as well. Campaigns informed by health psychology have targeted tobacco use. Those least able to afford tobacco products consume them most. Tobacco provides individuals with a way of controlling aversive emotional states accompanying daily experiences of stress that characterize the lives of deprived and vulnerable individuals. Practitioners emphasize education and effective communication as a part of illness prevention because many people do not recognize, or minimize, the risk of illness present in their lives. Moreover, many individuals are often unable to apply their knowledge of health practices owing to everyday pressures and stresses.

A common example of population-based attempts to motivate the smoking public to reduce its dependence on cigarettes is anti-smoking campaigns. Health psychologists also aim at educating health professionals, including physicians and nurses, in communicating effectively with patients in ways that overcome barriers to understanding, remembering, and implementing effective strategies for reducing exposures to risk factors and making health-enhancing behaviour changes. There is also evidence from occupational health psychology that stress-reduction interventions at the workplace can be effective. For example, Kompier and his colleagues have shown that a number of interventions aimed at reducing stress in bus drivers has had beneficial effects for employees and bus companies.

The Effects of Disease

Health psychologists investigate how disease affects individuals' psychological well-being. An individual who becomes seriously ill or injured faces many different practical stressors. The stressors include problems meeting medical and other bills; problems obtaining proper care when home from the hospital; obstacles to caring for dependents; having one's sense of self-reliance compromised; gaining a new, unwanted identity as a sick person; and so on. These stressors can lead to depression, reduced self-esteem, etc.

Health psychology also concerns itself with bettering the lives of individuals with terminal illness. When there is little hope of recovery, health psychologist therapists can improve the quality of life of the patient by helping the patient recover at least some of his or her psychological well-being. Health psychologists are also concerned with identifying the best ways for providing therapeutic services for the bereaved.

Critical Analysis of Health Policy

Critical health psychologists explore how health policy can influence inequities, inequalities, and social injustice. These avenues of research expand the scope of health psychology beyond the level of individual health to an examination of the social and economic determinants of health both within and between regions and nations.

The individualism of mainstream health psychology has been critiqued and deconstructed by critical health psychologists using newer qualitative methods and frameworks for investigating health experience and behaviour.

UNFORTUNATELY OF POWER OF MIND

There is tremendous power inherent in the mind. Unfortunately, few people realise that they possess this power and they behave as if they were weak and have nothing to contribute to this world and their own happiness. If they would study their own mind they would find the strength in it and they would be able to use it to their own advantage and for the benefit of others.

All of the achievements of human society are the direct result of the power of mind. Scientific discoveries are made because of intellectual power. The scientist concentrates his mental forces on his work; he gets sudden flashes of knowledge. He applies his findings in experiments and contributes something to the world for the control of nature. Primitive man was frightened and mystified by the forces of nature. He identified them with divine power and worshipped them. Today with his intellectual achievements modern man challenges the forces of nature without fear. He controls and uses them for both constructive and destructive purposes.

All the joys that people have in life—aesthetic, artistic, poetic, literary—are direct contributions of the human mind. Primitive man did not know how to use his mind; consequently, he was completely oblivious of his mental powers and he could not share his ideas. He might have felt inspiration from the beauties of nature but he was unable to express it. In a cultured society the sense of beauty can be communicated. The poetry of Browning. Wordsworth, Keats, Shelley, and of Shakespeare above all, the works of Hindu poets and dramatists like Kalidas and Girish Ghosh, or German writers like Goethe and Schelling, and French writers like Moliere and Racine, give an intense aesthetic intellectual satisfaction. The masterpieces of some of the great composers of Europe are tremendously inspiring. The religious music of the Hindu composers Tansen, Surdas, Mirabai, and Tagore is wonderful and transports one to a higher plane of consciousness.

Although an individual has the greatest joy in life when he uses fully his powers of mind, many people are not aware of this. Most people are still frightened by nature; consciously or unconsciously, the primitive tendency lingers because of ignorance of the physical constitution.

Many persons are frightened by disease. It is true that influenza, colds, virus infections, and such diseases are prevalent all over the world. Cancer, malaria, tuberculosis, and bubonic plague are destructive ailments. People have reason to be afraid of them. Fear of them disturbs the mind, creating many functional diseases. Little do they understand that the mind has the power at least to overcome psychosomatic diseases, as we explained in the book. So even from a medical point of view it is worth while to remember that the mind is inherently powerful. If people do not manifest that mental power, they succumb to all kinds of little disturbances and cannot even keep their bodies healthy. The question will arise: If it is an accepted fact that everyone possesses a powerful mind, then why don't they use it?

The answer is that most people are not aware that they possess it. Suppose that a man leaves his friend a legacy of a million dollars in the bank. If the friend does not know that he possesses this money he will not use it. He will not be benefited by it even though it may be in his name. Only when he knows about it can he do anything with it. The same is true of mental power. Then also a man must know how to use what is in his possession and not dissipate it. The parable of the prodigal son is an illustration of this point.

And not many days after the younger son gathered all together, and took his journey into a far country, and there wasted his substance with riotous living. And when he had spent all, there arose a mighty famine in that land; and he began to be in want.

A man may possess wealth but he can dissipate everything by not knowing how to make the best use of it. Similarly, even if a person knows that he has power of mind and can use it, he can still direct it for destructive purposes, as we find in the case of many scholars and scientists who misused that power by discovering implements for the destruction of humanity during the last World War. It is true that theoretical scientists like Einstein and others gave the basic ideas of atomic energy, yet other men with great mental powers used them for destructive purposes and thereby helped to demoralise humanity. Other scholars have become disintegrated themselves and have had to be hospitalised as the result of inordinate ambition and emotional tension, due to improper use of their minds. Dr. Carl Binger and others, discussing the principles of psychosomatic medicine, indicate what a devastating effect the misuse of the mind has on the human personality.

In a mysterious way human beings remain oblivious of what they possess. The Hindus call this ignorance *Maya* or nescience, a cosmic ignorance which coven man's true nature and gives rise to something else. They give a pertinent illustration. On a dark night when a person sees the trunk of a tree, he takes it to be a ghost, thief, friend, policeman, and so forth, according to his preconceived notion. When people have preconceived notions about certain things they interpret them as they like. Suppose someone has an idea that certain types of persons are no good. The moment he sees a man of that type he jumps to the conclusion that the man is no good. He does not have the objectivity to discriminate.

Recently the editor of a religious journal requested us to write an article showing the relationship between the Hindus and the Christians. An eminently devout person wrote a letter criticising the article, not from an objective or an intellectual point of view, but by attacking the personality of the writer. He did not know the writer at all, but he had formed an idea that certain persons are undesirable; therefore, he thought that a Hindu must be a bad person. He had no real knowledge of the writer's actual character. What can be done with such preconceived notions? Certainly, you cannot find the truth with them.

When people are hypnotised by themselves and by others, they cannot know what they are. If they have been constantly told that they are weaklings; that they are helpless; that they have nothing to contribute to themselves and to the world; how can they know what they possess? From out infancy our well-meaning parents, with their preconceived notions about the ways and behaviour of children, impose certain ideas on us. Often we hear the remark' "Oh, this child does not know anything. He doesn't understand what is happening." How do they know how much the child understands? It is amazing to observe the intuitive or instinctive power of a child.

When one of our brother Swami was very young, his older sister died during a cholera epidemic in India, leaving a little baby. Many other members of the family also died, leaving only an old grandmother and grandfather. That this little child felt what bad happened to her life was indicated by the mariner in which she behaved. She was actually afraid to meet anyone. It was interesting to observe how a little child, a few months old, could sense her loss. She could not be told that her mother and other relatives had died, as she was so young. Yet that baby knew what was missing in her life. People do not realise how much a child senses and feels, yet they say: "This child does not understand anything." They inculcate certain habits in the children because of their own actions. Take lying, for instance. Parents may often lie, riot thinking that the child will learn to do the same thing. When a telephone call comes, the mother tells Johnnie: "Say that Mother is out." He is taught to lie without thinking about it. Then when lie lies in some other way the mother scolds and disciplines him. In an unintentional way negative ideas are given to the children. Parents often almost hypnotise them with wrong impressions and ideas. Later on the children show them in their behaviour pattern and their reactions to the world. They gradually lose the power to control, guide, or develop their own mind.

On the other hand, we know of parents or guardians who have encouraged their children tremendously. The hypnotic spell of "good for nothing" was broken. These children developed a great deal of power in their lives as adults. In an Indian story there was a princess who was well-versed in Vedantic doctrines of life, immortality of soul, and divine power of man. When she was bringing up her little child, she would always sing the great words of Vedanta, "Thou art That, thou art divine." This little boy used to hear his mother humming over and over, "Thou art divine; thou art divine." As a result, when he grew up he manifested tremendous power of mind.

Just as negative ideas hynotise an individual, the positive, constructive, creative ideas dehypnotise him. He can bring out his latent power and show what he really is. Everyone needs to re mind himself of the power that he possesses. If some modern scientists can control physical nature, we do not see why an individual cannot control his own physical nature. Whatever is in the macrocosm is in the microcosm also. If the forces of atomic energy can be controlled with the help of intelligence, surely a man can control the particles of his own body. Of course, even the scientists who have been using this atomic energy are now frightened by it themselves. They are afraid because they are not sure what the other fellow is doing; and they are oblivious of their own power.

Everyone should have the full knowledge of the power that he possesses as well as a proper understanding of its use. Most people are not able to express their power of mind even when they know they have it, because their will power is weak and their emotions disintegrated. Unfortunately, mere intellectual knowledge of mental power is not sufficient. Otherwise, the world would not be what it is today. At a recent conference, a philosopher said that the Sermon on the Mount has been taught to us for the last two thousand years; yet see what we have been doing. People may have intellectual knowledge of the Sermon on the Mount; they may have intellectual knowledge of the Gospel of Buddha or other such teachings; yet if their emotions are not integrated, their inner power cannot be manifested.

That is the reason that people have to go through certain types of psycho-physical exercise in order to maintain and develop their mental powers. There may be a question that the term "psycho-physical," implies a parallelism between the mental and physical processes, as Professor Hugo Munsterberg and others in the West have thought. We wish to make our position clear that there is no dualism between mind and body; these two are not independent entities. They are interrelated and are the functioning of the same force in grosser and subtler forms. For the sake of understanding, we can safely say that for the time being the mind is dependent upon the body. When the body is disturbed or agitated, the mind is also disturbed. On occasions when the nerves are disturbed, the mind is also jumpy; and when the mind is in this state the nerves become shattered. When the mind is serene the nerves behave properly; it works both ways.

Can the mind act independently of the nervous system? First, let us think of the things that we observe through the nervous system with our sense organs and instruments. A person sees a flower and smells the fragrance. This experience stimulates the nervous system and consequently the mental process.

The individual thinks; he has an emotional or intellectual reaction, good or bad; and when the reaction is strong, he acts. These three functions: thinking, feeling, and willing, go together. They are interrelated and are constantly stimulated by certain sense perceptions. The mind functions in this way now, but there comes a time in the life of an individual when the mind can act independently of the nervous system. It does not then depend on direct sense perceptions. In this connection, we think of what some Western psychologists call extrasensory perception. The mind possesses the power to see things, not through the medium of sense contact yet just as directly and immediately as things are ordinarily perceived through the senses.

The mind possesses the power to perceive what is going on in distant places and also on a subtle plane beyond the range of ordinary perception. These subtle powers are popularly known as psychic and occult powers. There are many fraudulent claims, yet many cases are authentic and have been verified. These experiences may be misconstrued by many objective scientists as illusory and imaginary; but the investigations of psychical research societies and psychologists, such as Professor Joseph B. Rhine, Professor Gardner Murphy, and their colleagues, suggest to us that these experiences are within the range of the human mind. Indian psychologists, like Patanjali and others, not only believe in the possibility of such experiences but also give methods for developing these subtle mental powers through the practice of concentration.

Indian psychologists are emphatic in their declaration of the existence of these subtle powers and of the possibility of developing them through exact scientific methods of subjective experimentation. When a man develops subtle powers of mind, he can perceive things directly and immediately without the medium of the sense organs and nervous system. That is the time the mind perceives things as they really are and not through interpretation. Even the great scientists, who are supposed to be objective, perceive things through interpretation of the mind. That is the reason that Professor A.S. Eddington, in his *Philosophy of Physical Science,* comes to the conclusion that even scientific objective knowledge is relative.

For the same reason philosopher Kant tells us that the thing-in-itself is unknown and unknowable. What we know of the world or of the thing is nothing but the interpretation of the way the thing-in-itself affects our consciousness. Professor Eddington comes to his conclusion from scientific observation while philosopher Kant gets his knowledge, understanding, or flash through the flight of intellectualism or reasoning. Both of them, practically, come to the same conclusion as some of the Hindu philosophers do, namely, that *Brahman* or Reality cannot be perceived by the mind. The Hindu philosophers go a little further and say that there comes a stage in the course of the mind's development when the transformed mind perceives the Reality. In its present state, the mind functions as the body dictates or as the nerves react. Today there is a little change in the climate or there is a little physical irritation and the person becomes sick, Tomorrow there may be some other disorder of the body and the person becomes irritable. We see how the experience of physical change colors his perception. He may think he is independent, but he is a slave to the body for the time being. That is the reason the great Hindu teachers tell us that we have to go through psycho-physical exercises for the time being, so that the body may remain fairly healthy. We say fairly healthy rather than perfect. Perfection of the body is a misnomer, for the body constantly changes. When the body is fairly normal, then it does not disturb a person's mind with too many ailments. This is the time to dehypnotise the mind and manifest its power.

When a person does certain spiritual exercises or practices concentration or meditation, he finds that the latent power of the mind emerges. As he goes through these practices his emotions become organised and unified. People may find it difficult to understand and control the emotions. We do not ask anyone to repress his emotions; rather we ask him to transform or change the course of these emotions and direct them to higher channels to the divine. When he gradually succeeds in doing this, then the mental forces and emotions will be purified. Along with this redirection of the emotions, comes the practice of concentration. This practice unifies all the mental forces. When the mind is focused on anything, it ha, to remain quiet. A man who is performing experiments in the scientific laboratory is absorbed there because all other thoughts or emotional reactions are eliminated. When a mother is giving attention to the child all other thoughts are eliminated from her mind. When an artist is painting a picture, all other ideas or emotions are temporarily put aside. When a man concentrates his mind on God, all other ideas, associations, and emotions are forgotten. Of course, it is difficult to attain to that state or remain in it. Yet through practice and detachment one can attain it. Sri Krishna tells us: "Without doubt.......the mind is restless, and difficult to control; but through practice and renunciation.......it may be governed." Again He says: "When the completely controlled mind rests serenely in the Self alone, free from longing after all desires, then is one called steadfast, (in the Self)." Similarly, Patanjali, the father of Hindu psychology. says that by these two methods of detachment and constant practice, the "uncontrollable" mind can be subdued.

All latent powers of the mind are manifested when integration takes place. We then know the real dynamics of the mind. At that time functional diseases vanish. When a man has no emotional conflict, frustration, sense of insecurity, he has no anxiety or worry and his mind is peaceful. He may have organic trouble because of his age; or his body may deteriorate; or he may get some other disease; but he will not have functional trouble produced by the disturbed condition of the emotions. His nerves will remain strong and he can accomplish what he wishes, fully controlling his physical reaction. Some people have seen cancer patients. The excruciating pain a patient suffers cannot be described. Sri Ramakrishna had cancer of the throat. When the doctors would go to treat it, He would say to them: "Wait a minute." After a short time He would add: "Now you can go on." He had withdrawn His mind completely from the body. Then the doctors could do anything for He could not feel it. We never saw Sri Ramakrishna; we saw His disciples. Swami Turiyananda, one of the disciples had to undergo a serious operation. His heart was weak because of age and long suffering. The doctors were hesitant about giving him an anesthetic. They reported this to Swami Brahmananda our Master, who was then President of the Ramakrishna Mission. Swami Brahmananda went to the bedroom of the sick Swami and said: "You will just have to endure!" The Swami replied: "Yes, Maharaj, certainly." And all the preparations were made for this major operation in his room. He began to talk about *Brahman* to some of the young Swamis who were present while the operation was going on. The surgeon was amazed. After finishing everything he asked: "Swami, can you sing a song?" And Swami Turiyananda sang a devotional song. His mind was completely withdrawn from the body. There was not the slightest distortion of the facial muscles during the operation.

Sri Ramakrishna used to say that when Jesus was crucified, He withdrew His mind completely from His body; He was in another state altogether, a state of *samadhi* or superconsciousness. The nails pierced through His body but the mind was unaffected. Sri Ramakrishna gave an illustration of how this could happen. When the coconut is not yet ripe, the fibers, kernel, and shell are inseparable. But when the coconut is ripe, the kernel becomes separate. You can shake it and feel the kernel jump around inside. When a person is thoroughly established in higher spiritual practices, his mind and body become separated. His soul is separate, too.

The objective of everyone should be to bring out his own mental power. Many of us may say that we are not like Christ, Sri Ramakrishna, or Swami Turiyananda. We are ordinary people. It is true that we are ordinary in the usual sense; but we still have that divine spark; we still possess that mine of power in us. The difference is that we have hypnotised ourselves and we are continuing to do so, However, we can be dehypnotised by constant, positive thoughts, like the child of the Indian princess. We should remind ourselves that we are divine. We should remind ourselves that there is a reservoir of strength within us. We should tell ourselves that the petty changes in the world should not affect our mind. How disturbed we become if a man looks this way or talks that way! How the little things disturb and agitate us and make our minds go to pieces! The more we give our attention to higher phases of life the less we shall be affected by adverse circumstances. We do not know if anyone can be found who is not subject to them. Even Jesus and Sri Ramakrishna had their sad experiences. Jesus, an incarnation of God, was crucified.

Can anyone think that there will not be any change of condition in this life? It is unthinkable to look at things in this light. We have to face conditions as they are. We have to be unaffected by them and manifest our hidden, latent power of mind. We have no reason for frustration and conflict. We can overcome anxiety and apprehension.

We possess the power to face the problems of life and internal and external changes; and we have the power to overcome all mental weaknesses. Then we can dehypnotise ourselves and gradually manifest our will power, so that we can carry out the ideas that we have in life for our own betterment and for the good of society. In giving attention to the Abiding Spirit we will find that mental power will be manifest. It is nothing unusual. The difference that we see between one man and another and their achievements is due to the degree of manifestation of mental power. Some cultivate and express it, in different spheres of life, while others dissipate it and become disintegrated. It is of primary importance for everyone to consider how to use the best we have in us to full advantage. Then alone can we contribute something worth while to our life and to the lives of others. No great contribution can be made to life by a disturbed mind. Disturbances of the mind can be fully controlled as we manifest the real power in us and become free. Then we can say: "Mind can bind one; mind can liberate one."

SENSOR MODALITIES: ELECTROMYOGRAPH

An electromyograph (EMG) uses surface electrodes to detect muscle action potentials from underlying skeletal muscles that initiate muscle contraction. Clinicians record the surface electromyogram (SEMG) using one or more active electrodes that are placed over a target muscle and a reference electrode that is placed within six inches of either active. The SEMG is measured in microvolts (millionths of a volt).

Biofeedback therapists use EMG biofeedback when treating anxiety and worry, chronic pain, computer-related disorder, essential hypertension, headache (migraine, mixed headache, and tension-type headache), low back pain, physical rehabilitation (cerebral palsy, incomplete spinal cord lesions, and stroke), temporomandibular joint disorder (TMD), torticollis, and fecal incontinence, urinary incontinence, and pelvic pain.

Feedback Thermometer

A feedback thermometer detects skin temperature with a thermistor (a temperature-sensitive resistor) that is usually attached to a finger or toe and measured in degrees Celsius or Fahrenheit. Skin temperature mainly reflects arteriole diameter. Hand-warming and hand-cooling are produced by separate mechanisms, and their regulation involves different skills. Hand-warming involves arteriole vasodilation produced by a beta-2 adrenegeric hormonal mechanism. Hand-cooling involves arteriole vasoconstriction produced by the increased firing of sympathetic C-fibers. Biofeedback therapists use temperature biofeedback when treating chronic pain, edema, headache (migraine and tension-type headache), essential hypertension, Raynaud's disease, anxiety, and stress.

Electro-dermograph

An Electro-dermograph (EDG) measures skin electrical activity directly (skin conductance and skin potential) and indirectly (skin resistance) using electrodes placed over the digits or hand and wrist. Orienting responses to unexpected stimuli, arousal and worry, and cognitive activity can increase eccrine sweat gland activity, increasing the conductivity of the skin for electrical current. In *skin conductance,* an Electro-dermograph imposes an imperceptible current across the skin and measures how easily it travels through the skin. When anxiety raises the level of sweat in a sweat duct, conductance increases. Skin conductance is measured in microsiemens (millionths of a siemens). In *skin potential,* a therapist places an active electrode over an active site (e.g., the palmar surface of the hand) and a reference electrode over a relatively inactive site (e.g., forearm). Skin potential is the voltage that develops between eccrine sweat glands and internal tissues and is measured in millivolts (thousandths of a volt). In *skin resistance,* also called galvanic skin response (GSR), an Electro-dermograph imposes a current across the skin and measures the amount of opposition it encounters. Skin resistance is measured in ku (thousands of ohms).

Biofeedback therapists use electrodermal biofeedback when treating anxiety disorders, hyperhidrosis (excessive sweating), and stress. Electrodermal biofeedback is used as an adjunct to psychotherapy to increase client awareness of their emotions. In addition, electrodermal measures have long served as one of the central tools in polygraphy (lie detection) because they reflect changes in anxiety or emotional activation.

Electroencephalograph

An electroencephalograph (EEG) measures the electrical activation of the brain from scalp sites located over the human cortex. The EEG shows the amplitude of electrical activity at each cortical site, the amplitude and relative power of various wave forms at each site, and the degree to which each cortical site fires in conjunction with other cortical sites (coherence and symmetry).

The EEG uses precious metal electrodes to detect a voltage between at least two electrodes located on the scalp. The EEG records both excitatory postsynaptic potentials (EPSPs) and inhibitory postsynaptic potentials (IPSPs) that largely occur in dendrites in pyramidal cells located in macro-columns, several millimeters in diameter, in the upper cortical layers. Neurofeed back monitors both slow and fast cortical potentials.

Slow cortical potentials are gradual changes in the membrane potentials of cortical dendrites that last from 300 ms to several seconds. These potentials include the contingent negative variation (CNV), readiness potential, movement-related potentials (MRPs), and P300 and N400 potentials.

Fast cortical potentials range from 0.5 Hz to 100 Hz. The main frequency ranges include delta, theta, alpha, the sensorimotor rhythm, low beta, high beta, and gamma. The specific cutting points defining the frequency ranges vary considerably among professionals. Fast cortical potentials can be described by their predominant frequencies, but also by whether they are synchronous or asynchronous wave forms. Synchronous wave forms occur at regular periodic intervals, whereas asynchronous wave forms are irregular.

The synchronous delta rhythm ranges from 0.5 to 3.5 Hz. Delta is the dominant frequency from ages 1 to 2, and is associated in adults with deep sleep and brain pathology like trauma and tumors, and learning disability.

The synchronous theta rhythm ranges from 4 to 7 Hz. Theta is the dominant frequency in healthy young children and is associated with drowsiness or starting to sleep, REM sleep, hypnagogic imagery (intense imagery experienced before the onset of sleep), hypnosis, attention, and processing of cognitive and perceptual information.

The synchronous alpha rhythm ranges from 8 to 13 Hz and is defined by its waveform and not by its frequency. Alpha activity can be observed in about 75% of awake, relaxed individuals and is replaced by low-amplitude desynchronized beta activity during movement, complex problem-solving, and visual focusing. This phenomenon is called alpha blocking.

The synchronous sensorimotor rhythm (SMR) ranges from 12 to 15 Hz and is located over the sensorimotor cortex (central sulcus). The sensorimotor rhythm is associated with the inhibition of movement and reduced muscle tone.

The beta rhythm consists of asynchronous waves and can be divided into low beta and high beta ranges (13–21 Hz and 20–32 Hz). Low beta is associated with activation and focused thinking. High beta is associated with anxiety, hypervigilance, panic, peak performance, and worry.

EEG activity from 36 to 44 Hz is also referred to as gamma. Gamma activity is associated with perception of meaning and meditative awareness.

Neuro-therapists use EEG biofeedback when treating addiction, attention deficit hyperactivity disorder (ADHD), learning disability, anxiety disorders (including worry, obsessive-compulsive disorder and post-traumatic stress disorder), depression, migraine, and generalized seizures.

Photo-plethysmograph

A Photo-plethysmograph (PPG) measures the relative blood flow through a digit using a photo-plethysmographic (PPG) sensor attached by a Velcro band to the fingers or to the temple to monitor the temporal artery. An infrared light source is transmitted through or reflected off the tissue, detected by a photo-transistor, and quantified in arbitrary units. Less light is absorbed when blood flow is greater, increasing the intensity of light reaching the sensor.

A Photo-plethysmograph can measure blood volume pulse (BVP), which is the phasic change in blood volume with each heartbeat, heart rate, and heart rate variability (HRV), which consists of beat-to-beat differences in intervals between successive heartbeats. A Photo-plethysmograph can provide useful feedback when temperature feedback shows minimal change. This is because the PPG sensor is more sensitive than a thermistor to minute blood flow changes. Biofeedback therapists can use a Photo-plethysmograph to supplement temperature biofeedback when treating chronic pain, edema, headache (migraine and tension-type headache), essential hypertension, Raynaud's disease, anxiety, and stress.

Electrocardiograph

The electrocardiograph (ECG) uses electrodes placed on the torso, wrists, or legs, to measure the electrical activity of the heart and measures the inter beat interval (distances between successive R-wave peaks in the QRS complex). The inter beat interval, divided into 60 seconds, determines the heart rate at that moment. The statistical variability of that inter beat interval is what we call heart rate variability. The ECG method is more accurate than the PPG method in measuring heart rate variability.

Biofeedback therapists use HRV biofeedback when treating asthma, COPD, depression, fibromyalgia, heart disease, and unexplained abdominal pain.

Pneumograph

A pneumograph or respiratory strain gauge uses a flexible sensor band that is placed around the chest, abdomen, or both. The strain gauge method can provide feedback about the relative expansion/contraction of the chest and abdomen, and can measure respiration rate (the number of breaths per minute). Clinicians can use a pneumograph to detect and correct dysfunctional breathing patterns and behaviours. Dysfunctional breathing patterns include clavicular breathing (breathing that primarily relies on the external inter costals and the accessory muscles of respiration to inflate the lungs), reverse breathing (breathing where the abdomen expands during exhalation and contracts during inhalation), and thoracic breathing (shallow breathing that primarily relies on the external inter costals to inflate the lungs). Dysfunctional breathing behaviours include apnea (suspension of breathing), gasping, sighing, and wheezing.

A pneumograph is often used in conjunction with an electrocardiograph (ECG) or Photo-plethysmograph (PPG) in heart rate variability (HRV) training. Biofeedback therapists use pneumograph biofeedback with patients diagnosed with anxiety disorders, asthma, chronic pulmonary obstructive disorder (COPD), essential hypertension, panic attacks, and stress.

Capnometer

A capnometer or capnograph uses an infrared detector to measure end-tidal CO_2 (the partial pressure of carbon dioxide in expired air at the end of expiration) exhaled through the nostril into a latex tube. The average value of end-tidal CO_2 for a resting adult is 5% (36 Torr or 4.8 kPa). A capnometer is a sensitive index of the quality of patient breathing. Shallow, rapid, and effortful breathing lowers CO_2, while deep, slow, effortless breathing increases it. Biofeedback therapists use capnometric biofeedback to supplement respiratory strain gauge biofeedback with patients diagnosed with anxiety disorders, asthma, chronic pulmonary obstructive disorder (COPD), essential hypertension, panic attacks, and stress.

Hemoencephalography

Hemoencephalography or HEG biofeedback is a functional infrared imaging technique. As its name describes, it measures the differences in the colour of light reflected back through the scalp based on the relative amount of oxygenated and un-oxygenated blood in the brain. Research continues to determine its reliability, validity, and clinical applicability. HEG is used to treat ADHD and migraine, and for research.

Applications

Incontinence: Mowrer detailed the use of a bed-wetting alarm that sounds when children urinate while asleep. This simple biofeedback device can quickly teach children to wake up when their bladders are full and to contract the urinary sphincter and relax the detrusor muscle, preventing further urine release. Through classical conditioning, sensory feedback from a full bladder replaces the alarm and allows children to continue sleeping without urinating.

Kegel developed the perineometer in 1947 to treat urinary incontinence (urine leakage) in women whose pelvic floor muscles are weakened during pregnancy and childbirth. The perineometer, which is inserted into the vagina to monitor pelvic floor muscle contraction, satisfies all the requirements of a biofeedback device and enhances the effectiveness of popular Kegel exercises.

In 1992, the United States Agency for Health Care Policy and Research recommended biofeedback as a first-line treatment for adult urinary incontinence.

EEG

Caton recorded spontaneous electrical potentials from the exposed cortical surface of monkeys and rabbits, and was the first to measure event-related potentials (EEG responses to stimuli) in 1875.

Danilevsky published *Investigations in the Physiology of the Brain*, which explored the relationship between the EEG and states of consciousness in 1877.

Beck published studies of spontaneous electrical potentials detected from the brains of dogs and rabbits, and was the first to document alpha blocking, where light alters rhythmic oscillations, in 1890.

Sherrington introduced the terms neuron and synapse and published the *Integrative Action of the Nervous System* in 1906.

Pravdich-Neminsky photographed the EEG and event related potentials from dogs, demonstrated a 12–14 Hz rhythm that slowed during asphyxiation, and introduced the term electro cere brogram in 1912.

Forbes reported the replacement of the string galvanometer with a vacuum tube to amplify the EEG in 1920. The vacuum tube became the de facto standard by 1936.

Berger (1924) published the first human EEG data. He recorded electrical potentials from his son Klaus's scalp. At first he believed that he had discovered the physical mechanism for telepathy but was disappointed that the electromagnetic variations disappear only millimeters away from the skull. (He did continue to believe in telepathy throughout his life, however, having had a particularly confirming event regarding his sister). He viewed the EEG as analogous to the ECG and introduced the term. He believed that the EEG had diagnostic and therapeutic promise in measuring the impact of clinical interventions. Berger showed that these potentials were not due to scalp muscle contractions. He first identified the alpha rhythm, which he called the Berger rhythm, and later identified the beta rhythm and sleep spindles. He demonstrated that alterations in consciousness are associated with changes in the EEG and associated the beta rhythm with alertness. He described interictal activity (EEG potentials between seizures) and recorded a partial complex seizure in 1933. Finally, he performed the first QEEG, which is the measurement of the signal strength of EEG frequencies. Adrian and Matthews confirmed Berger's findings in 1934 by recording their own EEGs using a cathode-ray oscilloscope. Their demonstration of EEG recording at the 1935 Physiological Society meetings in England caused its widespread acceptance. Adrian used himself as a subject and demonstrated the phenomenon of alpha blocking, where opening his eyes suppressed alpha rhythms.

Gibbs, Davis, and Lennox inaugurated clinical electro-encephalography in 1935 by identifying abnormal EEG rhythms associated with epilepsy, including interictal spike waves and 3 Hz activity in absence seizures.

Bremer used the EEG to show how sensory signals affect vigilance in 1935. Walter (1937, 1953) named the delta waves and theta waves, and the contingent negative variation (CNV), a slow cortical potential that may reflect expectancy, motivation, intention to act, or attention. He located an occipital lobe source for alpha waves and demonstrated that delta waves can help locate brain lesions like tumors. He improved Berger's electroencephalograph and pioneered EEG topography.

Kleitman has been recognized as the "Father of American sleep research" for his seminal work in the regulation of sleep-wake cycles, circadian rhythms, the sleep patterns of different age groups, and the effects of sleep deprivation. He discovered the phenomenon of rapid eye movement (REM) sleep with his graduate student Aserinsky in 1953.

Dement, another of Kleitman's students, described the EEG architecture and phenomenology of sleep stages and the transitions between them in 1955, associated REM sleep with dreaming in 1957, and documented sleep cycles in another species, cats, in 1958, which stimulated basic sleep research. He established the Stanford University Sleep Research Center in 1970.

Andersen and Andersson (1968) proposed that thalamic pacemakers project synchronous alpha rhythms to the cortex via thalamocortical circuits.

Kamiya (1968) demonstrated that the alpha rhythm in humans could be operantly conditioned. He published an influential article in *Psychology Today* that summarized research that showed that subjects could learn to discriminate when alpha was present or absent, and that they could use feedback to shift the dominant alpha frequency about 1 Hz. Almost half of his subjects reported experiencing a pleasant "alpha state" characterized as an "alert calmness." These reports may have contributed to the perception of alpha biofeedback as a short-cut to a meditative state. He also studied the EEG correlates of meditative states.

Brown (1970) demonstrated the clinical use of alpha-theta biofeedback. In research designed to identify the subjective states associated with EEG rhythms, she trained subjects to increase the abundance of alpha, beta, and theta activity using visual feedback and recorded their subjective experiences when the amplitude of these frequency bands increased. She also helped popularize biofeedback by publishing a series of books, including *New Mind, New body* (1974) and *Stress and the Art of Biofeedback* (1977).

Mulholland and Peper (1971) showed that occipital alpha increases with eyes open and not focused, and is disrupted by visual focusing; a rediscovery of alpha blocking.

Green and Green (1986) investigated voluntary control of internal states by individuals like Swami Rama and American Indian medicine man Rolling Thunder both in India and at the Menninger Foundation. They brought portable biofeedback equipment to India and monitored practitioners as they demonstrated self-regulation. A film containing footage from their investigations was released as *Biofeedback: The Yoga of the West* (1974). They developed alpha-theta training at the Menninger Foundation from the 1960s to the 1990s. They hypothesized that theta states allow access to unconscious memories and increase the impact of prepared images or suggestions. Their alpha-theta research fostered Peniston's development of an alpha-theta addiction protocol.

Sterman (1972) showed that cats and human subjects could be operantly trained to increase the amplitude of the sensorimotor rhythm (SMR) recorded from the sensorimotor cortex. He demonstrated that SMR production protects cats against drug-induced generalized seizures (tonic-clonic seizures involving loss of consciousness) and reduces the frequency of seizures in humans diagnosed with epilepsy. He found that his SMR protocol, which uses visual and auditory EEG biofeedback, normalizes their EEGs (SMR increases while theta and beta decrease toward normal values) even during sleep. Sterman also co-developed the Sterman-Kaiser (SKIL) QEEG database.

Birbaumer and colleagues (1981) have studied feedback of slow cortical potentials since the late 1970s. They have demonstrated that subjects can learn to control these DC potentials and have studied the efficacy of slow cortical potential biofeedback in treating ADHD, epilepsy, migraine, and schizophrenia.

Lubar (1989) studied SMR biofeedback to treat attention disorders and epilepsy in collaboration with Sterman. He demonstrated that SMR training can improve attention and academic performance in children diagnosed with Attention Deficit Disorder with Hyperactivity (ADHD). He documented the importance of theta-to-beta ratios in ADHD and developed theta suppression-beta enhancement protocols to decrease these ratios and improve student performance.

Electrodermal System

Fere demonstrated the exosomatic method of recording of skin electrical activity by passing a small current through the skin in 1888.

Tarchanoff used the endosmotic method by recording the difference in skin electrical potential from points on the skin surface in 1889; no external current was applied.

Jung employed the galvanometer, which used the exosomatic method, in 1907 to study unconscious emotions in word-association experiments.

Marjorie and Hershel Toomim (1975) published a landmark article about the use of GSR biofeedback in psychotherapy.

Musculoskeletal System

Jacobson (1930) developed hardware to measure EMG voltages over time, showed that cognitive activity (like imagery) affects EMG levels, introduced the deep relaxation method Progressive Relaxation, and wrote *Progressive Relaxation* (1929) and *You Must Relax* (1934). He prescribed daily Progressive Relaxation practice to treat diverse psychophysiological disorders like hypertension.

Several researchers showed that human subjects could learn precise control of individual motor units (motor neurons and the muscle fibers they control). Lindsley (1935) found that relaxed subjects could suppress motor unit firing without biofeedback training.

Harrison and Mortensen (1962) trained subjects using visual and auditory EMG biofeedback to control individual motor units in the tibialis anterior muscle of the leg.

Basmajian (1963) instructed subjects using un-filtered auditory EMG biofeedback to control separate motor units in the abductor pollicis muscle of the thumb in his Single Motor Unit Training (SMUT) studies. His best subjects coordinated several motor units to produce drum rolls. Basmajian demonstrated practical applications for neuromuscular rehabilitation, pain management, and headache treatment.

Marinacci (1960) applied EMG biofeedback to neuromuscular disorders (where proprioception is disrupted) including Bell Palsy (one-sided facial paralysis), polio, and stroke.

"While Marinacci used EMG to treat neuromuscular disorders, his colleagues only used the EMG for diagnosis. They were unable to recognize its potential as a teaching tool even when the evidence stared them in the face! Many electro-myographers who performed nerve conduction studies used visual and auditory feedback to reduce interference when a patient recruited too many motor units. Even though they used EMG biofeedback to guide the patient to relax so that clean diagnostic EMG tests could be recorded, they were unable to envision EMG biofeedback treatment of motor disorders."

Whatmore and Kohli (1968) introduced the concept of dysponesis (misplaced effort) to explain how functional disorders (where body activity is disturbed) develop. Bracing your shoulders when you hear a loud sound illustrates dysponesis since this action does not protect against injury. These clinicians applied EMG biofeedback to diverse functional problems like headache and hypertension. They reported case follow-ups ranging from 6 to 21 years. This was long compared with typical 0-24 month follow-ups in the clinical literature. Their data showed that skill in controlling misplaced efforts was positively related to clinical improvement. Last, they wrote *The Pathophysiology and Treatment of Functional Disorders* (1974) that outlined their treatment of functional disorders.

Cardiovascular System

Shearn (1962) operantly trained human subjects to increase their heart rates by 5 beats-per-minute to avoid electric shock. In contrast to Shearn's slight heart rate increases, Swami Rama used yoga to produce atrial flutter at an average 306 beats per minute before a Menninger Foundation audience. This briefly stopped his heart's pumping of blood and silenced his pulse.

Engel and Chism (1967) operantly trained subjects to decrease, increase, and then decrease their heart rates (this was analogous to ON-OFF-ON EEG training). He then used this approach to teach patients to control their rate of premature ventricular contractions (PVCs), where the ventricles contract too soon. Engel conceptualized this training protocol as illness onset training, since patients were taught to produce and then suppress a symptom. Peper has similarly taught asthmatics to wheeze to better control their breathing. Schwartz (1971, 1972) examined whether specific patterns of cardiovascular activity are easier to learn than others due to biological constraints. He examined the constraints on learning integrated (two autonomic responses change in the same direction) and differentiated (two autonomic responses change inversely) patterns of blood pressure and heart rate change.

Schultz and Luthe (1969) developed Autogenic Training, which is a deep relaxation exercise derived from hypnosis. This procedure combines passive volition with imagery in a series of three treatment procedures (standard Autogenic exercises, Autogenic neutralization, and Autogenic meditation). Clinicians at the Menninger Foundation coupled an abbreviated list of standard exercises with thermal biofeedback to create autogenic biofeedback. Luthe (1973) also published a series of six volumes titled *Autogenic therapy*.

Fahrion and colleagues (1986) reported on an 18-26 session treatment programme for hypertensive patients. The Menninger programme combined breathing modification, autogenic biofeedback for the hands and feet, and frontal EMG training. The authors reported that 89% of their medication patients discontinued or reduced medication by one-half while significantly lowering blood pressure. While this study did not include a double-blind control, the outcome rate was impressive.

Freedman and colleagues (1991) demonstrated that hand-warming and hand-cooling are produced by different mechanisms. The primary hand-warming mechanism is beta-adrenergic (hormonal), while the main hand-cooling mechanism is alpha-adrenergic and involves sympathetic C-fibers. This contradicts the traditional view that finger blood flow is exclusively controlled by sympathetic C-fibers. The traditional model asserts that when firing is slow, hands warm; when firing is rapid, hands cool. Freedman and colleagues' studies support the view that hand-warming and hand-cooling represent entirely different skills.

Vaschillo and colleagues (1983) published the first studies of HRV biofeedback with cosmonauts and treated patients diagnosed with psychiatric and psychophysiological disorders. Lehrer collaborated with Smetankin and Potapova in treating pediatric asthma patients and published influential articles on HRV asthma treatment in the medical journal *Chest*.

Pain

Budzynski and Stoyva (1969) showed that EMG biofeedback could reduce frontalis muscle (forehead) contraction. They demonstrated in 1973 that analog (proportional) and binary (ON or OFF) visual EMG biofeedback were equally helpful in lowering masseter SEMG levels.

Budzynski, Stoyva, Adler, and Mullaney (1973) reported that auditory frontalis EMG biofeedback combined with home relaxation practice lowered tension headache frequency and frontalis EMG levels. A control group that received non-contentious (false) auditory feedback did not improve. This study helped make the frontalis muscle the placement-of-choice in EMG assessment and treatment of headache and other psychophysiological disorders.

Sargent, Green, and Walters (1972, 1973) demonstrated that hand-warming could abort migraines and that autogenic biofeedback training could reduce headache activity. The early Menninger migraine studies, although methodologically weak (no pretreatment baselines, control groups, or random assignment to conditions), strongly influenced migraine treatment.

Flor (2002) trained amputees to detect the location and frequency of shocks delivered to their stumps, which resulted in an expansion of corresponding cortical regions and significant reduction of their phantom limb pain.

McNulty, Gevirtz, Hubbard, and Berkoff (1994) proposed that sympathetic nervous system innervation of muscle spindles underlies trigger points.

PSYCHOLOGY IN HEALTH

Robust evidence has accumulated in recent years about the effectiveness of psychological interventions in managing a wide range of health conditions.

At the same time, there has been a growing recognition of the importance of psycho-social factors in illness and a strengthening commitment to the prevention of ill health. The positive contribution that psychology can make to the health service has become an increasing feature of reports from national guideline organizations.

These have highlighted the important role of psychology, particularly in the management of chronic diseases which are set to become more prevalent as the number of older people increases.

Major health problems are increasingly related to lifestyle choices such as smoking, alcohol consumption, exercise, diet and other factors such as stress, work life balance, personal confidence and self worth. Applied psychology, as the science of attitude and behaviour change, can help in all of these areas. It also has a role to play within the NHS itself by helping staff to manage change, improving their motivation and engagement and addressing issues they have through occupational health support.

The NHS has much to gain by incorporating psychological models and thinking across the broader health-care system, and by extending the concept of psychological interventions beyond their traditional base within Mental Health and into the arenas of health improvement and physical health care. However there has, to date, been very limited exploitation of the discipline's wider potential. There are a number of reasons for this, including lack of psychology input at policy making and strategic planning levels, relatively small numbers of appropriately trained staff, and service models which were not designed to maximise the transmission of psychological skills to other health professionals.

Although psychology has historically been one of the smallest professions within the NHS, it has exerted an influence out of proportion to its size and has expanded progressively its potential sphere of influence. It has done this, in part, by developing innovative models of service delivery and working collaboratively with others. However, continuing progress will depend on expanding the workforce. This is necessary to capitalise on the available knowledge base, to ensure the quality of psychological interventions, and to make an impact on strategic planning and service development. Future workforce planning and training arrangements must focus on the issue of capacity to deliver effective, high quality psychological interventions. This is the essential paradox facing psychological services in Scotland today: there is the potential to achieve a great deal, particularly in areas such as chronic disease management, health improvement, mental health and preventative approaches to lifestyle, but there are limitations and restrictions that prevent psychology from progressing. How can this problem be resolved?

That was the purpose of this conference. It set out to examine where psychology stands in the NHS at the moment and how it can move forward. It was important the discussions reflected the political and strategic objectives of NHSScotland.

To that end, the conference was attended by a wide range of stakeholders including representatives from the Scottish Executive, NHS Board management, Community Health Partnerships, local authorities, academic institutions, user and carer groups, The British Psychological Society and health professionals from a number of different backgrounds. It marked the beginning of a process to establish a consensus around the key issues that need to be addressed. This report is the first step along that road. It seeks to summarise the main points examined over the two days and promote wider consultation. Once feedback has been received, a framework based on all the responses will be developed. It will then be used by NHS Education for Scotland (NES) to establish future priorities for training and development.

The ultimate goal is to make the most effective use of psychological expertise to help improve the health of people in Scotland. That will require matching the skills and resources psychologists possess to the needs of the service and the job that needs to be done.

There is a clear demand for more psychologists and that is being addressed by NES and the Scottish Executive. There will be more psychologists available to the service in the future. However, that process will take several years. The more pertinent question facing the NHS in the short term is not how does it go about meeting the demand for more psychologists, but how will it meet the demand for more psychology?

The Future

Psychology can help the health service deliver more effective and efficient solutions to many of its current and future demands. There was agreement that realising the potential of psychological services will require action on a number of fronts including:

- political lobbying to raise the profile of the profession
- expanded programmes to train more psychologists
- the acceptance of greater responsibility for training other professions in psychological principles.

There are positive developments to build on. Psychological services already benefit from having a highly motivated, committed, innovative, flexible trained workforce.

There has been increased investment in training and innovations introduced in Scotland in the form of "flexible" trainees. Psychology also benefits from having a large pool of potential recruits. Psychology is the second most popular undergraduate degree and research in Scotland has shown that many of these graduates would consider taking up posts in the NHS if the opportunities were there for them. Psychologists also enjoy the good will of users of services and their carers.

Psychology into Practice-Key Themes

Many of our current health problems are related to lifestyle issues. Preventing ill health and encouraging health improvement requires attitude and behaviour change among both members of the public and health-care professionals. Psychologists are experts in long-lasting attitude and behavioural change and have an important contribution to make in this area. There is already evidence of effectiveness in many areas.

APPLICATIONS OF HEALTH PSYCHOLOGY

Improving Doctor-Patient Communication

Health psychologists attempt to aid the process of communication between physicians and patients during medical consultations. There are many problems in this process, with patients showing a considerable lack of understanding of many medical terms, particularly anatomical terms (e.g., intestines). One main area of research on this topic involves "doctor-centred" or "patient-centred" consultations. Doctor-centred consultations are generally directive, with the patient answering questions and playing less of a role in decision-making. Although this style is preferred by elderly people and others, many people dislike the sense of hierarchy or ignorance that it inspires. They prefer patient-centred consultations, which focus on the patient's needs, involve the doctor listening to the patient completely before making a decision, and involving the patient in the process of choosing treatment and finding a diagnosis.

Improving Adherence to Medical Advice

Getting people to follow medical advice and adhere to their treatment regimens is a difficult task for health psychologists. People often forget to take their pills or are inhibited by the side effects of their medicines. Failing to take prescribed medication is costly and wastes millions of usable medicines that could otherwise help other people. Estimated adherence rates are difficult to measure; there is, however, evidence that adherence could be improved by tailoring treatment programmes to individuals' daily lives.

Ways of Measuring Adherence

Health psychologists have identified a number of ways of measuring patients' adherence to medical regimens:

- Counting the number of pills in the medicine bottle—although this has problems with privacy and/or could be deemed patronizing or showing lack of trust in patients
- Using self-reports—although patients may fail to return the self-report or lie about their adherence
- Asking a doctor or health worker—although this presents problems on doctor-patient confidentiality
- Using 'Trackcap' bottles, which track the number of times the bottle is opened; however, this either raises problems of informed consent or, if informed consent is obtained, influence through demand characteristics.

Managing Pain

Health psychology attempts to find treatments to reduce and eliminate pain, as well as understand pain anomalies such as episodic analgesia, causalgia, neuralgia, and phantom limb pain. Although the task of measuring and describing pain has been problematic, the development of the McGill Pain Questionnaire has helped make progress in this area. Treatments for pain involve patient-administered analgesia, acupuncture (found by Berman to be effective in reducing pain for osteo-arthritis of the knee), biofeedback, and cognitive behaviour therapy.

Biofeedback

Biofeedback is the process of becoming aware of various physiological functions using instruments that provide information on the activity of those same systems, with a goal of being able to manipulate them at will. Processes that can be controlled include brain waves, muscle tone, skin conductance, heart rate and pain perception.

Biofeedback may be used to improve health or performance, and the physiological changes often occur in conjunction with changes to thoughts, emotions, and behaviour. Eventually, these changes can be maintained without the use of extra equipment. Biofeedback has been found effective for the treatment of headaches and migraines.

Definition

Three professional biofeedback organizations, the Association for Applied Psychophysiology and Biofeedback (AAPB), Biofeedback Certification Institution of America (BCIA), and the International Society for Neurofeed back and Research (ISNR), arrived at a consensus definition of biofeedback in 2008: "Biofeedback is a process that enables an individual to learn how to change physiological activity for the purposes of improving health and performance.

Precise instruments measure physiological activity such as brain waves, heart function, breathing, muscle activity, and skin temperature. These instruments rapidly and accurately 'feed back' information to the user. The presentation of this information — often in conjunction with changes in thinking, emotions, and behaviour — supports desired physiological changes. Over time, these changes can endure without continued use of an instrument."

4

Personality Disorder and Clinical Psychology

CHARACTER DISORDERS

In the *character disorders*—called "personality trait and pattern disturbances" in the official classification—some distortion of the personality develops early in life and persists as a person's style, as the characteristic way in which he copes with his environment and defends himself. A character disorder may never be experienced as something abnormal or intrusive, and may therefore never give rise to anxiety once it becomes established. It is the bent twig of childhood which distorts the form of the personality and gives rise to compensatory changes to offset the distortion.

The end-result may be an adult who seems always inhibited in certain areas of function, or who shows exaggerations of certain personality characteristics, or who stands chronically apart from the affairs of the marketplace, or rushes impetuously into every quickening stream that passes near him.

If such an adult and those who are close to him accept his peculiarities as simply his nature he is not likely to find them disturbing or seek to change them. He may be proud of them and consider them, not incorrectly, as signs of his individuality. It is only when a person with a character distortion realises that something is wrong with him, with his attempts at adaptation, defence, mastery and satisfaction, that he experiences his difficulties as ego-alien, usually without knowing precisely what they are or why he feels as he does. The realisation often comes with repeated failures and dissatisfactions which a person cannot explain away. It may come because new circumstances force a person to compare himself with others, and the comparison raises self-doubt, dissatisfaction and perhaps anxiety. He may even recognise that some of what he has regarded as his special virtue or his mark of individuality may be in fact a pathological need, fear or incapacity. He may find, for example, that his vaunted firmness rests upon a rigidity which keeps him from changing even when a change is necessary, or that his widely known affability is actually a fear of displeasing anyone, or that his willingness to compromise stems from an inability to take a firm stand.

One of the simplest ways of illustrating how a character disorder may be mistaken for a virtue is to look into the motives and the methods of conforming. Every child learns to conform to what is expected of him. This is an integral part of growing up from babyhood through childhood and adolescence to adulthood. It is also the basis of cross-cultural differences in adult personality. The child in each different society is provided with unique models for identification and with adult guidance in learning to conform to these models.

A child in any culture may learn to conform gladly and willingly, but still without achieving normal, effective adulthood. If, for example, a parent demands unquestioning conformity of a child, regardless of the circumstances and of the child's changing needs, the child is most likely to be what he is compelled to be, even if this means serious distortion in his personality or character organisation. If a child receives love in return for self-effacement, and if no other significant adult counteracts this trend, he will grow to adulthood as a chronically self-effacing person who even seek out a marital partner who will also reward his self-effacement. This may be an acceptable situation, satisfying to all concerned, but it is riot a normal personality organisation. Neither is the personality organisation normal that is built around the *masochistic acceptance of punishment or restraint* as *an inevitable part of parental love,* nor one built around *infantile dependence.* Nevertheless if a parent treats a child consistently with *sadistic affection,* the child is likely to develop a reciprocal *masochistic acceptance of sadistic affection* which may last into adult life, as we have seen in some of our neurotic and psychotic patients. If a parent keeps a child consistently in a state of *infantile dependence,* no matter how this is rationalised, the child may always seek out situations and persons that encourage his lifelong pattern.

The important point here is that unquestioning conformity, self-effacement, masochistic suffering and infantile dependence are often acceptable and even sometimes highly valued by society. That is, persons who are themselves relatively free of character distortions often admire them in others, without stopping to consider why these others have them while they themselves do not. It is self-evident that persons who cannot he comfortable unless they are conforming, who enjoy self-effacement and masochistic suffering, or who live contentedly in infantile dependence, are not likely to get into trouble unless they carry their characterological needs to extremes. To avoid common misunderstandings, it is essential to state here that courage, integrity, dependability, normal self-sacrifice and the ability to accept dependence upon others are not signs of character disorder. It is only when these seeming *qualities* turn out to be *demands,* upon a human environment which does not want them, and does not gain in warmth or understanding from them, that we call them disorders rather than virtues.

If a person with a character disorder seeks therapeutic help it is because he has for some reason become dissatisfied with the way he is organised, or with the way he operates, and because he hopes through therapy to acquire a different, happier and more effective way of living. Nowadays it is this hope that motivates a large percentage of patients who turn spontaneously to psychotherapy and psychoanalysis. The hope is an ambitious one. It implies the possibility of making fundamental changes in a personality organisation that has determined the patient's very style of life, perhaps from early childhood. Sometimes such a hope can be fulfilled; more often it cannot. If a patient's hope can be so modified that he expects improvement rather than a radical change, his chances of reaching his goal will be greatly increased, and the chances of therapeutic disillusionment will be correspondingly lessened.

Classification. The problem of classifying character disorder has not yet been solved. We have today two competing systems of classification. Neither of them is satisfactory and the two overlap. One of them takes off from the principle of erogenous zonal development. A recent presentation equates genital or phallic traits with hysterical character, anal-sadistic traits with compulsive character, and oral narcissistic traits at least in part with depressive character. The other system is the one adopted by the official classification. It recognises *compulsive, paranoid, cyclothymic (manic-depressive)* and *schizoid personalities,* to which we shall add *hysterical personality.* Because of the overlapping of these two systems, and because of the still unsettled state of the grouping, we shall follow the official classification to the extent that it parallels neurotic and psychotic reactions.

Before going on to discuss the major varieties of character disorder it might be well to state in what way these differ from neurotic and psychotic reactions. They differ in representing a variety of personality structures which are in some way distorted but manage to achieve a stability that includes the distortion. For example, a compulsive personality or character is so organised that the person having it can operate—as an overconscientious, inhibited, rigid individual—without developing symptoms of an acute conflict, such as we saw in the cases described under obsessive compulsive reactions. Similarly, a manic-depressive (cyclothymic) personality may exhibit unmistakable mood swings that carry the person to euphoric heights and depressive depths, without his becoming psychotically or even neurotically manic or depressed.

In short, there is a distortion of character which more or less permanently alleviates anxiety but leaves a person with less flexibility, less maneuverability than normal.

Under stress, such a distorted personality organisation may develop its own characteristic peculiarities to the point where a neurotic or psychotic or psychosomatic illness appears, with symptoms which are only exaggerations of the distortion. For example, an overconscientious, inhibited, rigid person may develop typical obsessive compulsive symptoms, thereby becoming frankly neurotic. There is also the possibility, repeatedly seen in practice, that such a person may regress under stress and develop a psychotic reaction.

This possibility is of more than theoretical interest. In entering upon the treatment of personality or character disorders one must bear in mind the risk of a psychotic regression resulting from therapeutic disturbance of the pathological equilibrium. Effective psychotherapy and psychoanalysis often involves risk, just as surgical interference does. The therapist who takes such inevitable risks into account is not to be blamed if, in spite of all reasonable precaution, they materialise in the course of therapy. He must be ready, of course, to change his methods and even to taper off therapy, if the dissolution of a character disorder seems to be leading toward psychotic regression has actually precipitated one. No surgeon makes an incision without thereby endangering his patient's health and life; but without this danger there can be no surgery. No Psychotherapist or psychoanalyst opens up the old conflicts crystallised in personality distortion without endangering his patient's equilibrium: but without this danger there can be no effective psychotherapy or psychoanalysis.

MOTILITY

Disorders of motility occur commonly in psychotic states. They may appear in voluntary movement or in posture. They may find expression in a generalised overactivity or in stereotyped repetitive movements of head or limbs. These disturbances can be seen in the consulting-room or in the hospital ward. Interruption of voluntary movement, after its initiation, is the counterpart to the obstruction of speech usually described as blocking of thought. In this motor blocking, patients become fixed at some stage of a voluntary movement, and it is not brought to completion. Sometimes it is easy to see that this interruption of movement is an expression of motor ambivalence (ambitendency).

The posture of some patients is awkward and unusual. Head, neck, and arms may be held rigidly in uncomfortable positions and repetitive movements of the limbs are often to be seen. Postural persistence is thus a common feature. Many of the automatic movements and stereotypes which occur in the schizophrenias can be regarded as due to motor perseveration. This form of perseveration consists of a compulsive repetition of a motor act. It may arise spontaneously or as a response to an instruction. It can be elicited by asking the patient to perform a simple act. The patient will continue with the movement indefinitely. A second form of motor perseveration can also be found in schizophrenic states. Here a response evoked under a first stimulus continues when a second stimulus is offered. This form of perseveration is not as common in the schizophrenias as it is in organic mental states.

Clinical observation alone can lead to the recording of all the disorders of motility. However, this may be possible only over an extended period of time and with the cooperation of nursing staff. What phenomena are to be looked for? Briefly, are there disturbances of voluntary movement? Is the patient able to act on and complete an intention or command? Does motor-blocking occur during the course of a voluntary act? Is there evidence of ambitendency? Note the presence of motor perseveration, repetitive movements, and echopraxia. Describe any disorders of posture. Note whether there is flexibilitas cerea or postural persistence. Are there periods when voluntary movement occurs normally? What kind of verbal content and affect are associated with the transition from abnormal to normal motility and vice versa? Note the fantasies associated with the disorders of motility if they can be elicited. Is voluntary movement disturbed by auditory or visual percepts?

In those circumstances where it is impossible to observe the patient over a long period of time, an assessment of the extent to which motility is disordered can be obtained by the administration of a series of simple tests. These tests are similar to those administered to patients suspected of suffering from organic brain disease (Luria, 1966). Their function is to elicit delay in response, postural persistence, perseveration, and disorganisation of voluntary movement.

SENSORI-MOTOR ORGANISATION

It is sometimes forgotten that the schizophrenic patient exhibits disturbances of bodily function which are reflected in physical signs. Several years ago, Shattock (1950) and Hoskins (1946) described changes which appear in the different bodily systems in the schizophrenias. More recently, interest has been revived in the neurological abnormalities which can be detected in some schizophrenic patients. There is some evidence in favour of the view that both positive and negative neurological signs are encountered significantly more often in schizophrenic patients than in healthy controls (Lemke, 1955).

Patients who demonstrate psychomotor phenomena almost always present disturbances at the sensori-motor level also. Although these phenomena are transient in nature and variable in expression, particularly in the recent case, it is essential to record their presence. On the motor side, hypotonia, hypertonia of the limb musculature, diminution or absence, accentuation, and asymmetrical reactions of the tendon reflexes have been recorded. The hyper-reflexia is sometimes associated with a tonic reflex response which can be most easily elicited during the examination of the biceps tendon reflexes. The biceps muscle progressively shortens with successive blows of the tendon hammer until the forearm is quite unsupported, making an angle of various degrees with the upper arm. Here there is a persistence of posture akin to the cataleptic phenomenon. It can, like the latter, be regarded as due to tonic or static perseveration. This can be contrasted with the other form of perseveration already described in the section on motility (clonic or kinetic perseveration), which occurs in the course of voluntary movement.

On the sensory side, inattention to tactile stimuli is a common finding in some cases of schizophrenia, and generalised analgesia may be encountered.

The localisation of tactile stimuli is often disturbed, displacement occurring from one body-part to another. This takes place at random, the stimulus not being transposed to the symmetrically opposite part of the body.

With regard to sensory organisation, schizophrenic patients have been found to show a face dominance when examined by means of double simultaneous stimulation. Sensory signs, like the motor phenomena, show a striking variability of response—a positive sign being obtained, disappearing, and then re-emerging at a later time.

In the course of a neurological examination special attention should be paid to the presence of tonus changes in the limb muscles—asymmetrical states should be noted. Similarly, a record should be made of hyper-reflexia and asymmetrical reactions of the tendon reflexes.

Attention should be paid to the possible presence of tonic reflex responses, particularly in those cases presenting with hypertonia of the upper limb musculature.

Similarly, investigation must be made of inattention to tactile and painful stimuli. Are there indications of displacement (disturbed localisation) of sensation from one body-part to another? Is there face dominance?

During the course of a routine neurological examination perseverative signs frequently make their appearance, particularly when the patient is asked to carry out simple instructions. Such signs should be recorded.

METHODOLOGY OF CLINICAL OBSERVATION

The collection of clinical observations in cases of psychosis presents many difficulties. The observing physician is rarely afforded the opportunity of witnessing the entirety of the clinical manifestations, as occurs in physical disease. In the psychoses there are few objective signs which can be recorded independently of the patient's cooperation.

Most of the clinical data consist of the patient's subjective experiences, much of which he is reluctant to communicate. This reluctance is often most pronounced with the psychiatrist and therefore it is necessary to know to whom the patient is willing to unburden himself, whether a fellow-patient, a nurse, or an occupational therapist.

The fact that the phenomena are psychological in nature means that there is a variability in the clinical picture far exceeding that which appears in somatic disease. Certain symptoms and behavioural features are present one day and not the next. They are revealed to one examiner and not to another. The presence of this variability demands that the patient shall be observed over a fairly lengthy period of time if a complete account of the condition is to be obtained.

It is well known that patients suffering from psychoses frequently make their strongest attachment to members of the nursing and ancillary staffs. It is to them that they reveal their thoughts and feelings. Additionally, the nurse and occupational therapist are with the patient for long periods of the day and are therefore in a position to observe his behaviour in all its aspects. The patient's attitude to the psychiatrist is a complex one and this interferes with the patient's ability and willingness to express himself.

Very often the psychiatrist becomes the recipient of fantasies which convert him into a punitive rather than a helpful figure. This may increase in intensity until he becomes part of a persecutory system. It is usually impossible to detach these fantasies by means of explanation because of the patient's lack of insight in to the fact that he is ill.

The collection of clinical information about psychotic states is therefore dependent on the establishment of a team approach to the patient and his illness. In this regard, the nurses and occupational therapists have a part to play as important as that of the psychiatrist; and it is essential that they should come to appreciate the significance of the phenomena with which they are confronted.

These data only become available when a constructive working relationship is achieved between psychiatrist anti nursing staff. With such a background it is possible, for example, to direct their attention to the importance of recording such behavioural items as unusual posture, difficulty in the initiation and completion of voluntary movements, compulsive repetition in writing, drawing, and speech, and echo reactions. They can also observe and note the manner in which the patient reacts to their approach and continuing interest. Is the patient attentive or inattentive, responsive or unresponsive?

Does he involve them in his delusional preoccupations? In order to systematise these and other observations a modified form of the examination scheme can be devised. Regular meeting can be held to discuss the scheme and foster familiarity in its use. Continuous practice with the scheme in discussions helps to provide some degree of control over the unreliability of observation that is inevitable in any descriptive technique.

The psychiatrist can gather information either by seeing the patient alone or by holding group sessions with a number of patients. Whatever method is employed, it is necessary for the observation to continue over at least a three-month period. The group situation has the advantage of providing a setting where the patient can be observed interacting with others, and there is often less restraint and more spontaneity than in the individual session.

Patients suffering from psychotic illness do not spontaneously provide recollections of childhood or adolescence, as do patients with neurosis. They appear to he preoccupied with their irrational ideas and this militates against the production of information about their current life experiences. Nevertheless, the individual session gives the observer a better chance of assessing the patient's capacity to relate and the extent of the non-psychotic process still intact. During the observation period, information obtained from all sources—psychiatrists, nurse, and occupational therapist—is pooled at weekly meetings.

It is inevitable that some degree of unreliability will always he a hazard of the clinical method when it is unaccompanied by the kinds of objective measure which are commonplace in clinical medicine—the biochemical and radiological examinations.

It is probably a mistake, however, to exaggerate what has come to be known as observer error in clinical examinations. This factor, observer error, will always influence the results of clinical observation, particularly in psychiatry. It can be partially controlled by the method described above where observers are adequately trained, have adequate trained, have adequate experience, and obtain familiarity with a recording instrument—the examination scheme in this case.

Objections can be made against the technique of observation and the method of recording, and the question can then be asked: 'How far is the method reliable? Beck (1967), criticising the author's observational approach (Freeman, 1967), wonders how, even where the observer has the necessary training to note the phenomena that are nosologically significant, the author and his colleagues go about evaluating their gathered information, and how important trends can be detected from the large file that must accumulate for each patient.

Beck is critical of the author's alternative to rating scales as a method of recording and assessing clinical data: if rating scales fail to provide essential detail, then can reliance be placed on the observations made by nurses and occupational therapists?

The need for control over clinical observation, whether made by psychiatrist, nurse, or occupational therapist, is absolutely essential, as Beck (1967) advocates. However, the objective 'statistical' approach is no less vulnerable to criticism, although of a different kind. It has difficulty in producing significant information about the patient beyond identifying the presence of certain signs and symptoms. It is uncertain what the method is extracting from the clinical milieu—a criticism that can to some extent be made also of the clinical approach, although here a degree of control is exercised over the attitudes of the observer. Again, the objective method is quite incapable of throwing light on those subjective experiences which may be associated with the data recorded on rating scales. Finally, this method takes no account of influences operating on patient and observer at the time of sampling.

The examination scheme described in this chapter is an attempt to begin a process of building a reliable and comprehensive method of recording and evaluating the manifestations of psychotic illness. The points that Beck (1967) has raised must be taken into account. It would, however, seem logical to begin with an account in qualitative terms of a scheme which has been built on the foundations of clinical experience with psychotic patients.

The research for the future would then consist of developing this scheme so that it would eventually achieve sufficient reliability to be employed to assess mental status before and during research procedures, or to estimate changes in symptomatology before and after therapy.

INTEGRATION OF PERSONALITY

The technique of integration of personality lies in knowing bow to handle the emotions properly and how to harmonise and unify the different functions of the total mind—emotion, intellect, and will. The man begins his emotional life like an animal. But man becomes man when he rises from the animal plane to the divine plane through the stages of human development. When he transforms his lower passions and integrates his emotions and makes his life altruistic, then alone does he function on the divine plane. As Professor Edgar S. Brightman says: "Spirituality is a life of harmony, unity, and integration."

In order to achieve transformation of personality, the first requisite is that an individual must have the desire to integrate his emotions. The growth of personality depends on the intensity of this desire. If the desire is strong and the person makes a strenuous effort for its fulfilment, he succeeds; if it is less intense and the effort less strenuous, his growth is affected accordingly.

Another factor to be considered is that many people do not have sustained desire and effort; they are unsteady and lukewarm and, consequently, integration is retarded. Sometimes circumstances create a kind of craving for development; glorious living examples of personal integration also inspire many people. However, this is often temporary and they do not seem to make any real progress. They become unstable in their efforts. Those who are unsteady in their desire for integration of personality and are temporarily motivated to attain it, through change in circumstances or casual ambition frequently have an emotional reaction. They lose all incentive for effort, feeling incapable of success. Often the basis for this reaction is lack of perseverance and tenacity rather than lack of capacity.

That is why some spiritual teachers feel it is useless to spend time with such persons in discussing methods and practices for spiritual life and emotional integration. On the other hand, there are some true lovers of mankind who are prepared to do everything for the unsteady persons who have temporary higher desires.

They know that their love, sympathy, and living example will gradually stimulate and stabilise the desire of these erratic people. Sri Ramakrishna, the great spiritual leader of nineteenth-century India, used to say that a piece of wet fuel kept near the fireplace for some time will become dry and fit for use. So these spiritual teachers feel that if disorganised and distracted people can remain in their company, and if they are given genuine love, the personality of the erratic ones will be changed and they will become tenacious in their efforts to integrate their emotions. Herein lies the utility of guidance and dynamic sympathy in the relationship between the integrated teacher and the seeker of integration.

A case in point is A, who became interested in the religious ideal through association with the spiritual teacher. This individual lost interest, in the course of time, because of emotional attractions which turned his mind into other channels. Nevertheless, the teacher continued to shower love and sympathy on the student, with deep understanding of the instability of human emotion. This gradually influenced the student who eventually became stabilised. Another person, B, was also associated with the religious teacher and became interested in the higher ideal. When other emotional attractions pulled his mind away, this individual had the misfortune to lose personal contact with the teacher through circumstances which compelled a separation. B had been devoted previously to the ideal; but when the dynamic and sympathetic influence of the teacher was withdrawn the effect on B's emotions was disastrous. There are a few methods of stabilising the desire for emotional integration. The constant association with an integrated personality, preferably a spiritual teacher, is important. This association stimulates a higher desire in the student and aspirant. We have seen many instances of radical transformation through such contacts. Again, there have been some individuals who, although they wished to develop themselves, lost their sustaining power of spiritual growth because they did not have the association of an integrated personality.

Two young men, C and D, had a mutual friend who persuaded them to go with him to visit a great spiritual person. Even though C was not so anxious to give up his old habits, he continued to go with his friend to see this great personality. As time went on, he went through a radical change and became emotionally integrated and spiritually inspired. On the other hand, D could not continue his association and as a result he lost all incentive to stabilise himself emotionally.

It is true that personalities of spiritual magnitude are not always to be found, so it is advisable for an individual to create the atmosphere himself through study of the teachings of the great religious leaders. In the course of time, this habit gradually inculcates a desire to change one's emotional structure and to evolve spiritually.

The second requirement for the integration of personality is that an individual must have a higher philosophy of life. Without this there is no possibility of integration. As we brought out aesthetic, intellectual, or national ideals may direct a person's emotions to one goal; yet these emotions may become destructive forces. Moreover, the hedonistic philosophy of life produces selfishness instead of unselfishness and gradually creates disintegration in the personality instead of unification. So again we suggest that the supreme goal of life should be regarded as the manifestation of the divine nature of man. This furnishes the real basis of self-control. By self-control we mean the control of disruptive emotions and the redirection of the so-called primitive urges (self-preservation, self-expression, sex pleasure, knowledge, and gregariousness) and the secondary emotions (greed, fear, envy, and so forth). It goes without saying that the personality cannot be integrated so long as man has tension within him, either because of the repression of any of these urges, lack of satisfaction, overstimulation of one or another of the urges at the cost of harmony in the emotional structure in the mind, or because of the malfunctioning of the emotions.

So it is necessary that there be a certain amount of control of the primitive urges. Their harmonisation and transformation is of vital importance for the integration of personality. Integration must be based on emotional stability and harmony; it cannot be accomplished by repression or unbridled and unregulated emotional satisfaction. That is the reason that a sound philosophy of life—that the human soul is potentially divine and we are the children of God and joint heirs with Christ, according to St. Paul—is absolutely essential for emotional stability. Unless this attitude is cultivated, there is no means for the control of the lower emotions. Control of the destructive emotions enables a person to fulfill the real purpose and supreme goal of life—the manifestation of divinity in man or love of God and neighbour.

In fact, this is the rationale behind the desire for the integration of personality. Mere intellectual, philosophical, theological, or sociological understanding of the establishment of the brotherhood of man does not have sustaining power nor does it integrate the emotions.

Many absolutist philosophers often lose their absolutism in actual life when their emotions are aroused. Theologians lose the conception of love of God and neighbour when national passions are stimulated. Great scientists, as we have observed previously, may become subservient to the national cause and lose sight of higher ideals. Many religious groups also in the name of religion have not hesitated to express most inhuman and brutal tendencies at different times in history. Such evidence shows that something more than intellectual understanding of the ideal is necessary. How sound is the statement made by Professor Brightman in his *Nature and Values:*

No philosophy which does not satisfy his whole mind will permanently satisfy man. Since Plato first saw this principle and used it as a pulverising weapon against sexual sin, it has been a cornerstone of any sound philosophy of life. But what is sound is not always immediately effective. A tragic feature of human life is displayed in the violence with which man opposes his own permanent good in the interest of his temporary good, or supposed good. Passion and greed are blind but intense: and they often sweep away the power of the truest and highest ideals as if they were no more than film air.

Professor Mowrer also declares: "Thus it is that we come to see that neurosis involves, basically, a learning deficit rather than a learning excess, but one which the individual is often unable to correct, spontaneously and unaided."

In our experience we have known persons who were intellectually inspired by high ideals but who could not carry them out. One such individual is E who did not have a proper understanding of the higher philosophy of life, even though she was inspired by personal contacts with the teacher. Neither did she apply and practice the steps outlined below. Her family life was affected by her selfish attitude and arrogance; yet she did not try to overcome this attitude and she failed to integrate her personality. F was inspired intellectually by a higher ideal but he continued to suffer with functional diseases because he lacked emotional stability and did not follow the required steps. Another man, G, continued to have functional ailments and was extremely unpopular among his associates because he failed to integrate his emotions or to follow the other steps. He, too, had intellectual ideals but was unable to carry them out in his daily life. So the third step—directing the emotions to God—is essential for emotional integration. Then a person can strike at the root of emotional disintegration and selfish urges. Human beings have various innate and spontaneous emotional expressions. Some naturally have the attitude of a child that loves his parents; others naturally feel and express conjugal love; again there are some who have parental love for children; while another group likes the comradeship of friends.

Those who have a predominantly emotional type of mind should be helped to establish one of these relationships with God, as it is easier for them to use their natural tendencies for this. They should think of God as their child, friend, mother, father, or beloved, and then express their emotions to Him through one of these relationships. In their devotional practices they should try to remember this relationship and accordingly act as if God were present in that particular form to receive their affectionate treatment and offering.

This very habit of doing something for God as their own friend, child, and so forth, will gradually intensify their feeling toward Him and consequently will unify all their other emotions. Even in their human relationships and interpersonal behaviour they should try to remember the presence of God in those whom they love. Through the cultivation of these inner faculties, one can gradually unify the emotions.

The saintly character among the Christians, Hindus, Jews, and others have demonstrated that integration of personality can be accomplished through proper handling of the emotions and directing them to God. St. Francis of Assisi, St. Anthony of Padua, St. Teresa of Avila, and St. Therese of Lisieux (The Little Flower), were great examples in the Christian tradition. The devotees of Brindaban, Mirabai, and Tulsidas of India, and many of the great disciples of Sri Ramakrishna of modern India, illustrate this point. Similar instances can be found in the tradition of other religions.

In the fourth step an individual must struggle in every action to express the consciousness of his divine nature. He must also try to see the presence of God in others. The moment the lower passions arise—either because of the weakness, disharmony, or destructive activities of other—that very moment he must try to see God in them and thereby overcome his passions. Anger cannot be conquered by anger and hatred cannot be conquered by hatred; it is love that conquers hatred, as Buddha declared. The more a person expresses anger and hatred the more these tendencies possess him. In other words, he intensifies those lower tendencies through their expression. Really and truly a man is the victim of his passion. According to Hindu psychologists, emotions can be more effectively controlled before they are expressed, when they are still in an incipient state. The founder of Indian psychology, Patanjali, says that the *samskaras* (the impressions or unconscious contents of the mind) must be controlled and transformed. According to him: "Their control is by practice and non-attachment." In his *Raja Yoga,* Swami Vivekananda equally stresses the control of these unconscious impressions so that they can be transformed from destructive to creative forces. He says:

...When a large number of these impressions is left on the mind they coalesce, and become a habit. It is said, "habit is second nature"; it is first nature also, and the whole nature of man; everything that we are is the result of habit. That gives us consolation, because, it is only habit, we can make and unmake it at any time. The Samskaras are left by these vibrations passing out of our mind, each one of them leaving its result. Our character is the sum total of these marks, and according as some particular wave prevails one takes that tone. If good prevails one becomes good, if wickedness, one becomes wicked, if joyfulness, one becomes happy. The only remedy for bad habits is counter habits; all the bad habits that have left their impressions are to be controlled by good habits, Go on doing good, thinking holy thoughts, continuously; that is the only way to suppress base impressions. Never say any man is hopeless, because he only represents a character, a bundle of habits which can be checked by new and better ones. Character is repealed habits, and repeated habits alone can reform character.

The fifth step is the cultivation of feelings opposite to anger, hatred and other disintegrating urges. The deliberate cultivation of higher qualities quiets the mind and gradually integrates the emotions. The more one expresses his higher emotions and altruistic tendencies, the more he overcomes the Opposite tendencies. Thereby he creates new unconscious contents in the mind.

This is what we call the formation of character. Hindu psychologists are most emphatic on the deliberate cultivation of other tendencies, even for the so-called destructive and disintegrated personalities. It has been found through experience that this not only integrates those who are controlling and redirecting their emotions but it also has a good effect on the persons to whom the emotions are expressed. The teachings of the Sermon on the Mount and the *Dhammapada* of Buddhistic tradition support our conviction. Sri Ramakrishna used to urge his followers to direct their emotions into higher channels. "Therefore one should direct them to God. If you must have desire and greed, then you should desire love of God and be greedy to attain him." It should be noted here that rather than repressing the emotions, this method enables one to control, regulate, and gradually to transform them. It goes beyond what some of the Western psychologists call sublimation. Moreover, it creates emotional satisfaction while a person is still struggling for the attainment of the goal.

The next step is the practice of concentration. The constant thought of God brings out all the latent powers of mind and thereby enables a person to carry out the spiritual philosophy of life in everyday activities. His will power is developed by this practice. Without will power he cannot apply his ideals in his activities. It stands to reason that when any kind of force is scattered it loses its vigour. On the other hand, when it is concentrated it becomes extremely powerful. Usually mental forces are scattered in various emotional urges, interests, and activities. The practice of concentration unifies them so that all the latent powers are manifested. Then a person can see God in himself and others and his attitude is changed in his interpersonal relationships. A man of integration whose will is unified never submits to lower passions. On the contrary, he becomes a centre of love and attraction.

When the integration of personality is accomplished through the application of the six steps—desire for integration, acceptance of a higher philosophy of life, direction of the emotions to God, expression of inner divinity, cultivation of higher tendencies, and the practice of concentration—the person becomes established in the idea. He is then a true altruist and can influence others to change their lives.

For instance, Krishna, Buddha, Jesus, Ramakrishna, and other great spiritual personalities changed people by their dynamic influence. Others like St. Paul and Swami Vivekananda also transformed many individuals. We have personally observed that even lesser personalities influence others if they have dynamic love and sympathy.

We have seen how disturbed and disintegrated persons were completely changed by outstanding spiritual personalities through the dynamic influence of sympathy and love. About forty years ago in India a man joined the Ramakrishna Order and went to live in the monastery near Calcutta. His brother, who was addicted to intoxicants and other undesirable habits, wanted to take him away. He went to the monastery in an intoxicated and, angry condition one day for this purpose. He was met by Swami Premananda, a great disciple of Sri Ramakrishna. It was a hot day, so the Swami sent for water and food for the man and fanned him, talking gently and kindly to him. After a while, the man became calm and decided to leave. As he was going, the Swami said: "Come again!" Although the man was drunk, those magnetic words made a deep impression on his mind. He had never experienced such love. The very next day he returned to the monastery, intoxicated as ever. But Swami Premananda greeted him affectionately and gave him more refreshments, talking gently with him all the while. As the man prepared to take his leave, the Swami repeated the words: "Come again!" The man returned to the monastery many times, for he could not resist that love. In a short while he gave up his unfortunate habits and asked if he might be allowed to remain in the monastery. He eventually joined the Order and did wonderful work for suffering humanity. He was changed into an altruist by the love and sympathy of Swami Premananda. Similar incidents can be noted from the lives of Swami Brahmananda and others whom we knew intimately. Other religions also record such incidents.

Love and sympathy are the most dynamic forces for changing the personalities of others. An illustration of this is seen in the life of a woman to whom we shall refer as H. She came to us in an erratic and disorganised condition when she was young. Her home life was seriously disrupted by conflict between her parents which ended in divorce. She did not have any real emotional satisfactions nor did she have any sense of security in the home. Her father remarried but the mother remained single. Unfortunately, neither of the parents seemed to be a stabilising influence in the girl's life. The only way she could get emotional satisfaction was to seek happiness outside. She had no stability of life in this, as she could not definitely form a goal to be achieved. Her only interest was to engage herself in social functions and entertainment.

Consequently, her whole future was threatened by inevitable frustration and consequent neurosis. When she came to us we tried gradually to convince her of the higher spiritual values of life and to show her that life was not meant for mere sense enjoyments and social functions, since these would sooner or later lose their attraction. She would need moral, intellectual, and spiritual values in order to sustain herself.

She was given a definite scheme of life so that she could gradually find satisfaction in intellectual, moral, and spiritual functions. She used to visit her teacher at least twice a week. She also took up spiritual practices of concentration, meditation, and repetition of the name of God. Gradually, she unified her will power so that she could live according to her new attitude. Constant sympathetic and loving encouragement was given to her so that her emotions gradually became stabilised. She had the desire to integrate her personality and she understood the higher philosophy of life, so with guidance she followed all the steps to the best of her ability. Redirection of her emotions to God transformed her personality; her life was thoroughly reorganised; and her activities became creative and constructive.

Another young woman was considerably disorganised due to a serious conflict between herself and her mother. The mother was an aggressive and domineering person. The girl was also self-expressive in her early adolescence. Naturally, there was serious conflict between them. The girl felt frustrated and thwarted by the mother's domination. Consequently, she sought satisfaction, self-expression, and security through other channels. The result was disastrous. The personality of the girl was seriously affected. Fortunately, in an almost unexpected way she developed a desire for integrated religious life. However, she needed considerable encouragement to sustain this temporary higher aspiration. She was given the higher values of life and was asked to do her daily duties in the spirit of service and consecration. She was also told that her real self-expression would be attained only when she could consecrate her activities, even her livelihood, and do everything in the spirit of service.

She was not told to crush her expression. On the contrary, she was requested to direct it through intellectual pursuits, higher growth in everyday life, and through spiritual realisation. She was also given systematic spiritual practices of concentration and meditation and other devotional exercises. She was encouraged to study the books which would sustain her desire for spiritual growth. She formerly came to see us frequently. Patience and loving understanding on the part of the teacher inspired her to go ahead with her spiritual practices in spite of her conflicts and unsteadiness. Old habits and unconscious urges persisted for some time, but the new inter-pretation of life and spiritual practices strengthened by encouragement and sympathetic understanding enabled her to change the course of her life.

A young man came to us about fifteen years ago. He had a mistaken idea that religious service meant giving up his usual employment and taking up social service work. He was frustrated because he wanted to marry and settle down in life, but the type of work he was doing did not enable him to maintain even himself. Had he married then, he and his family would have become a burden to society. Fortunately, he listened to our advice which was to qualify himself for greater achievement in life. He was also told that daily duties can be converted into worship.

There was no reason to think that business and household duties were necessarily secular, He was given an understanding of the relative values of life in relation to the supreme goal of religious achievement. He was also given systematic spiritual practices.

According to our advice he began to practice meditation on a particular aspect of God that was suited to his temperament. He also practiced certain forms of prayer and repetition of the name of God and he spent time in daily scriptural study. He was tenacious and enthusiastic in his understanding of the new ways of life and in his religious exercises. He went ahead and qualified himself for a secular position in life. His frustration vanished and he is now doing something worth while.

Many of the self-expressive and egocentric modern aspirants dislike to be told that they need to change the course of their lives or that they need to go through necessary technical training of the mind or that certain kinds of activities and achievements are harmful for them. They often try to find excuses to go their own way, even though they want help and support from the teacher. They even try to get the sanction of the teacher for their activities. In many cases, a spiritual teacher should be wise enough not to allow the students to feel that their ego is to be crushed. Otherwise, the purpose of spiritual guidance will be wholly defeated in certain sections of modern society. If the teacher can pursue the tactful method of guidance with a great deal of sympathy and love, and without letting the student feel that the teacher is interfering, he can accomplish much in the long run in stimulating a desire for integration of personality on the part of the student.

We have often noticed how tactfully Swami Brahmananda, our peat master, would handle some individuals. He often would say that a certain type of person would only accept tactful hints for their own good. How true this statement was has been verified by our later experiences. There was a teacher who was harsh and tactless to some of his students, even though he thought only of their welfare. The effect was disappointing.' In fact, he actually defeated his purpose with some of his students. As we go through the experiences of spiritual instruction, we fully realise how far-sighted Swami Brahmananda was in his handling of human personalities who seemed to be interested in the integration of their lives. Time and again his tact and unlimited love and patience gradually changed them. The spiritual teacher who really' wants to further the welfare of his students and the therapist who really wants to help his patients and clients will remember this important point. Otherwise, they will actually defeat their own purpose. This is not what Carl Rogers calls non-directive counselling. Our method is based on the teacher's deep spiritual understanding of the student and on his love for him. We admit that this type of treatment requires time. But no human integration is possible without the need for time.

Freud and his followers advocate "transference" in order to do therapeutic work. This means that the patient consciously or unconsciously must establish a relationship with the therapist, in order for the psychotherapy to be effective. Freudian transference has some value in this connection, but psychotherapists should realise that the basis of transformation ought to be at least sympathy. Their influence could become more effective if they themselves would try to integrate their personality. It is true that they go through psychoanalysis. However, psychoanalysis cannot and does not properly integrate a person, no matter how helpful it may be in the treatment of disorganised persons. Individuals also need definite mental training, as we have suggested in the various steps. Only when the psychotherapists are integrated and have sympathy and love for their patients can they become dynamic forces in the process of integration. Any person who wants to help disintegrated or unstable individuals must have deep sympathy and love. Only then is he able to inspire the people to adopt and apply a higher ideal in life.

We are a little concerned by the emphasis of Dr. Robert W. White on the technique of non-directive counselling, standard psychoanalysis, and brief psychoanalysis. It seems to us that the greatest emphasis should be given to the development of personality and not merely to the technique of training psychologists or counsellors. Mere technical knowledge of the method does not help the client or patient to reconstruct his personality, but we appreciate the points Dr. White brings out. They are worth the consideration of every psychotherapist and religious counsellor. He writes:

There are four important aspects of the therapeutic situation. (a) The therapist is *expert,* in the sense that he possesses special training, experience, and knowledge about maladjusted and disordered behaviour. (b) The therapist is *permissive,* in the sense that he serves only the interests of health and makes no censorious judgments upon the patient's acts or feelings. (c) the therapist is *interested and friendly,* communicating in this way a certain warmth that makes the relationship more personal than is ordinarily the case in a professional consultation. (d) The therapist is a *source of encouragement....* the effect of his presence is to increase courage.

It is gratifying to note what an outstanding psychiatrist, Dr. David G. Wright, has to say about the qualifications of a psycho-therapist. He has had a great deal of therapeutic and administrative experience. According to him:

Unfaltering follow-through of treatment efforts, no matter what the difficulty is, and no matter what the time consumed, is necessary. To do this, capacity for, and training towards, self-understanding and un-wavering determination to aim for the completion of the patient's personality redevelopment, and never for anything less, is required.

He goes on to say: "In connection with the qualifications of therapists, the first phase of therapy is that of making and maintaining contact; of becoming a meaningful part of the patient's word." Dr. Wright does not express this view merely from an intellectual standpoint but also out of the depth of his own experience in the treatment of patients. He deserves a great deal of appreciation for the fact that he continued regular treatment of his patients at one time in spite of a serious illness of his wife. Such adamantine tenacity and sense of responsibility and feeling for the patients is needed in a counsellor, therapist, and religious leader.

On the other hand, the emphasis on technical knowledge of counselling and other types of psychotherapy is often discouraging. To illustrate this we present one incident. A minister who took up the technique of counselling used to call on an elderly man. The man was isolated and depressed as he had no one to visit with him, so the religious leader used to smile and talk with him. After a while, the old man became encouraged and he used to look forward to the weekly visits. As a result of these contacts he showed a great change. Thereupon, the religious counseler discontinued his visits.

This upset the old man immensely and made him worse than he was in the first place. We do not imply that all religious counsellors and therapists behave like this. But we have evidence enough to prove that mere emphasis on the understanding of technique alone is often advocated. A situation to illustrate this is that of a young girl of twenty-two years of age who was a patient in a reputable private mental hospital in New England. She happened to be known to us through her father, so we began to visit her in the hospital. She told us that she was not confiding all her problems to the doctor. "I don't tell him my problems because he doesn't care for me," she said. Her expression was significant Dr. Wright fully realises this point, which he has expressed in his paper as well as in his personal treatment of his patients. There must be feeling for the patient, client, or student who is seeking stability and integration and above all spiritual development.

It seems that many outstanding religious leaders who advocate the necessity of pastoral counselling feel that religious ministers or counsellors should go through deep analytical therapy in order to be of help to their parishioners and clients. Dr. Seward Hiltner, one of the leading personalities in this field, suggests that the pastors should undergo psychoanalysis as part of their training, just as the professional psychiatrists do. He also says:

Even a relatively brief series of consultations with a good therapist can be valuable to the minister, both personally and professionally. Professionally speaking such personal therapy is important not so much in teaching one how to counsel, as in teaching him what to expect from counselling and therapy.

However, he indicates that it is not absolutely necessary for a minister to seek the services of a therapist. He writes:

Of course, the number of therapists is small; it costs money to go to them—though not an excessive amount usually; and they are sometimes ignorant of philosophy and blindly antitheological. We do not say a minister must have such consultations. But if he has the time and means and accessibility and interest, he will get something that profits him both personally and professionally. He will still, however, need training in pastoral counselling.

It goes without saying that Dr. Hiltner wants to help the people and also to teach the young pastoral counsellors. We would have appreciated finding passages in his book advocating the direct mental training of religious counsellors,

Technical training and mere knowledge of the causes of mental disturbances and disintegration do not integrate the personality and change the behaviour pattern even of those personalities who are not totally disintegrated. Emotional reconstruction needs a sympathetic, patient, and loving emotional relationship between the helper and the helped, as well as an understanding of techniques and causes. The reconstruction must be achieved by the person himself, but we agree with Dr. Wright and such others that help is needed not only by the disorganised persons but also by the fairly normal persons. Clinical psychologists and religious counsellors should recognise that their own personality has a tremendous effect on their clients, patients, or students. If they are loving and sympathetic, then their clients will react in one way, but if the counsellors are indifferent and treat their clients as mere cases, they will react in another way. People who do not have affection and sympathy cannot touch the emotional life of those they are trying to help. Religious counsellors especially should remember this fact; otherwise, their aggressive and non-directive counselling will mean little where the integration of personality is concerned.

A question may arise about the effect of the integrated personality on society at large. Therefore, it should be noted that the principles which are applicable to individual integration are also applicable to social integration. Social integration and stability depend on the kind of philosophy adopted by a society and its application by the leading personalities. It is impossible to integrate a society unless its leaders are integrated. The dynamics of the individual mind affect the group. The lives of great reformers like Krishna, Buddha, Jesus, and Ramakrishna, and St. Francis and Swami Vivekananda have already proved that the dynamic, integrated personality can transform cultural patterns in society by changing the individual thought currents and lifting the people to a higher plane of consciousness. So it is the individual integrated personalities who build up an integrated and harmonious culture.

PERCEPTION OF THE SELF, SELF-REGARD, AND PERSONAL IDENTITY

In order to overcome difficulties in the comprehension and usage of the term 'cathexis of the self' and the associated concept of narcissism, this section of the examination scheme has been designated 'Perception of the Self, Self-regard, and Personal Identity'. It would be unfortunate if a psychoanalytical concept i.e. narcissism so valuable in description and explanation, were to be relegated to a position of secondary importance. Here again, the investigator encounters the problem of how far it is justified to separate observation and interpretation. Cut off from explanatory concepts, observational data frequently appear disconnected and meaningless. On the other hand, excessive attachment to interpretation can lead to a stereotyped explanation of clinical phenomena and to inattention to significant data.

Descriptive psychiatry has drawn attention to the various phenomena which reveal how the patient experiences the self in psychotic illness. However, the tendency here has been to categorise the various phenomena under separate headings—for example, depersonalisation, transivitism, etc.—and this has led to their appearing separate from one another and without any interconnections. Psychoanalysis has corrected this static tendency by suggesting that the disorders affecting the mental and bodily self can be understood as the result of disturbance in distribution of libido between self and object. Such a state of affairs implies the presence of a state of pathological narcissism.

Many of the phenomena that appear in psychosis can be classified under the heading of narcissism because they possess so many characteristics similar to those encountered in the course of childhood development. Psychoanalytic theory proposes two narcissistic phases in childhood: First, there is the stage of primary narcissism, where bodily and mental experience are syncretic in nature. Alteration in the condition of one implies alteration in the condition of the other. As development proceeds beyond early infancy, object relations are established and this primary form of narcissism becomes progressively limited.

Nevertheless in childhood it reveals its presence in a cognitive and affective egocentrism. It is this egocentrism that is universally encountered in psychotic state—sometimes obviously libidinised, sometimes not. The advent in childhood of an awareness of personal and sexual identity, with an implication of stable identifications, constitutes the stage of secondary narcissism. In contrast to the primary phase, objects exist in their own right although they can still be the recipients of narcissistic cathexes. The psychosis is characterised by a dissolution of adult mental functions.

This leads to the exposure of mental processes which have limited adaptive value: in this case, phenomena which reveal a disorder of perception of the self, self-regard, and personal identity. These phenomena, regarded by psychoanalysts as narcissistic, have long been the subject of discussion and controversy. What is their nature? Their resemblance to certain forms of childhood thinking and behaviour has already been referred to. Does this mean that in psychosis there is the reappearance of narcissistic phases of development—particularly of primary narcissism—due to fixations occurring at an early infantile period, or is this pathological narcissism something different only brought to light by the disease process? The latter was the view taken by Schilder (1926). Such a view dispenses with the need for regression and fixation. While this problem is not particularly relevant in the present context, it stresses the importance of taking into account the known facts of development when approaching the symptomatology of the psychoses for the purposes of classification.

With such considerations in mind, the following questions may be asked: is there an adequate investment of the boundaries of the self and the self-representations? If so, is this constant or is it subject to derangements during the course of the illness? Is there evidence of a loss of stability of the self as reflected in disturbances of self-object discrimination, resulting in a projection (externalisation) of self-representations and/or a merging with the object leading to transient identification? Are there specific changes in the physical characteristics of the body as experienced subjectively, and loss of autonomy of the self as indicated by such phenomena as flexibilitias cerea and automatic obedience? Is there a disturbance of personal and sexual identity? Are there indications of a disorder of the self as evidenced in increase in intensity of bodily sensations, perceptions, thought, and affect, in hypochondriacal preoccupations, in changes in the body-image, in an over-valuation of the self, and in an exaggerated belief in the effect of thought and action? Is there an awareness of disintegration of the self, a weakness or loss of bodily or mental functions?

COMPULSIVE PERSONALITY OR CHARACTER

There are some compulsive trends in every normal person. They appear as automatic orderliness, neatness, frugality and obstinacy, and as automatic conformity, inhibition and conscientiousness. Without these relative inflexibilities a stable society would be impossible. Even taking pleasure in being neat, orderly and frugal, in standing one's ground, in conforming, in practicing inhibition and being conscientious *is* in itself far from abnormal. Such pleasure is one of the major sources of satisfaction in being an acceptable member of society. Its roots are in the child's early need to be a member of his family, of his later need to belong to neighbourhood and school groups, and of his pressing adolescent need to be one of the crowd.

We speak *of a compulsive personality* or *character* only when these trends are so pronounced and insistent that severe anxiety appears when people or circumstances interfere with their exercise. It is this threat of severe anxiety that forces tine people to practice extreme conformity, to be excessively conscientious, and to exhibit crippling inhibitions in areas where initiative or active participation is essential for normal function, especially in sex and aggression. People with compulsive personality or character distortions suffer from life-long unwarranted concern over conforming, over conflicts as to what is good and bad, right and wrong, clean and dirty. They may overcompensate for their compulsive trends by immersing themselves in work to the virtual exclusion of relaxation and recreation. These are the "driven" persons. One sees examples of such overcompensation in business and professional men, in housewives and mothers, who neglect all the other phases that would make their lives we' balanced by filling up their time completely with overwork. One sees other examples in persons whose rigid conformity to some set of standards, sometimes the standards of a rebellious group, makes them incapable of an intelligent flexibility in meeting new situations which society actively fosters.

There are advantages in recognising extreme rigidity in dealing with everyday life, or with a personal or social crisis, as part of a character distortion built into the compulsive personality. It makes the inflexibility and insistence of compulsive relatives, friends, and public officials easier to understand and accept. It also prepares us for the possibility that a person with a life-long compulsive distortion, if he is exposed to more stress than he can tolerate, may develop a fullblown obsessive compulsive reaction easily. He may, instead, develop an anxiety reaction, or a serious phobia to protect himself from anxiety. The anxiety reaction and the phobia will be contaminated by obsessive compulsive symptoms like those in the case of Ramona M.

Traditionally, the compulsive personality or character has been linked to anal-sadistic trends. Its origins have been located in the childhood struggle with parents over bowel control, and in a childhood regression after failure to solve edipal conflicts at a genital level.

This is not difficult to accept if we recall how some of our clinical cases of obsessive compulsive reactions were outspokenly and intolerably anxious (ever contamination, feces and soiling. We had no reason for hesitating there in relating such compulsive concern with a partial regression to childhood levels of conflict over bowel control and the struggle for independence from parental figures. In some of the cases no inferences were necessary. The patients spontaneously recalled the unreasonable demands made upon them in these universal childhood adaptations.

In *obsessive compulsive neuroses* we see the failure of repression and the emergence in acute form of anal-sadistic impulses and of ego defences against them—reaction formation, displacement, isolation, undoing, countermeasures, doubt and rumination. In *compulsive personality* or *character distortions* we see the same kind of symptomatic structure; but the symptoms are neither extreme nor acute, and they are built into the adult personality. In the case of Sally J. we saw a person with an obvious *personality* or *character distortion,* evident even ill early childhood, who suffered an *acute obsessive compulsive' reaction* when sexually aroused.

The great majority of compulsive personality or character disorders never break down in an acute neurosis or psychosis. They remain inhibited, rigid, obstinate, excessively neat and orderly, overconscientious; or they flux some of these compulsive characteristics with their opposites to form a contradictory picture. Thus, compulsive disorderliness and dirtiness may coexist with inhibitions, rigidity and obstinacy. The same man may be compulsively stingy and a compulsive spendthrift.

Hysterical Personality or Character

This common clinical variety was unaccountably omitted from the official classification. It is characterised by a lifelong tendency to be histrionic, exhibitionistic, narcissistic and emotionally shallow. We are retaining the old term *hysterical* both because the clinical picture is close to the commensense meaning of the word, and because neither conversion nor dissociative reactions—the successors to hysterical reactions—can be equated with this histrionic, narcissistic personality or character distortion which we are about to describe.

There are some hysterical trends in most normal persons just as there are compulsive trends. Without some tendency to be dramatic, boastful or frivolous on occasion a normal personality would seem dull, solemn and emotionally uninvolved. The person who can be "the life of the party" is often a person with normal dramatic or frivolous trends. A narcissistic, boastful enthusiasm over what one is doing can be entertaining to others and lift their morale. The origins of such behaviour are in the normal "showing off" and silliness of little children, who have been allowed a limited, healthy expression by parents who understand a child's need to be childishly gay. Its normal adult product is sometimes the artist of screen, stage or television, the scientist, the politician and the writer, those who remain stable and develop their talents as their profession.

We speak of hysterical personality or character only when histrionic narcissistic, exhibitionistic display continues into adulthood almost as it appeared in childhood, and when criticism of display or interference with it provokes unreasonable anger, sullenness or self-depreciation. In mild instances, "the life of the party" soon becomes a public nuisance. In more pronounced cases, the person with hysterical personality or character seems never to have grown up. He seems always to be an actor who insists upon being the centre of attention. He does things to shock, amuse or impress people, not so much because he needs self-expression—everybody needs self-expression—but because of a pathological narcissism, a consuming need to be noticed, to be admired or feared, but always to be conspicuous. His fleeting and shallow emotional attachments are to some extent the consequence of such a general orientation, and to some extent its cause. The impression of instability, insincerity and superficiality is also a consequence of an orientation which places attention-getting at the top of the motivational hierarchies.

Traditionally, the hysterical personality or character has been linked with failure to resolve edipal conflicts and with fixation in a phallic phase of sexual development. The contrast is striking between compulsive hostility, with its concern over contamination, and the erotic display of a great many hysterical characters. Hysterical personalities or characters conform more closely to normal feminine patterns of needing to be attractive, to be noticed and to be loved, than to the masculine patterns of aggression, initiative and relative independence. It is for this reason that we find hysterical distortions of personality or character much more frequently among women than among men.

The decompensation of a hysterical personality may lead to one of several regressions. Among these is. of course, the development of an outspoken conversion reaction. Here display takes the form of a disabling symptom which, even though unconsciously produced, serves the purpose of forcing people to pay continual attention to the patient. Another possibility is that needs for narcissistic supplies may become powerful enough to lead to a depressive illness, neurotic or psychotic, when they are frustrated. A third possibility is that deeper and more diffuse fixations may result in the transformation of hysterical distortion into a schizophrenic reaction. This last possibility, more prominently discussed a few decades ago than now, is still something to remember in dealing therapeutically with hysterical personality or character distortion.

Paranoid Personality

The paranoid personality is one that has its origin in a lack of basic trust. There is evidence that in many cases the paranoid person has received sadistic treatment during early infancy and that he has, in consequence, internalised sadistic attitudes toward himself and others. Because of his basic lack of trust in others the paranoid personality must be vigilant in order to safeguard himself against sudden deception and attack. He is exquisitely sensitive to traces of hostility, contempt, criticism or accusation in the attitudes of other people.

These traces, often slight and usually unconscious, the paranoid personality treats as though they were fully conscious and of prime importance. His lack of basic trust hampers the paranoid personality in carrying out reality testing operations. He magnifies unconscious hostility or unconscious homosexual trends in other persons: and he always assumes that what is clear to him must also be clear to other people. At the same time, the paranoid person is characteristically unaware of his own hostile, contemptuous, critical and accusing attitudes. Consequently, he is unable to understand why anyone else should behave toward him with resentment or hostility.

The exquisite sensitiveness of the paranoid personality toward relatively slight and often wholly unconscious trends in others comes from his readiness to detect aggression, seductiveness and deceit in his surroundings. This in turn orianiates in early childhood experiences of being treated sadistically, or at least in experiencing whatever treatment he received as being sadistic, belittling, critical and accusing.

We can assume that the lack of basic trust in infancy interfered with the development of a normal symbiotic relationship with the available mother figure. This, in turn, means that ego and later superego identifications would not lead to the formation of effective ego boundaries, or to the normal maturation of the superego and the ego ideal. Defective ego boundaries and an immature superego, with its ego-ideal component, interfere grossly with reality-testing so that the paranoid personality cannot distinguish effectively between what is external shared social fact and what is internal imagined private fantasy. On the other hand the essentially neurotic fixations present in paranoid persons keep them in better overall contact with external reality than is the case with depressive and schizoid personalities.

A significant result of the defective ego boundaries is that the paranoid personality must depend heavily upon denial and projection. Denial, as an ego defence, is called into action when something has managed to penetrate into preconscious or conscious organisation. Denial, in other words, repudiates something which is already present, and projection changes it into something that appears to come from the outside. This maneuver is certainly primitive and childlike; but it is the maneuver of preference for a great many otherwise mature persons. These persons exhibit a paranoid distortion, a personality or character structure which leaves them unusually prone to suspicion, envy, jealousy and obstinacy.

The degree and the manner in which homosexuality enters into the organisation of the paranoid personality is still the subject of controversy. We have elsewhere reviewed some of the significant literature, beginning with Freud's dynamic interpretations, and proceeding with the part played by excessive love to counteract excessive hate, by delusional masochism, by sadism and a very early superego, by superego nuclei, by denial, projection and the pseudocommunity.

Objections to assuming a central role for homosexuality in the paranoid personality have, been spelled out by MacAlpine and Hunter in their introduction to the translation of Schreber's *Memoirs of My Nervous Illness* and in their discussion of Freud's views which appears at the end of their translation. These objections have been reinforced by the observation that whereas paranoid men complain of homosexual advances and homosexual persecution, paranoid women complain principally of accusations that they are prostitutes. Further objections have been raised in relation to paranoid psychoses and narcissism, with considerable emphasis upon the work of Federn, which would seem to carry paranoid experiences back to phases of development earlier than edipal conflicts. The genuineness of homosexuality in paranoid mechanisms has also been called into question. The question of the role of homosexuality in paranoid personalities must still be considered a moot one. It is even possible that male and female homosexuality have different bases, since the evolution of sexuality in the two sexes follows different lines. In any case, a differentiation between latent and manifest homosexuality still needs to be emphasised. Delusions and hallucinations, like manifest dreams, are conscious and preconscious experiences which may require interpretation before their evidence can be accepted. This caution applies both to the pro's and con's of the basic question.

CYCLOTHYMIC (MANIC-DEPRESSIVE) PERSONALITY

The existence of a cyclothymic or manic-depressive personality is based upon the presence in some persons of a mood fluctuation which is apparently not paralleled by external events that justify the fluctuations. It is also based upon the persistence in some persons of a euphoric or a depressed mood without fluctuations. The official classification implies that the warmth, friendliness and generosity of cyclothymic persons is only apparent or superficial. It seems to accept the time-worn view that depressive and manic moods are endogenous, that is, generated from within, presumably independent of or almost independent of external factors and internal conflicts or fantasies.

This is no place to join the battle over endogenous and exogenous personality disturbances. The view that manic and depressive moods are of metabolic or other biochemical origin is both ancient and honourable. It has been reviewed a number of times within recent years. One critical review emphasises the statistical decline of manic and depressive illnesses in the United States and other countries, and weighs carefully ecological, cultural and social factors which may play a part in the apparently rapid decline in the United States. These figures apply strictly to psychotic developments; but they are not without relevance to problems of origin and incidence of fluctuating moods as character disorders or of persistent hypomanic and depressive moods without psychosis. The depressive personality has already been discussed, on psychotic depression. Manic reactions have been discussed, both in relation to historical perspectives and to mania as a defence against threatening depression, on manic reactions and manic-depressive cycles.

Schizoid personality. The schizoid personality, like the paranoid, is presumed to originate in a lack of basic trust, which dates back to the symbiotic mother-child relationship of early infancy, and in anxieties, fears and sadism aroused during and after this early phase. The character of the childhood and adolescence of schizoid personalities, suggests strongly that they have never felt fully accepted, even in the direct form of close body contact during infancy, and that, unlike paranoids, they have not been allowed to express the rage they must have felt, in many instances not even ordinary normal aggression.

They are often described as having been quiet, shy, obedient children, oversensitive to the criticisms and rejections of others, shrinking from interpersonal relationships while at the same time feeling lonely and out of things.

Many such children avoid competitive games and the close relationship of their peers. They may be looked upon by their peers as odd, queer or snobbish. Consequently they are often the targets for teasing which wounds them more than it should. They may take refuge in omnipotent and often vengeful fantasies. Many of them are avid readers, lone students of nature, or poets or artists. Most schizoid personalities have a defective defensive system: and this keeps them in closer contact with primary process material than average. Some are able to make use of their "intuitive" feelings in their fantasy, their poetic or artistic endeavours, and their unity with nature. Nevertheless, all schizoid personalities pay for whatever intuition they may have by remaining detached, uncomfortable with others, lonely and aloof. This is not the picture of primitive joy but of a pervasive loneliness for which the schizoid child, adolescent and adult try to compensate as best they can.

The adulthood of the schizoid personality seems to be simply a continuation of early' childhood trends in more mature forms. In adolescence there may be a period of active, hostile rebellion, of angry distrust and obstinacy; or there may be a period of heightened asceticism with moralising and intolerance for the behaviour of others. This is only an exaggeration of what adolescence brings out in a large proportion of normal persons. The adult schizoid personality is typically aloof, unsociable, secretive and uncomfortable in the close proximity of others, especially of members of the opposite sex. He sometimes gives an impression of being self-sufficient, but this impression arises from a defensive refusal to trust anyone, to confide in anyone.

Unlike the paranoid personality, the schizoid cannot as a rule express hostility or even ordinary aggression. For this reason, and because of his distrust, he usually avoids open competition. He is the prototype of the ivory tower detached and abstract thinker. His relative lack of interaction with others may make him semi a colourless person, which he may actually be, but it is also possible that he has a rich and vivid fantasy life behind the drawbridge and the moat of his solitary castle. Occasionally a schizoid person is able to pour out feelings in writing or drama which astonish those who know him personally. Usually, however, the isolation of a lifetime leaves the interior of the castle bleak. If a schizoid person meets losses, frustrations or intrusion which he cannot handle, there is always the possibility that he will regress into a schizophrenic reaction.

SOCIOPATHIC PERSONALITY DISTURBANCES

This group corresponds to what used to be called *psychopathic personality* and is now called *sociopathic personality disturbance* in the official classification. We have, however excluded sexual deviations and the addictions because, as Cleckley has pointed out, these disorders are not necessarily related in actual clinical cases. The *sociopathic personality* seems unable to learn, that is, to profit by his experiences, in certain areas of interpersonal relationship. He may be of average or superior intelligence. Yet he repeatedly acts out in such a way as to invite social ostracism and often legal prosecution, without being able to change his impulsive behaviour. As a rule the sociopathic person cannot fully realise that what he does is socially wrong or dangerous, or that he has any responsibility to society to control his behaviour.

It is common experience among therapists who work in this field to find the sociopathic person expressing apparently deep remorse and sincere good intentions, only to repeat what he has just been reprimanded or punished for, as though his remorse and sincerity were pure sham. Sometimes his expressions are sham, often they are not.

When they are not, the sociopath seems to have conscious, but shallow and fleeting, feelings of remorse and good intentions. He cannot, however, control unconscious impulses to repeat what he has been repeating, regardless of his words and the punishment inflicted upon him. The exasperation that others feel over this apparent deception is easy to understand. Even experts in this field often express exasperation in their clinical reports. Sometimes this is what the patient wants the therapist and others to feel. Their defeat and despair are his strange triumph and revenge.

During the nineteenth century there was a great deal of interest in the persons we now call sociopathic. They were stigmatised a century ago as moral imbeciles or as being morally insane. These names were intended to distinguish between intellectual deficit and moral deficit. In harmony with prevailing conceptions at that time, the sociopath was considered to be suffering from an inborn, incurable character defect which nothing could modify. The original change of terminology to *psychopathic personality* was intended to escape the implication of moral condemnation, which is foreign to modern psychiatry. Unfortunately the old conviction that the disorder was innate and unmodifiable clung to the new name and has persisted down to the present time. In once again changing the name, to *sociopathic,* we have reasons for hoping that the old pessimism may lift since, as we shall see in a moment, a beginning has been made toward understanding the dynamics underlying adult sociopathic distortions.

It should be said at the outset that current psychotherapy and psychoanalysis have little success in dealing with adults in this group. Nevertheless, it is worth reflecting that seventy years ago the neuroses were generally regarded as untreatable. Moreover, as the records show all too clearly, neurotic patients used to exasperate clinicians then in much the same way that sociopathic personalities do today. It is difficult for a therapist to tolerate situations in which therapeutic failure is so consistent and the disorder seems so completely irrational. It is also worth remembering that thirty years ago there were few who regarded psychotic patients as amenable to psychotherapy or psychoanalysis, and that today a great many psychiatrists are seeking occult physiological disturbances for the psychoses, just as a great many psychiatrists blamed physiological disturbances for the neuroses before psychodynamic therapy demonstrated the genetic and unconscious origins of neurotic symptoms which we all accept today.

When a gross distortion of organisation turns out not to be explicable in terms of inheritance or the accidents of intrauterine life and birth traumata, the clinician and the research worker turn to the conditions of childhood which may have produced the adult distortion. We see this as established practice in research and clinical therapy when one deals with adult deformities of body structure. The aim of such work, of course, is to prevent the occurrence of the adult distortion.

This is the situation today with regard to sociopathic disturbances. Since the adult sociopath seems to be little benefitted by psychotherapeutic and psychoanalytic procedures, with few exceptions, we look to childhood conditions in the hope that these may be changed in such a way as to prevent the development of sociopathic distortions. Perhaps while progress is being made in this direction there may also be progress made in relation to helping the adult.

A major obstacle to therapeutic success is the patient's own attitude, especially when he insists that there is nothing wrong with him, that he does not need help and will not accept it. It has been said in this connection that you cannot sentence a person to psychotherapy. This obstacle is not limited, however, to the treatment of sociopathic persons. Every clinician sees patients who seem to do everything they can to make themselves worse. You cannot, for example, sentence a cardiac patient to keep his weight down or bo rest and exercise as he should. Such problems are also psychological ones, and as every practitioner knows they can defeat both therapist and patient.

Within these limitations, optimism has been aroused in the last two decide by the new light shed upon conditions in childhood which seem responsible for adult sociopathic distortions. This new light has come from the simultaneous psychotherapeutic—in some patients psychoanalytic—treatment of parent and child. The therapeutic advances have been definite but modest; the therapeutic understanding which the clinicians have gained in been great. As one worker in this field has put it, "The genesis of some of the human characteristics included in the definition of psychopathic personality (sociopathic personality) is no greater mystery than other syndromes in psychopathology." He goes on to say that when both parent and offending child are studied therapeutically at the same time it is almost always possible to reconstruct the chief dynamics involved. In actual cases studied, the more significant parent—usually hut not always the mother—has been observed encouraging amoral or antisocial behaviour in the child without consciously realising it. Evidently tine neurotic needs of the parent—domineering, dependent, hostile or erotic—were finding vicarious gratification in the child's behaviour. In some cases reported, a parent showed unmistakable relish while the child was telling the therapist about his misdeeds, as though the recital were pleasurably wicked, but once the tale was told the parent turned immediately moralistic and condemned it and the child. In some instances the parent egged the child on with his story, supplying hints and missing bits of information which he or she had been treasuring up. In still others, the parent said angrily or shouted what the child was not to do, often thereby suggesting something which the child had not thought of doing. In one case, the child reporting alone to the therapist said, "That's what she *wants* me to do!" In another, both parents openly enjoyed and laughed about the petty thefts and lawbreaking of their children, but could not understand how these children, grown to adolescence, could possibly commit delinquent crimes showing disregard for other people's safety and property.

The questions posed by these and many other studies and observations seem directly concerned with adult sociopathic personality disturbances in which some distortion interferes with the integration of ego-superego standards. How is a child who has openly ambivalent and often unconsciously corrupting parents to develop consistent ego and superego attitudes himself? Early in life the significant parent or both parents must be the main sources of identification, and therefore the chief determinants of his personality structure. Faced with such inconsistent, ambiguous or even corrupting attitudes, how is the child to know which he shall internalise, or whether to internalise them all? Every child, early in life, has only parental approval and disapproval, parental love and parental rejection, to guide him in what he selects. If a significant parent, while perhaps voicing strong disapproval, at the same time shows so much relish that even strangers pick it up, what can he or she expect of the child who inevitably senses both? When, for example, a parent insists upon hearing every detail of a misdeed, listens with rapt attention, and then angrily condemns the child, what sort of confusion does this introduce into the child's perception of reality. Early in life children are especially sensitive to unconscious attitudes, which often strike them with a clarity denied to adults. If these are furtively corrupting, the child will probably be corrupted. Like his parent, he may himself come to condemn verbally what he secretly and perhaps unconsciously enjoys. Another possibility, which we see actualised in some sociopathic personality disturbances, is that as a child grows up in such an atmosphere, he becomes unable to take any social injunction seriously and even fails to establish any stable emotional relationship.

At first glance it may seem that the two opposed forces present in the ambiguous behaviour of a parent are about equal. This may be true objectively. But we must remember that when a small child is forming his basic identifications he is at the same time struggling with forbidden impulses and fantasies from within. Shall he go along with these asocial or antisocial impulses and fantasies or shall he resist them?

What is reality saying to him from the outside, an "outside" which he scarcely recognises as separate from himself? When there is no unified superego, and while the superego is still rudimentary or immature, the child needs a lot of outside help in handling the powerful impulses of the moment. He needs help that is unambiguous, clearcut and without anxiety or ulterior motive. At such a time the child is testing reality, constructing his world and constructing a social self within himself. If he is confronted by grossly inconsistent, ambiguous or corrupting identification models, he can hardly escape constructing his world and himself in distorted ways. All this we have known for a long time. It remained for the simultaneous study of the child offender and the parent to reveal actual observation confirming such interrelationships.

Theoretically, the child whose identification figures—the significant parents—are capricious, inconsistent or emotionally neglectful should grow into adulthood with irresponsible or emotionally shallow and meaningless attitudes toward others. This picture we actually see in many sociopathic personalities. If a child receives verbal rebukes and nonverbal encouragement for acting out his nonsocial and antisocial impulses or fantasies—and every little child experiences such impulses and fantasies—we should expect theoretically that he would grow to be an adult who says all the right things and does all the wrong ones. This, also, we know to be a leading characteristic of many sociopathic personalities.

If, after a child's nonsocial and antisocial acting out is covertly encouraged and vicariously enjoyed by a parent, the child is suddenly punished when the parent realises what is happening, he is likely to grow up not only inconsistent or antisocial but also with a deep resentment toward authority figures in general.

If, as happens perhaps more often in sexual deviation than in sociopathic personality disturbance, a parent unconsciously or consciously seduces a child in the direction of acting out forbidden impulses and fantasies, and repeatedly frustrates the child, the child may be expected to develop serious superego defects as well as deep resentment. There are cases among sociopathic personality disturbances in which the patient approves of everything he does, no matter what it is, and uses secondary processes mainly in providing rationalisations for whatever behaviour is socially inacceptable. This is not delusional behaviour, but it seems to be close to it.

The question is often raised as to why only one child in a family of several should grow up with a sociopathic personality disturbance. We could say, as we do also in relation to neuroses and psychoses, that in all genetic and dynamic development there is involved a multiplicity of factors. This is true; but some of the case studies of sociopathic disturbances in children have also shown that, for some as yet unknown reason, a whole family seems to select one child as the scapegoat. The child is chosen as the one to act out the forbidden impulses and fantasies of parents and siblings, while they may be able to enjoy vicariously what the scapegoat does without themselves experiencing responsibility or guilt for it.

This observation confirms others made especially in the family relationships of schizophrenic patients. Here, also, one child may seem to have been predestined from an early age to act out the delusional fantasies of a potentially psychotic parent, sometimes with the abetment of other siblings who call attention to anything strange about the selected child. Attempts at treating such a patient, grown to psychotic adulthood, are often met clinically by anxious resistance on the part of the parent. Sometimes the threat of recovery in the patient precipitates a parental crisis, in some cases amounting to an outspoken psychosis. Once more, we find that there are comparisons possible at genetic and dynamic levels between sociopathic personality disturbances and the neuroses and psychoses. Such a relationship is likely in the future to stimulate further efforts at finding suitable therapy for sociopathic personality disturbances.

We shall turn now to a descriptive account of sociopathic personality disturbances. Classification within the group is highly unsatisfactory, in part because we do not understand these disturbances well, in part because in the, past they have been comparatively neglected by dynamically oriented therapists, just as used to be the case with the psychoses. The three types we shall distinguish are not dynamically established. They are merely descriptive subgroups whose characteristics to a large degree overlap.

INADEQUATE AND UNSTABLE PERSONALITIES

Under this general heading we shall discuss a miscellaneous group of personality disorders that do not belong with the character disorders which we have just described. Chronically inadequate and unstable personalities seem to have their origins early in life, and they persist throughout adulthood. Some investigators take this to mean that the defects are congenital, perhaps hereditary. Others take it to mean that the defects come from very early infantile experience, including early disturbances of physiology. The work of Spitz and others, who have demonstrated the baneful influences of early infantile deprivation upon personality integration, makes it all the more difficult to differentiate the hereditary or congenital from the experiential.

For our purposes this differentiation is not crucial. It would be unreasonable to assume that everyone starts out in lift with the same degree of biological fitness, or with the same potentialities for emotional response. It would be equally unreasonable to assume that infantile experiences do not sometimes determine the course of further development, including further physiological development. Either factor or both may be involved in the development of inadequacy or instability. We shall leave the task of making such distinctions to the investigations now in progress and to those which are currently proposed. In the virtual absence of conclusive findings we shall confine ourselves in this section to a brief description of inadequacy and instability.

Inadequate Personality

In this group the official classification places persons whose response to the ordinary demands of life—intellectual, emotional, social and physical—are generally ineffectual. These persons seem not to be grossly deficient according to mental tests and physical examinations. Nevertheless, they are inept in life, show poor judgment continually, are usually improvident and lacking in a normal sense of responsibility. They are often good-natured, easy-going and no trouble to others, except for their inability to persevere in anything, even when they are in sight of reward. In spite of normal or above-normal intelligence, the inadequate personality pursues immediate pleasure like a child, unable to postpone it in the interest of the reality principle. He is usually described as lacking in physical as well as in emotional stamina, a description that suggests the old conception of the "constitutionally inferior psychopath."

There can be no question that the inadequate personality is for some reason unable to carry through a normal maturing process that would lead to a responsible adulthood. There is room for doubt, however, that physical inadequacy explains the syndrome, if indeed the inadequate personality really constitutes a syndrome. As matters stand today, the inadequate personality whose physical and intellectual defects do not show up in tests and examinations remains one of our many unsolved psychopathological and psychodynamic problems. The study of actual cases reveals a pervasive immaturity which seems to be a result of abnormalities in the family structure. The inadequate personality reflects ineffectualities in personal interaction within the family that reared him. It seems more than ever doubtful today that he can be dismissed as "poor stuff," as he used to be before the age of psychodynamics.

Emotionally Unstable Personality

Like the inadequate personality just discussed, the emotionally unstable personality is described in the official classification as a failure to achieve mature self-control, without considering possible psychodynamic origins. Emphasis is upon the presence of strong and poorly controlled hostility, guilt and anxiety, which together with impulsiveness make it impossible for the emotionally immature person to establish and maintain meaningful, stable interpersonal relationships. The emotionally' unstable person is said to react at times with explosive intensity' to relatively slight external stress. In the course of such an emotional reaction he may shout, threaten, assault others or destroy things. He is described as being jealous and quarrelsome in relation to persons of the opposite sex. He may even attempt suicide to relieve himself of an intolerable situation. When he is not emotionally disturbed he may be outgoing and friendly.

The impression one gets from clinical descriptions suggests an adult who is impulsive, unpredictable, hostile and sometimes dangerous to himself and others. These descriptions also suggest that perhaps the emotional instability of the patient is contagious. Much that is described fits into the frame of paranoid reactions and paranoid personality. It seems to be the immaturity of emotional control that leads to this diagnosis of emotionally' unstable 'personality. The patient appears to suffer from a child's impulsiveness and lack of emotional control; and he expresses himself episodically with all the physical power, but not the emotional integration, of an adult. There have been attempts to give these emotionally unstable persons the benefit of a psychodynamic approach. Perhaps such studies will enable us to understand them and classify them more intelligently.

Passive-aggressive Personalities

In this subgroup the official classification includes a continuum of immature dependent personalities which are divided into three types. The *passive dependent type* is openly passive and childishly dependent. The *passive aggressive type* shows aggression in passive ways, comparable to civil disobedience and the sit-down strike. The *aggressive type,* although deeply dependent beneath the surface, is reactively hostile and provocative. A few words will be sufficient to describe each of these three types.

Passive dependent type. These persons seem to be helpless, indecisive and clinging, as though they' were still small children. In spite of an underlying hostile attitude toward others, they avoid the show of aggression, appear fearful and timid, and shrink from situations expressing hostility. They appear to be frightened, angry grown-up babies.

Passive aggressive type. These persons act out in their personal lives the principles of civil disobedience. Their passive aggression can be as infuriating to their associates as the sit-down strike is to employers. Civil disobedience and the sit-down strike were utilised by persons who felt badly used by authority figures against whom they could not employ violence without provoking the authority figures to violent countermeasures. Adults who are not actually in the same danger, but who are emotionally miniature, may behave as though they actually were. They become sullen and stubborn, use inefficiency and procrastination to defeat their superiors complain of bad treatment and tend to demoralise others. Underneath it all, these are fearful, anxious persons who treat authority, and even their equals, as though they were domineering tyrants.

Aggressive type. The aggressive persons in this group arc fundamentally no less fearful and dependent than the others. Their aggression is purely reactive and defensive. It is more like that of a rebellious child or adolescent than of an adult. The aggression takes the forms familiar to anyone who has worked with rebellious children and adolescents. Sarcasm, provocative acts and talk, argumentativeness, competitiveness and demands for special attention are common components of the picture. Some if the members of this group seem constantly irritable, develop temper tantrums and become destructive with relatively little provocation. Often they seem to encourage others to retaliate. Some individuals arc ambitious and some indulge in grandiose daydreams. The fact that these persons are not actually adolescent, and that they seem to persist in their reactive aggressive behaviour no matter what others do, makes them difficult problems for their adult associates and for authority figures. It is probable that a great many of these and some of the previously discussed types are paranoid or schizoid personalities. It would be instructive to have follow-up studies made of these groups to see what happens to them as time goes on and their dependency needs and frustrations continue to grow.

STATUS OF THE COGNITIVE FUNCTIONS

In the Adult Personality Profile cognitive functions are described under the ego. This is consistent with the psychoanalytic theory of the ego, which regards it as a '.....Coherent organisation of mental processes' (Freud, 1923, p. 17) much of which is unconscious in both the descriptive and the dynamic sense. The organised and differentiated ego-functions are contrasted with the unorganised, undifferentiated processes of the id. Attention, concentration, speech, thinking, perception, judgement, memory, motility, and defence are designated ego-functions.. Here attention is directed only to those phenomena which indicate a disturbance of cognition. Motility and defence are described in later sections of this examination scheme. The title of this section has been altered from the earlier one of 'Cognitive Dysfunction' (Freeman *et al.*, 1965) to 'Status of the Cognitive Functions'. The reasons for this alteration are that there is no definite knowledge of the nature of the disturbance and that the changes are rarely consistent or uniform.

In psychotic states, with the exception of manic-depression, there is loss of high-level discrimination in the use of words, in thinking and perceiving, and in memory. Words may be altered in their form quite apart from changes in their meaning. Neologisms and paraphasias are not uncommon. Concepts are altered so that they are no long autonomous and independent of wishes and affects. Similar considerations apply to percepts. This trend was explained as resulting from the intrusion of a primitive mode of mental function — the primary process. In this approach interpretation is subordinated to accounts of abnormal cognitive function as encountered in psychosis. The following inquiries must be made.

(a) Is there a disorder of verbalisation as expressed through speech? Is grammatical construction adequate? Is there obstruction or 'derailment' or omission in the flow of associations? Are words changed in form? Is there a naming difficulty? Do paraphasic phenomena occur? Is there evidence of perseveration of speech content? Does echolalia occur? Are there indications of a fluctuation between normal and abnormal speech? Does obstruction of speech ever give way to fluent verbalisation? What is the content of speech when this occurs? What are the conditions under which blocking becomes manifest? Is there any indication that the patient fails to comprehend the speech of others?

(b) Information should be sought about those instances where thinking has assumed a magical, omnipotent quality. Examples should be provided of cases where concepts have lost their independence and gained new meanings as a result of condensation. Note should be made of instances of concrete thinking.

(c) Is the patient able to sustain attention for purposes of ordered thinking and for appropriate reactions to environmental stimuli? Are there signs of distractibility? Does this distractibility emanate from the patient's attempt to understand his experiences or is the external stimulus registered passively outside consciousness, only secondarily making its appearance in speech? Is there a fluctuation between states of inattention and purposive directed thinking? Is the change to normal attention related to the anticipation of the satisfaction of a need or to delusional or hallucinatory experiences?

(d) What is the state of the perceptual functions? Are the modalities adequately differentiated? Is there evidence of synaesthesiae? In the sphere of visual perception, is there any disturbance of size, shape, or distance constancies? Is the stability of visual perception influenced by bodily movement? Are percepts experienced more intensely than normal—for example, noise or colour? Are percepts experienced concretely? Does the eye or ear have a symbolic significance for the patient? Does the patient perceive a physical change in his body? Can he discriminate one individual from another? Are there condensations of visual percepts and memory traces leading to misidentifications? Is there evidence of hallucinations in one or more of the sensory modalities?

(e) Is there any obvious defect of short-term or remote memory? Are memories deranged with respect to their temporal sequence? Is there a repression of significant life experiences prior to the onset of the illness? Do memories make their appearance in the hallucinations or delusions?

(f) Is there faulty judgement arising from anxiety or guilt—leading to various forms of misinterpretation of environmental events?

5

Clinical Psychology and Mental Health

ROLE OF THE CLINICAL PSYCHOLOGIST

In the preceding, we traced the development of clinical psychology. From a historical perspective, it is clear that major changes have occurred during the profession's brief lifetime. Not only has clinical psychology gained in popularity as shown by the geometric increase in the number of professionals—but the scope of its activities has grown dramatically. As a result, the role of clinical psychologists has become more varied and flexible, while their prestige in many institutional settings has been enhanced. Of course, with an expanding role, clinical psychology has sometimes encountered difficulties and resistance from other professional groups (e.g., psychiatry). However, this is only natural when one expanding professional group is perceived as encroaching on the territorial rights of another.

In this chapter, we will examine the role of the clinical psychologist today in a variety of educational, research, clinical, and community settings. First, let us consider what the term *role* means. Like McGinnies (1970), we believe that "The concept of role is a convenient shorthand for designating certain well practiced behaviours that are specific to situations in which particular individuals are involved. To 'play a role' is simply to perform in a manner that has been reinforced in certain classes, or categories, or situations". Also, as Blanchard and Barlow state, (1976) "*role* refers to the expectations persons hold in common toward any person occupying a slot or position in a system. It is impossible to view a role apart from its relationship to other roles because the expectations of one role specify behaviours toward other role incumbents.....". These definitions should be kept in mind when the relationship of clinical psychology to other professions or other areas within psychology is discussed. We will first look at three traditional areas within clinical psychology; teaching, research, and clinical practice. We will consider job satisfaction and the typical work week of several clinical psychologists in each area. In addition, we will deal with new areas in clinical psychology in the 1970s and 1980s.

Next, we will consider the clinical psychologist's professional identity, discussing the psychologist's relationship to the APA and other professional groups (e.g., Association for advancement of Behaviour Therapy [AABT]; Society of Behavioural Medicine). We will also be concerned with publications specifically designed for clinical psychologists. Then we will look at the ethical considerations of the clinical psychologist. Some of the principles of the APA Code of Ethics will be summarised and reported violations described. Finally, we will turn to the relationship between clinical psychology and psychology in general, and finally to other professional groups. Some of the problems inherent in these relationships will be outlined and discussed. Issues of certification, licensing, and other relevant legislative action regarding accreditation will be examined.

Before describing the variety of roles carried out by clinical psychologists, we might point out that most of us in this field find the profession to be rewarding, exciting, and stimulating. Many doors are opened with the Ph.D. in clinical psychology. Consider the clinical psychologist working in a pediatric setting who helps parents adjust to their child's chronic illness; doing psychotherapy with dying patients; or working in industry to select managerial personnel and setting up institutes to improve staff relations. These, of course, are some of the more unusual activities carried out by clinical psychologists. But they all are possible!

THE CLINICAL PSYCHOLOGIST AS EDUCATOR AND RESEARCHER

Many clinical psychologists work in settings where education is a primary responsibility. Of course, the type and amount of teaching required will vary both within and across settings. For example, in university psychology departments, teaching is often formal, with the clinical psychologist preparing and delivering lectures to large undergraduate classes several times a week (e.g., abnormal psychology, introduction to clinical psychology, tests and measurement). Generally, at the undergraduate level (particularly in the more basic courses), there is less interchange between professor and students than in graduate seminars. This, unfortunately (for both), is often the result of large class size.

At the graduate level, teaching is often less formal, with both students and professor presenting material to the seminar group. This formal creates considerable interest, interchange, and lively discussion. Also at the graduate level, the apprenticeship model is often followed, with the professor providing direct research and clinical supervision (on a one-to-one basis) in specially designed tutorials. However, in other topic areas (notably statistics), the lecture method usually prevails.

The clinical psychologist's teaching load in the university psychology department varies with the size of the school and the professor's rank. In smaller, poorly funded departments, the load is heavier than in larger, well-endowed departments. Also, the higher the academic rank (instructor, assistant professor, associate professor, professor), the lighter the teaching load. Generally, those with higher ranks (associate professor and professor) are assigned (by clinical directors and chairpeople) fewer courses so that they may pursue other professional interests (e.g., research, consultation, and direct clinical service to clients).

To give a clearer idea of what the academic clinical psychologist does day to day, we include an actual schedule of an associate professor from a large, well-established psychology department. This individual is also director of the psychology clinic in his department.

He has a light teaching load, which permits him to pursue his research interests. Primary teaching duties consist of clinical practicum supervision, one graduate behaviour therapy seminar that meets twice weekly, and research supervision of graduate students. In addition to research-related activities, he spends time in meetings and clinical consultation at a local Veterans Administration hospital.

Had this person been associated with a junior college rather than a large university, the course load would have been larger, would have consisted of teaching undergraduate students, and of course would have left much less opportunity for doing research.

Clinical psychologists associated with medical schools. VA hospitals, general hospitals, community mental health centres, and institutes for retarded persons also teaching. However, teaching, by its very mature, tends to be very different in such settings. The focus is on providing direct services. Hence, with some exceptions (i.e. medical schools and hospitals affiliated with medical schools), teaching is less academic and theoretical, more pragmatic and applied. Although some formal lectures (to medical students and nurses) and seminars (to psychology interns and psychiatric and medical residents) are offered, most of the teaching consists of one-to-one supervision of diagnostic and therapeutic activities. Moreover, in such institutional settings, the clinical psychologist spends a fair amount of time training paraprofessionals. Indeed, as their prestige in medical settings has increased, clinical psychologists have offered fewer direct services to clients and patients and have become more active in training nondegreed and B.A.-level mental health workers (Cohen, 1974).

Let us now consider the schedule of a young clinical psychologist employed in a research-oriented psychiatry department in a large medical school. This clinical psychologist (an assistant professor), working on an inpatient service for highly disturbed children, is almost totally devoted to research. From this schedule, it appears that no direct service is being offered. Rather, the clinical psychologist is serving as a consultant to staff (nurses, nursing assistants, special education teachers, research assistants), to enable them to carry out intervention programmes.

In settings that emphasise clinical service, a junior clinical psychologist undoubtedly would spend a lot of time assessing and treating clients (in individual, family, and group psychotherapy). This certainly would be true of the clinical psychologist employed in a community mental health centre (cf. Hollingsworth and Hendrix, 1977).

Before describing clinical psychologists as practitioners, let us consider their role as researchers. In later chapters, we will present a more comprehensive analysis of the kinds of research carried out. Here, however, we should note that in most cases, the setting and the availability of subjects will influence the type of research that a given clinical psychologist is able to pursue. For example, the clinical psychologist in a university setting will probably carry out theoretical analogue research with college students. By contrast, the individual in a hospital setting is more likely to do research with seriously disturbed patients that has clinical import. Such research could involve diagnostic comparisons or the effects of specific treatment. Individuals working with retarded subjects may focus on developmental factors, while those working with outpatients in community mental health settings may wish to assess how well the programme serves the community at large.

In any event, the possibilities for doing research are limited only by the availability of subjects, research supports, time, and ingenuity. Among the areas in which clinical psychologists have made a major research contribution are epidemiology, personality, psychopathology, assessment and diagnosis, psychotherapy evaluation, and programme evaluation.

THE CLINICAL PSYCHOLOGIST AS PRIVATE PRACTITIONER

In the Garfield and Kurtz (1976) survey of clinical psychologists, 23 per cent were in full-time private practice. Further, 47 per cent had at least part-time private practice. Thus, the private sector of clinical psychology is a sizable proportion.

As a private practitioner, the clinical psychologist offers certain services to the public, much as a dentist or general medical doctor does. Office hours are established, and patients (i.e., clients) are seen for assessment, diagnosis, and psychotherapy. Fees are charged for services rendered. This, of course, is in contrast to the clinical psychologist who is hired by an institution where the same services may be performed for a yearly salary).

There are many myths about the practices of clinical psychologists. In a tongue-in-cheek description entitled "Demythologizing Private Practice," Taylor (1978) accurately points out that "Today, many of the children seen are Medicaid beneficiaries. The fathers are commonly deceased or missing and the mothers frequently migrant. There are middle-class children referred for the treatment of active ulcers resistant to medication. There are the military dependents, predominantly the families of enlisted men living in mobile home parks and often eating with the help of food stamps. I am a consultant to two children's homes, working with staff and residents in a population that has been exposed to both economic and educational deprivation, has been frequently abused sexually and otherwise, has spent portions of its youth on the run, and is emerging from jail or other confinement". This can hardly be considered the glorious upper-middle-class practice so often much like the kind of private practice one of the authors had when he did this on both a full-time and a part-time basis.

By contrast, Taylor (1978) adds, "Or course we all 'know' of the psychologist working a 35-hour work week at $60 per hour. His clients are movie stars, successful writers, and the wives of corporate executives, with maybe a sprinkling of high-level bureaucrats. They come in three to five times a week for 6 or 7 years, so he only needs about 10 referrals a year. He hasn't learned anything lately and the clients won't either. We know he is out there. Have you met him yet?". The authors of this book have known a very few that might fit this description. However, they are in the minority.

What do clinical psychologists in private practice actually do? Perhaps this can best be answered by looking at the schedule one of the authors followed when he was in full-time private practice in a suburban community in Connecticut. In addition, this practicing clinician (like many others in the community) also consulted at a local VA facility, supervising psychology interns in their diagnostic assessments of patients. His schedule often extended through Saturday. In some instances, when married couples were seen together, later evening appointments were required, particularly for working couples.

Let us consider the sources of information that clinicians use in the consulting room. These sources are diverse. Some data may come from an analysis of the case history, with the patient, relative, friend, or employer as the main informant. They may be confirmed by psychological testing or by direct observation during the assessment. At times, home visits may be indicated. This is time-consuming (i.e., travel to and from office) and costly, but may be necessary when dealing with aporaphobics (i.e., patients whose symptoms will not permit them to leave home) (cf. Emmelkamp. 1979). Other sources of data include school and medical records and other psychiatric records on the client.

The clinical psychologist in individual practice should be certain that the psychological complaint does not have a medical basis. This is particularly important since there are some medical disorders that have major effects on psychobiological functioning (e.g., hypothyroidism or pancreatic cancer masking as depression). In most cases, then, clients should first have a medical evaluation to rule out such possibilities, even though they are rare. Also, severely psychotic and depressed patients are referred to clinical psychologists in private practice. In these cases, biological treatment is indicated (e.g., antipsychotics, antidepressants). The clinical psychologist here would be remiss in not referring the patient to a competent physician (e.g., psychiatrist) for that aspect of the treatment. However, the clinical psychologist can still continue providing psychotherapeutic treatment to the patient together with the biological approach. Of course, for the suicidal or homicidal patient, hospitalisation will be required.

The Clinical Psychologist as Consultant

Although almost no clinical psychologists are full-time consultants, many do supplement their income with consultative work. Such services may be offered to VA facilities, state hospitals, state facilities for the retarded, prisons, community agencies (e.g., group homes, halfway houses, juvenile correctional facilities, police departments, courts), and industry. In working for any of these agencies, the clinical psychologist is expected to offer certain expertise that, for many reasons, may not be available.

Thus, as consultant, a specific segment of the clinical psychologist's skills is being purchased. For example, a VA hospital psychiatry department may be interested in applying behaviour modification techniques to given patients. The clinical psychologist who is an expert in behaviour modification may be hired one-half day per week to teach behavioural principles to staff, show them how to implement techniques, and teach them how to assess the effects of the new treatments. This may be done through formal lectures, suggested reading lists, direct personal supervision, and actually modelling of the behavioural technique.

Consultative work may be geared to assessment, treatment, research, staff relations, or the design and implementation of entire programmes. For example, as consultants, the authors have been asked to lend their expertise to develop and implement behaviour modification strategies in several psychiatric settings. The authors know one clinical psychologist who does personality evaluations of candidates for positions in a city police department. Research clinical psychologists are frequently asked by the National Institute of Mental Health and the Veterans Administration Research Service to consult and help evaluate grant proposals. Sometimes a hospital department torn by dissension may ask the clinical psychologist to implement a staff relations training programme to reduce the discord and promote better role adjustment for both supervisers and supervisees.

Whatever the consultant's assignment, a particular set of skills is needed. First, of course, the consultant should indeed be an expert in the area. Second, the consultant must be political and sensitive to the needs and interests of the consultees. This is critical when the consultant has been hired by an administrator (e.g., a hospital director) of a given setting, institution, or programme. Very often, this has not been discussed with the staff. Hence, such consultation, regardless of its value, may be viewed as an imposition and resented. This could lead to subtle non-compliance with the consultant's advice or even open defiance. Such a situation might occur when the goals of the staff (who work directly with patients) and those of the director differ.

For this reason, Bellack and Franks (1975) have argued on behalf of the "soft-sell" approach: The consultant should be pragmatic and specific in making recommendations; should model the behaviour desired; and should use a minimum of technical jargon. These suggestions apply most clearly when the consultant is dealing with staff rather than peers (i.e., nondoctoral professionals and paraprofessionals). Of course, when consulting with peers, the consultant might keep these points in mind without insulting the intelligence of colleagues (jargon may be less a problem here). Obviously, being a consultant is a demanding job. In addition to requiring relevant knowledge, the individual needs political acumen, interpersonal adeptness, and good timing. It is necessary to be quick on one's feet, especially when put to the test. Often the consultant will be asked to solve very difficult problems. This may be done because no one else has succeeded or simply to test the consultant's expertise. Thus, in the role of consultant, the clinical psychologist with less experience will probably be less successful. The seasoned consultant, in contrast, is fully aware of the kinds of "games" consultees play. Indeed, the role of consultant is one of the most difficult that the clinical psychologist will be asked to perform. However, when done well, it can be quite rewarding.

Other Roles and Specialisation

As the number of clinical psychologists has increased and the profession has matured, so have its role boundaries. The role of the clinical psychologist today far exceeds that described in Harrower's (1965) excellent summary statement. For example, 19 per cent of all community mental health centres now have a clinical psychologist as their executive director. In the late 1950s and early 1960s, the notion of the clinical psychologist as administrator had little credence. Indeed, most directors of mental health establishments held the M.D. degree. In addition, many clinical psychologists now serve as ward administrators in mental hospitals. Others now are working in the emergency rooms of general medical and surgical hospitals (Barlow, 1974). This contrasts sharply with the more subservient role of clinical psychologists after World War II (i.e., psychological assessor in relation to the psychiatrist, who was administrator-therapist).

The role of clinical psychologists has continued to expand. They have begun to work with lawyers in judicial areas of mutual concern (e.g., the use of corporal punishment; patients' rights). For example, they have collaborated in developing standards for using aversive techniques in institutional settings. More clinical psychologists are employed in pediatric hospitals than in the past (Drotar, 1977), as well as in dental schools. The advent of behavioural medicine (i.e., the application of psychological-behavioural principles to the treatment of medical disorders) has opened up new areas for clinical psychologists in hospital departments (e.g., medicine, urology, neurology) formerly considered off limits. An example here might be the use of behavioural techniques in treating bedwetting in children. Other innovative career opportunities are outlined in a volume edited by Woods (1976).

In the 1970s and beyond, specialisation in all fields has become the norm. This holds true for clinical psychology as well. In addition to acting primarily as an educator, researcher, or provider of direct service, the clinician's roles have become more clearly defined. There are fewer and fewer generalists as time goes on. Even if a clinical psychologist calls himself a behaviour therapist, that label will not fully characterise the activities carried out with particular types of clients. Some behaviour therapists specialise in the treatment of children. Others are more concerned with adult neurotics. Some work with inpatients, others with psychiatric outpatients or medical patients (e.g., application of biofeed-back techniques). Still others specialise in the treatment of geriatric populations. And finally, some clinical psychologists specialise in group or family therapy or in the assessment and treatment of a given disorder (e.g., obesity, alcoholism, drug addiction).

Regional and Local Associations

Up to now, in discussing journals of interest to clinical psychologists, we have listed those published by the APA and Division 12. However, there are many others; some of these are present. Several of them are sponsored by associations, whereas others are directed by independent editors and published by large companies.

In addition to the national APA, there are a number of local, state, and regional associations that may be affiliated. Thus, a clinical psychologist living in Pittsburgh may simultaneously be a member of the Pittsburgh Psychological Association, the Pennsylvania Psychological Association, the Eastern Psychological Association, and the APA. A clinical psychologist practicing in rural Florida may belong to the Florida Psychological Association, the Southeastern Psychological Association, and the APA. By belonging to a local professional association, the clinical psychologist is able to support clinical psychology in that community, state, or area of the country. Also, by belonging, exchange of information with colleagues is facilitated. Mutual concerns, problems, and issues may be discussed, often leading to enhancement of the profession.

Other Associations

There are many multidisciplinary associations that hold particular interest for clinical psychologists. Although their members include some psychiatric nurses, social workers, and psychiatrists, clinical psychologists are generally in the majority. Let us briefly consider two associations that are well established at the time of this writing and a third that is growing. First, the Association for Advancement of Behaviour Therapy (AABT) (about 3,000 members) is, as its title implies, an interest group for those concerned with the application of behaviour principles to treatment, educational, medical, and social problems. The AABT holds a national convention in the late fall and publishes two journals *(Behavioural Assessment; Behaviour Therapy)* and a newsletter *(The Behaviour Therapist).*

Second, the Society for Psychotherapy Research is a somewhat smaller organisation that is cross-disciplinary and cross-theoretical in nature. This organisation is devoted to the scientific study of the psychotherapeutic process and its outcome. Third is a new organisation. The Society of Behavioural Medicine.

According to its founding statement, "Behaviour medicine is the *interdisciplinary field* concerned with the development and integration of behavioural and biomedical science, knowledge and techniques relevant to the understanding of health and illness and the application of this knowledge and these techniques to prevention, diagnosis, treatment and rehabilitation.... The Society of Behavioural Medicine is an open organisation founded to serve the needs of all health professionals interested in the integration of the behavioural and biomedical sciences in clinical areas." The goals of this society are consistent with the expanded role of clinical psychology in dealing with overall health problems. For this reason, it undoubtedly will continue to attract many clinical psychologists as members.

INTRAPROFESSIONAL AND INTERPROFESSIONAL RELATIONSHIPS

Clinical psychology may best be described as the "stepchild" of psychology and of the mental health professions. That is, in each instance clinical psychology appeared second and has acted as an interloper. Thus, it has at times been viewed with considerable suspicion by both academic nonclinical psychologists and practicing psychiatrists.

Let us first consider the relationship between clinical psychology and academic psychology. Hunt (1965) noted that "The basic scholarly and research orientations of psychology as a science make many psychologists suspicious of the service function and reluctant to see the growth of psychology as a profession". Indeed, there are several renowned universities where psychology departments have never had a clinical division (e.g., Brown University; Princeton University) or where the clinical programmes were recently dropped from the curriculum (e.g., Harvard University; Stanford University). The feeling here, again, is that the major mission of an academic department is to pursue knowledge. Application of such knowledge to specific problems is given much less credence.

A second concern of nonclinical psychologists in the early 1950s and 1960s was that clinical psychology was nonscientific. Given the critiques of projective testing and loosely defined psychotherapies, this position was understandable. With the advent of behavioural assessment and therapy and scientific clinical psychology in the 1960s and 1970s, greater rapprochement and improved intradepartmental relationships have ensued (cf. Russell, 1973). However, in the eyes of many purists, clinical psychology is still viewed askance, despite its improved scientific status. Turning now to interprofessional relationships, we should note that, as professionals, clinical psychologists interact with members of many disciplines (education, nursing, social work, dentistry, medicine, law, and psychiatry). Needless to say, these interactions are sometimes very complex. However, we believe that some general statements are in order. We will present our own interpretation of these relationships, since the data are not always clearly defined for such purposes.

With education, the relationship has been cordial and complementary to some extent. However, at times there has been dissension over the control of training programmes at the graduate level (cf. Hunt, 1965). With nursing the relationship, on the whole, has involved clinical psychologists presenting lectures and seminars to nurses and nursing students. Thus, this relationship tends to be one-sided (i.e., nonreciprocal). In some cases, nurses working in psychiatric settings have been caught in the psychology-psychiatry conflict. With social work, the relationship can best be described as cordial but a bit distant. Although clinical psychologists and social workers are part of the so-called "mental health team," there has been little formal interaction between the two disciplines. Most recently, the barrier seems to be breaking down in those graduate schools where teaching of courses may be shared by the two departments (e.g., the behavioural programmes at the University of Michigan and the University of Wisconsin).

With dentistry the relationship has been cordial, but until recently little interaction has occurred. Presently, greater interest in joint academic and research endeavours is evident (cf. Mclamed, 1979), especially behavioural applications promoting dental hygiene. Similarly, with medicine there now is an upsurge in collaboration, particularly with the advent of biofeedback and behavioural medicine. Undoubtedly these collaborative efforts will yield important results for clients, patients, and society. With law the relationship has always been good, with joint interest devoted to patients' rights and forensic psychology. The most complicated interprofessional relationship exists between clinical psychology and psychiatry. The history dating back to World War II, has often been filled with dissension and animosity. Let us briefly consider these events and the reasons for the problems.

At first the great conflict between clinical psychology and psychiatry was over whether clinical psychologists had the right to conduct psychotherapy independently, without medical supervision. However, before World War II this was not a problem. Clinical psychologists were rarely employed in medical settings; they restricted their activities to teaching, research, testing, and vocational counselling. During and after World War II, clinical psychologists began to assume roles that previously had belonged to psychiatry (diagnosis and psychotherapy). In the late 1940s and early 1950s, despite wide variations in training experiences (i.e., graduate schools for clinical psychologists, medical schools for psychiatrists), clinical psychologists and psychiatrists found themselves in overlapping roles, vying for territorial dominance. Moreover, clinical psychology internships increasingly were begun in medical settings (initially on a very large scale in the VA hospitals).

Most psychiatrists preferred the older model, in which the clinical psychologist was basically an x-ray technician (tester) vis-a-vis the psychiatrist. However, seeing the opportunities (undoubtedly deserved) for an expanded role, more and more clinical psychologists were trained to conduct psychotherapy, not only in medical settings presumably under medical supervision but independently in private practice in direct competition with psychiatrists. (No matter how the arguments are phrased, the competition for private patients and the financial rewards can never be discounted as the real basis for conflict between the disciplines.)

Clinical psychologists, on the other hand, argue that they, because of their training in psychology, are better able to deal with psychological and interpersonal problems. Medical education is definitely not oriented that way. Hence, the psychiatrist is at a distinct disadvantage here. Kiesler (1977) argues that a strong reason for choosing a psychologist "...is the more extensive background of the psychologist in the study of human behaviour and another is the formal training in science which should lead the psychologist to be up-to-date on scientific findings and produce a healthy skepticism about current fads".

In the 1960s and 1970s some of these arguments died down, clinical psychologists pursued their independent practices, and legislation was enacted to certify and license them. Still, there was considerable opposition from some psychiatrists. For example, Kiesler (1977) points out that quite recently the president of the Apa "argued that only psychiatrists should be considered qualified to receive reimbursement under national health insurance". So the battle continues, but on different fronts.

Despite the obvious differences between clinical psychology and psychiatry, however, the picture is not totally bleak. There has been much amity and cooperation between the two disciplines. Thus, areas of disagreement may be considered political in nature. At the interpersonal level, cooperation is no different from that between and among clinical psychologists. That is, it is quite variable.

On a day-to-day basis, most clinical psychologists and psychiatrists who are employed in the same settings get along fairly well. For example, in departments of psychiatry, clinical psychologists often find excellent employment opportunities (in terms of professional possibilities and remuneration). In such departments, they teach and supervise medical students and residents. In these same departments, psychiatrists have an important role in teaching psychology students and interns. In dealing with patients, clinical psychologists and psychiatrists work together to ease the problems. Each discipline obviously has unique skills and expertise that may help to eliminate patient psychopathology. Also, a perusal of many psychiatric and some psychological journals shows the results of joint research by clinical psychologists and psychiatrists. Finally, although psychiatry as a whole has resisted the clinical psychologist's assuming the role of mental health administrator both at the ward level and for entire mental health system (e.g., director of community mental health centre; state commissioner of mental health), the more enlightened psychiatrists recognise that possessing an M.D. degree is not synonymous with being an effective administrator. As time goes on, the competent mental health administrator is increasingly recognised, regardless of the degree held. We view this as a healthy trend.

Training of Clinical Psychologists

The Boulder Model, which called for the training of clinical psychologists as scientist-professionals, was almost universally adopted after the conference report was published. It remains the dominant approach to training today. However, it has come under increasing fire in recent years, and new models have been offered. The basic question is, is it feasible to train people to be both scientists *and* professionals? Given the growing doubts, many strictly professional programmes have been proposed. In fact, the most recent national training conference, held at Vail, Colorado, in 1973 (Korman, 1976), advocated that practitioners and researchers be trained independently. In this section, we will describe and compare these alternative models and provide examples of the types of graduate programmes they produce.

MENTAL HEALTH PROFESSIONAL

A mental health professional is a health care practitioner who offers services for the purpose of improving an individual's mental health or to treat mental illness. This broad category includes psychiatrists (D.O. or M.D.), clinical psychologists (Psy.D or Ph.D.), clinical social workers (MSW or MSSW), psychiatric nurses, mental health counsellors, professional counsellors, pharmacists, as well as many other professionals. These professionals often deal with the same illnesses, disorders, conditions, and issues; however, their scope of practice differs. The most significant difference between mental health professionals are the laws regarding required education and training across the various professions.

PROFESSIONAL DISTINCTIONS

Comparison of American Mental Health Professionals

Mental health professionals exist to improve the mental health of individuals, couples, and families. Because mental health covers a wide range of elements, the scope of practice greatly varies between professionals. Some professionals may enhance relationships while others treat specific mental disorders and illness. Often, as with the case of psychiatrists and psychologists, the scope of practice may overlap.

Most qualified mental health professionals will refer a patient or client to another professional if the specific type of treatment needed is outside of their scope of practice. Additionally, many mental health professionals may sometimes work together using a variety of treatment options such as concurrent psychiatric medication and psychotherapy. Additionally, specific mental health professionals may be utilized based upon their cultural and religious background or experience.

Increasingly, primary care providers, such as internists, pediatricians, and family physicians, provide many initial components of mental health diagnosis and treatment for children and adults. In particular, family physicians are trained during residency in interviewing and diagnostic skills, and may be quite skilled in managing conditions such as ADHD in children and depression in adults. Likewise, many (but not all) pediatricians may be taught the basic components of ADHD diagnosis and treatment during residency. In many other circumstances, primary care physicians may receive additional training and experience in mental health diagnosis and treatment during their practice years.

Psychiatrist

Psychiatrists are physicians and one of the few professionals in the mental health industry who specialize and are certified in treating mental illness using the biomedical approach to mental disorders including the use of medications.

Psychiatrists may also go through significant training to conduct psychotherapy and cognitive behavioural therapy; however psychologists and clinical psychologists specialize in the research and clinical application of these techniques. The amount of training a psychiatrist holds in providing these types of therapies varies from programme to programme and also differs greatly based upon region.

Specialties of Psychiatrists

As part of their evaluation of the patient, psychiatrists are one of only a few mental health professionals who may conduct physical examinations, order and interpret laboratory tests and EEGs, and may order brain imaging studies such as CT or CAT, MRI, and PETscanning. A medical professional must evaluate the patient for any medical problems or diseases that may be the cause of the mental illness.

Historically psychiatrists have been the only mental health professional with the power to prescribe medication to treat specific types of mental illness. Currently, Physician Assistants and advanced practice psychiatric nurses may prescribe medications, including psychiatric medications. Clinical psychologists have gained the ability to prescribe psychiatric medications on a limited basis in a few U.S. states after completing additional training and passing an examination.

Educational Requirements for Psychiatrists

Typically the requirements to become a psychiatrist are substantial but differ from country to country. In general there is an initial period of several years of academic and clinical training and supervised work in different areas of medicine, in order to become a licensed medical doctor, followed by several years of supervised work and study in psychiatry, in order to become a liceensed psychiatrist.

In the United States and Canada one must first complete a Bachelor's degree. Students may typically decide any major subject of their choice, however they must enroll in specific courses, usually outlined in a pre-medical programme. One must then apply to and attend 4 years of medical school in order to earn their MD or DO and to complete their medical education. Psychiatrists must then pass three successive rigorous national board exams (United States Medical Licensing Exams "USMLE", Steps 1, 2, and 3), which draws questions from all fields of medicine and surgery, before gaining an unrestricted license to practice medicine. Following this, the individual must complete a four-year residency in Psychiatry as a psychiatric resident and sit for annual national in-service exams. Psychiatry residents are required to complete at least four post-graduate months of internal medicine (pediatrics may be substituted for some or all of the internal medicine months for those planning to specialize in child and adolescent psychiatry) and two months of neurology, usually during the first year, but some programmes require more. Occasionally, some prospective psychiatry residents will choose to do a transitional year internship in medicine or general surgery, in which case they may complete the two months of neurology later in their residency. After completing their training, psychiatrists take written and then oral speciality board examinations. The total amount of time required to qualify in the field of psychiatry in the United States is typically 4 to 5 years after obtaining the MD or DO (or in total 8 to 9 years minimum). Many psychiatrists pursue an additional 1–2 years in subspecialty fellowships on top of this such as child psychiatry, geriatric psychiatry, and psychosomatic medicine.

In the United Kingdom, the Republic of Ireland, and most Commonwealth countries, the initial degree is the combined Bachelor of Medicine and Bachelor of Surgery, usually a single period of academic and clinical study lasting around five years. This degree is most often abbreviated 'MBChB', 'MB BS' or other variations, and is the equivalent of the American 'MD'. Following this the individual must complete a two-year foundation programme that mainly consists of supervised paid work as a Foundation House Officer within different specialties of medicine. Upon completion the individual can apply for "core specialist training" in psychiatry, which mainly involves supervised paid work as a Speciality Registrar in different subspecialities of psychiatry. After three years there is an examination for Membership of the Royal College of Psychiatrists (abbreviated MRCPsych), with which an individual may then work as a "Staff grade" or "Associate Specialist" psychiatrist, or pursue an academic psychiatry route via a PhD. If, after the MRCPsych, an additional 3 years of specialization known as "advanced specialist training" are taken (again mainly paid work), and a Certificate of Completion of Training is awarded, the individual can apply for a post taking independent clinical responsibility as a "consultant" psychiatrist.

Clinical Psychologist

A clinical psychologist studies and applies psychology for the purpose of understanding, preventing, and relieving psychologically-based distress or dysfunction and to promote subjective well-being and personal development. In many countries it is a regulated profession that addresses moderate to more severe or chronic psychological problems, including diagnosable mental disorders. Clinical psychology includes a wide range of practices, such as research, psychological assessment, teaching, consultation, forensic testimony, and programme development and administration. Central to clinical psychology is the practice of psychotherapy, which uses a wide range of techniques to change thoughts, feelings, or behaviours in service to enhancing subjective well-being, mental health, and life functioning. Unlike other mental health professionals, psychologists are trained to conduct psychological assessment. Clinical psychologists can work with individuals, couples, children, older adults, families, small groups, and communities.

THE ORIGINS OF MENTAL HEALTH

The mental hygiene movement

The origin of the mental hygiene movement can be attributed to the work of Clifford Beers in the USA. In 1908 he published A mind that found itself 4, a book based on his personal experience of admissions to three mental hospitals. The book had a great repercussion and in the same year a Mental Hygiene Society was established in Connecticut. The term "mental hygiene" had been suggested to Beers by Adolf Meyer 5 and enjoyed a quick popularity thanks to the creation in 1909 of the National Commission of Mental Hygiene. From 1919 onwards, the internationalization of activities of this Commission led to the establishment of some national associations concerned with mental hygiene: in France 6 and South Africa 7 in 1920, in Italy 8 and Hungary 9 in 1924. From these national associations the International Committee on Mental Hygiene was created and later superseded by the World Federation of Mental

Health. The mental hygiene movement, in its origins and reflecting Beers' experience in mental hospitals, was primarily and basically concerned with the improvement of the care of people with mental disorders. In Beers' own words: "When the National Committee was organized, in 1909, its chief concern was to humanize the care of the insane: to eradicate the abuses, brutalities and neglect from which the mentally sick have traditionally suffered."

It was at a later stage that the Committee enlarged its programme to include the "milder forms of mental disability" and a greater concern with preventive work. The rationale behind this shift was the belief that "mental disorders frequently have their beginnings in childhood and youth and that preventive measures are most effective in early life", and that environmental conditions and modes of living produce mental ill health.

By 1937, the US National Committee for Mental Hygiene stated that it sought to achieve its purposes by: a) promoting early diagnosis and treatment; b) developing adequate hospitalization; c) stimulating research; d) securing public understanding and support of psychiatric and mental hygiene activities; e) instructing individuals and groups in the personal application of mental hygiene principles; and f) cooperating with governmental and private agencies whose work touches at any point the field of mental hygiene. Thus, the mental hygiene movement had initially a para-psychiatric nature, directing its efforts towards the improvement of psychiatric care. The inclusion of preventive activities among its interests did not distinguish it from psychiatry: the movement aimed at maximizing what was accepted and proposed by the most advanced psychiatrists of the epoch in the USA, most of whom followed a psychoanalytical orientation.

According to the group which launched it, the mental hygiene movement "visualized, not a single patient, but a whole community; and it considered each member of that community as an individual whose mental and emotional status was determined by definite causative factors and whose compelling need was for prevention rather than cure. The Mental Hygiene Movement, then, bears the same relation to psychiatry that the public-health movement, of which it forms a part, bears to medicine in general. It is an organized community response to a recognized community need." 4. On the other hand, it was also stated that: "At the present time both psychiatrists and mental hygienists are more than ever conscious that their objectives are in fact identical and that each group needs the other for the fulfilment of their common task."

The World Health Organization

From its very beginning, the WHO has always had an administrative section specially dedicated to mental health, as an answer to requests from its Member States. The first Report of the WHO's Director General 10, in its English version, refers to an administrative section called "Mental Health". However, the French version of the same report calls it "Hygiène Mentale". Well until the 1960s we find hygiène as the French translation of health in some WHO publications and in some instances we find also mental hygiene used interchangeably with mental health in the English version of some documents. The volume no. 9 of the WHO's series Public Health Papers was published in 1961 in English with the title Teaching of Psychiatry and Mental Health 11, in 1962 in French with the title L'enseignement de la Psychiatrie et de l'Hygiène Mentale 12 and in 1963 in Spanish with the title Enseñanza de la Psiquiatria y de la Salud Mental 13.

In the preamble to the WHO Constitutions, it was stated that "health is a state of complete physical, mental and social wellbeing and not merely the absence of disease or infirmity" 14, a now widely quoted definition. This definition is clearly a holistic one, intended to overcome the old dichotomies of body vs. mind and physical vs. psychic. It is also a pragmatic one, insofar as it incorporates into medicine a social dimension, gradually developed in Europe during the 19th century.

It should be noted that mental, in WHO's definition of health (as well as physical and social) refers to dimensions of a state and not to a specific domain or discipline. Therefore, according to this concept, it is incongruous to refer to physical health, mental health or social health. Should one wish to specify a particular dimension, the most appropriate noun to designate it should be wellbeing and not health (e.g., mental wellbeing or social wellbeing). This negligent use of the word health seems to have been also in operation when mental hygiene (a social movement, or a domain of activity) was replaced by mental health (originally intended to designate a state and later transformed in a particular domain or field of activity).

The International Congress of Mental Health

The First International Congress of Mental Health was organized in London by the British National Association for Mental Hygiene from 16 to 21 August, 1948. Starting as an International Conference on Mental Hygiene, it ended with a series of recommendations on mental health. Throughout the proceedings of the conference, hygiene and health, qualifying mental, are used interchangeably, sometimes in the same paragraph, without any clear conceptual distinction. However, in the 17 pages of the recommendations of the conference, hygiene is very sparingly used. At the end of the congress, the International Committee on Mental Hygiene was superseded by the World Federation for Mental Health. In addition to the wording employed in the proceedings of that congress, gradually replacing hygiene by health, some of its recommendations were also influential at other levels. An example is recommendation 6 to the WHO that "as soon as practicable, an advisory expert committee be established, composed of professional personnel in the field of mental health and human relations".

The conference had been convened under the theme "Mental Health and World Citizenship". From a conceptual point of view, nevertheless, and perhaps reflecting an immediately post-war situation, discussions over world citizenship prevailed over those on mental health. Only one concept of mental health was put forward, by J.C. Flugel, Chairman of the Conference's Programme Committee: "Mental health is regarded as a condition which permits the optimal development, physical, intellectual and emotional, of the individual, so far as this is compatible with that of other individuals."

Echoing concerns about the absence, or rather limited number of, participants from places such as Far East, South America and the Soviet Union, the hope was expressed that "mental health as understood in Western countries [is not] necessarily at variance with the sense in which it is understood in other countries" 15. In a more detailed way, some delegates elaborated on what was summarized as the "four levels of mental health work: custodial, therapeutic, preventive and positive". It is not difficult to see a considerable overlapping between this proposal and the one already implemented by the mental hygiene movement. At the closing session, O.L. Forel, Lecturer in Psychiatry at the University of Geneva, answering to criticisms that mental hygiene, as understood in that conference, went beyond the medical and scientific framework, made a clearly political (in Plato's sense) statement by saying that: "I dare hope to be your interpreter in expressing our pride that so many scientists came here not at all to develop their respective sciences, but to have them at men's service".

Reading through the proceedings of this congress gives one a feeling of the tensions between a pragmatic approach, developed by the mental hygiene movement (basically defended by delegates from the USA), and a more politically-oriented approach, proposed by other participants, perhaps translating the experiences of some delegates from European countries, which had severely suffered from the war. In the end this latter approach prevailed, with the transformation of the mental hygiene movement into the mental health movement. Perhaps as a reflection of this basically political movement, in 1949 the National Institute of Mental Health started its activities in the USA.

RECENT DEVELOPMENTS

After half a century of the mental health, and almost a century of the mental hygiene movements, some developments can be perceived. On a more general level, the WHO's very concept of health has been recently questioned; formulated half a century ago, it is no longer felt by some as much appropriate to the current situation 16,17.

On the whole, mental health continues to be used both to designate a state, a dimension of health – an essential element in the definition of health – and to refer to the movement derived from the mental hygiene movement, corresponding to the application of psychiatry to groups, communities and societies, rather than on an individual basis, as is the case with clinical psychiatry. However, mental health is, quite unfortunately, still viewed by many as a discipline, either as a synonym of psychiatry, or as one of its complementary fields.

A recent trend has been the addition of the qualifier public to either mental health or to psychiatry, as it can be seen in a WHO document entitled Public mental health 18, or in a journal named Psiquiatría Pública, published in Spain since 1989. This is very much in line with the concept of mental health as a movement rather than a discipline.

In 2001, the WHO dedicated its annual report (The World Health Report - Mental health: new knowledge, new hope) to mental health 19. In that same year, the theme of the World Health Day was Stop Exclusion – Dare to Care, a quite clear political statement, that I am sure would have immensely pleased Clifford Beers.

In the message from the WHO Director-General that opens that report, Gro H. Brundtland summarizes the three main knowledge areas covered by the document: a) effectiveness of prevention and treatment, b) service planning and provision, and c) policies to break down stigma and discrimination and adequate funds for prevention and treatment.

If one allows for the semantic variations between the beginnings of the 20th and the 21st centuries, the same concerns of the origins of the mental hygiene movement, discussed earlier on, can be found in the mental health content of the World Health Report. Perhaps the biggest difference between these two political platforms is the emphasis on the improvement of hospital care in the former (the only form of treatment available by then), and the contemporary emphasis on distancing mental health from psychiatric hospitals and placing it in the community.

However, one must admit that, unfortunately, what was high in Beers' agenda in 1909, namely, an improvement in the standards of mental health care and an eradication of the abuses to which people with mental disorders are usually subject, is still a major concern of the most progressive and advanced agenda of people interested in the promotion of mental health around the world.

Onflict and Frustration

Some scientific studies clearly indicated that the feelings of continual conflict and frustration will have a negative effect upon our well-being. The chronic inability to be successful, meet one's goals, or even know one's goals is weakened. Unhappiness, frustration and unresolved needs and desires cause great emotional unhappiness.

The conflict and frustration may be on a conscious level or subconscious level. There may often be conflict in our emotions and attitudes between the conscious and the subconscious mind. For example, an individual may appear to be calm and happy, yet underneath that mask of calmness could be repressed anger and hurt that is hidden. A shy person may actually be full of rage.

The individual tries to maintain his or her life in a way that keeps the mask of the calm person or shy person in place. When there is conflict, and the person cannot predict and be secure in his or her world, then there may be fear and pain for the individual. He or she may not be able to cope. When there is too much conflict between the conscious and subconscious mind, disease may occur, and other emotional problems may appear. Therefore,

always be calm and collective in most problems of life and try to face them head on with full determination.

Frustration

We strive to gratify our wants and desires, our goals, aims, and ambitions. Introspection and self-knowledge make this much self-evident; experience with others confirms the generalization. Moreover, we are often unable to satisfy our desires or accomplish our goals. Sometimes our ambitions exceed our abilities, or we misperceive the possibilities. But sometimes we are blocked by an external barrier that precludes gratification. This may be a traffic jam preventing us from reaching an appointment, a college rule prohibiting us from taking a particular course, an amorous neighborhood tom cat interrupting our sleep, or our race restricting professional advancement. Whatever the barrier, we are frustrated. All of us are so frustrated from time to time.

In addition, we all have experienced irritation and anger at some frustrations. A long line preventing us from seeing an eagerly awaited movie, a crush of shoppers hindering the purchase of some simple necessities, a slow driver obstructing a narrow road, probably have aroused in all of us that familiar flush of annoyance, even anger. That frustration of our desires and goals occasionally leads to anger is a commonplace. It is subjectively unquestionable—a fact of our existence.

Of course, not all frustrations lead to anger. Indeed, it is more common to accept frustration—the blockage of our wants or goals—as feedback suggesting that we adjust or alter our aims. We do this automatically, hour by hour, day by day. Frustration signals the error in the trial-and-error process by which we dialectically adjust our perspectives to external powers and potentialities. To live, to assert oneself, is to be hindered, to face difficulties, to be *opposed*.

My desire to write this section uninterruptedly is hindered by construction noise in the background; my desire for physical comfort is defeated by the summer heat; my search for the right words to express my "understanding" is blocked by the barrier between structured language and unstructured "insight" and feelings. Moreover, when I let my consciousness stroll through the nested levels of my existence, I am also aware of a multitude of frustrations that reach consciousness like a flock of pheasants startled out of tall grass. Frustrations associated with family, research, teaching, politics, and the growing structure of coercive rules and laws. As I write, my life is within a matrix of such frustrations, high and low, large and small, significant and trivial.

Yet at the moment I am content, relatively happy, and feel no irritation, no anger.

Besides our desires and goals, our frustrations and anger, there are two other commonplace facts of life. We sometimes desire or aim to injure or hurt others, and behave in such a manner, sometimes because of our frustrations. Again, in our subjective world, these two facts are incontestable. Our awareness of them enables us to better perceive others[1] to adjust our interests and interactions, and to develop predictive expectations.

We can then understand why on a hot day in slow city traffic, one motorist will attack another for blocking his path, why a parent whose losing bridge game is interrupted for the fifth time by a child will vigorously spank him, and why a mistress cast off by her lover will send poison pen letters to his wife.

In the late 1930s, the commonplace enabling us to understand such behavior in certain contexts was erected into an invariant law of nature by a group of Yale psychologists (Dollard et al., 1939). First, they equated aggression with the desire to hurt or injure others. This effectively confused the various forms of aggression with one overt manifestation and confounded the bases of aiming to harm another, which may be instrumental (as in spanking a child), defensive (as in kicking an attacker), or hostile (as in spreading malicious gossip). Were one to equate love with kissing, the conceptual, cognitive confusion would be no less.

Second, frustration was defined as interference with a goal *response,* thus keying frustration to an objective barrier or difficulty, and to manifest behavior.[2] Interference was felt to be through punishment or goal inaccessibility, further confusing frustration as blockage with frustration as deprivation.

Conflict Helix

The relationship of relative deprivation-turned-injustice vector to the process of conflict is easily clarified. Injustice vectors—the moral sense of deprivation relative to others—are part of the conflict situation. These are vectors of interest, the opposition of which creates the conflict situation. Here, awareness (or perception) and the situation give context and meaning to the opposing interests; expectations of behavioural outcomes interrelate the injustice vector and its drive to action with the capability of the other and our expectation of his behavior. In other words, the situation of conflict involves our interests and their justness; our perception of others and our sense of injustice by comparison; and our beliefs about the capabilities of others and the outcomes of our actions. Within the framework of the helix, the conflict situation comprises the variables important to transforming the potential for collective violence into the potential for class violence and, finally, into manifest violence. At the collective level, the injustice vector fundamentally defines the class consciousness necessary to the class struggle within all organizations, including the state.

The initiation phase of manifest conflict involves a trigger provoking the will to action, and the occurrence of such a mechanism depends on the balance of powers an individual perceives between himself and others. Consequently a sense of injustice is no guarantee of action. This is also true of Gurr's model, in which the transformation of potential to manifestation depends on a balance of powers.

But deprivation theory does not explain what happens after the manifest conflict or violence ensues, while the conflict helix is in mid-ascent. Out of manifest conflict a balance is formed among the diverse interests held by people on the basis of their capability and wills. There ensues adjustment among the diverse vectors of injustice, an adjustment based on subjective perception and expectations honed by the reality of others. Conflict and the resulting balance form a structure of expectations that enables different views of injustice and different classes to live together.

In time these expectations may become incongruent with the underlying balance; a person may develop new reference groups, have new experiences, be the object of an ideological campaign ("workers are oppressed"). The sense of injustice may change such that the previous class balance (between workers and management in a factory) no longer reflects the parties' interests, or the underlying capabilities or wills of the parties may alter (bureaucratic dissension may weaken governmental control over dissidents). Then a trigger, such as an event provoking a rearoused or newly inflamed sense of injustice may provoke a turn of the conflict helix, a new balancing of powers and injustices, of classes.

At the *ontological and empirical levels* the nature of the psychological field and the conflict helix seems to answer the question, What is social justice? Just wants and injustice vectors vary considerably among people. Such interests and feelings are diverse, multidimensional, and *personal*. Moreover, the amount willingly sacrificed to satisfy just wants or to right a sense of injustice varies across individuals. People have different expectations, capabilities, interests, and wills. And the overriding superordinate goal, self-esteem, is intrinsic to the individual.

Then how, apparently, do we determine what is just? How do we balance different views of what is just? Given the diversity of human beings, this question can only imply two alternatives: we force our view of social justice on someone else (say, through governmental coercion), or people settle for themselves and among themselves their own balance. If the conflict helix as a field process operates at all levels without the imposition of an antifield on it, the diverse views of social justice will compromise and balance in terms of interests, capabilities, and wills. This seems to argue for the maximum freedom, for a precondition of the conflict helix is that each is free to pursue his just wants and to square his sense of injustice against others. The precondition of social justice is therefore freedom. Or, so it seems.

But this is a factual conclusion about an ethical question, which is not logically possible. Facts can be heuristic, they can provide some guidelines to thought, but they cannot make the argument themselves. To fully and logically answer the question we must consider the nature of ethics and then the ethical nature of social justice. Ultimately, we will have to use ethical arguments to determine what is socially just. And this I will do in the concluding volume of this series, *Vol. 5: The Just Peace*. There we will find that at the level of ethics we arrive at a conclusion similar to that we found ontologically and empirically: as a matter of ethics, social justice is the maximization of the freedom of individuals to choose the principles that govern them, even if they choose to be unfree.

Social unrest

The general condition of the community in which milling is both frequent and widespread and in which rumour is recurrent is the crucible in which the more highly organized forms of collective behaviour develop. This condition, known as social unrest, can lead to outbursts of violence. The American urban black uprisings of the 1960s were preceded and accompanied by social unrest in the form of a rise in tensions in black communities throughout the country; the Russian Revolution was preceded by several years of constant unrest and turmoil, involving random assassinations, strikes, and riots.

There are several distinguishing characteristics to social unrest. First, there is a general impairment of collective life routines. People find it difficult to concentrate on their work or even to adhere to rules in playing games. Any occasion to abandon routines is welcomed. Second, people are hyperreactive. The magnitude of the response is out of proportion to the usual meaning of any stimulating incident. A small police provocation elicits a major outcry of police brutality; a trivial success is the occasion for large-scale celebration. Milling and rumour abound because incidents that would normally pass with little notice become occasions for both. Third, social unrest is marked by contagiousness. When restlessness is strictly individual, one person's restlessness merely annoys another. But when restlessness becomes a shared experience, people are highly suggestible to one another. Questioning and exploring alternative courses of action are reduced to a minimum. Fourth, social unrest is not specific with respect to grievances or activities. When there is social unrest in a school, students complain of both restrictions on their behaviour and the lack of clearly defined rules; they find fault both with school administrators and with their fellow students. Finally, social unrest is perhaps the most volatile of collective states. Unlike rumour or milling, it does not remain focused on an issue or problem. Unlike crowd behaviour or fads, it has not yet been channeled into one main direction. Although social unrest may eventually die down without any serious aftermath, it is a condition in which people can be easily aroused.

CLINICAL PSYCHOLOGY VERSUS OTHER MENTAL HEALTH PROFESSIONS

In addition to clinical psychology, there are many professional and subprofessional groups which provide mental health services to the public. In some cases their roles, activities, and responsibilities vary with their training and skills. Frequently activities overlap, causing confusion about the differences between groups and their areas of competence.

Clinical psychologists earn the Ph.D. or Psy.D. degree after four or more years of graduate school training beyond the bachelors degree. They also have a full-time, one-year internship (or two years half-time) to refine their clinical skills. They are trained to do research and to conduct psychological assessment and treatment. Some clinical psychologists seek postdoctoral training to become proficient in a specialised area (e.g. nuropsychological assessment). When clinical psychologists work with other her professionals on an interdisciplinary "team," they typically are uniquely qualified to perform psychological assessments and to plan and conduct research (e.g., to evaluate the quality of services or determine the types of patients who profit from specific services).

Psychiatrists are physicians who specialise in psychiatry. They receive M.D. degrees after attending medical school to receive a general medical education. Following a one-year internship, they take a three-year psychiatric residency, during which they learn the skills of the field of psychiatry. Since they are physicians, psychiatrists are legally permitted to prescribe medication. They are also specially skilled in diagnosing medically related psychiatric difficulties and in treating severe psychopathology. Some psychiatrists receive training in verbal psychotherapy (especially psychoanalysis), and some are trained to conduct research. However, they are uniquely qualified to use biological treatments (i.e., drug therapy).

Psychiatric social workers generally earn the Master of Social Work (M.S.W.) degree after two years of graduate training. While some are trained in a variety of psychological treatments, most concentrate on family case work. They conduct extensive family interviews, visit clients of their homes, and attempt to help by using relevant community resources (e.g., finding jobs for ex-patients). *Psychiatric nurses* also perform psychotherapeutic interventions. More often, they provide general nursing care and supplemental treatment services for psychiatric patients (e.g., helping to foster social interaction).

Development of the Profession

The field of clinical psychology has no clear trail of milestones or discoveries which mark its early development. Rather, it evolved slowly but of other disciplines and bodies of knowledge in an almost random and coincidental fashion. Interest in human behaviour, especially maladaptive or pathological behaviour, can be traced back through history. For example, William Shakespeare was a brilliant observer of human nature and motivation; many of his character sketches are valid today. Philosophical analyses and arguments about human nature, such as those of Hobbes and Locke, are also part of the background of clinical psychology. Similarly, Darwin exerted an important influence by bringing the study of humanity into the arena of science. In fact, the somewhat conflicting values of science and philosophy are a continuing major source of controversy for clinical psychology.

More direct lines for the development of the field are usually traced back to the later nineteenth century (Watson, 1953). After Wundt's development of the first psychology laboratory in 1879, the systematic, scientific study of human behaviour became more important. This importance was shown by the so-called "psychometric tradition"—the emphasis on careful and specific measurement. In 1890, James McKeen Cattell coined the term "mental tests" to refer to the procedures for measuring psychological processes such as sensation and perception. This was the unofficial beginning of the *testing movement*. Mental testing became not only the backbone of the field but also the major source of activity and professional identity for clinical psychologists for the next sixty years. One milestone was the first useful intelligence test, published by Alfred Binet in 1905. Developed for use in the Paris school system, this test (by Binet and his colleague, Simon) showed that children could be compared and classified according to intellectual level. Previously they were had been categorised as only normal or retarded. As a result of this refined measurement, Binet's work also led to new training programmes for the more educable mentally retarded. This gave impetus to applied psychological in general.

The second major source in shaping the field was the "dynamic tradition"—the interest in human motivation, needs, drives, and psychological processes. This emphasis was stressed by William James and G. Stanley Hall two of the important academic psychologists of their time. However, the most significant influence was the work of Sigmund Freud. Freud's work, of course, had a tremendous impact on the entire mental health field. His emphasis on intrapsychic processes and psychodynamics was revolutionary at the time. Curiously, his initial impact was much greater on psychology than on psychiatry (Garfield, 1965). His writings created much interest in the psychological basis of behaviour, as well as in the possibilities of using psychological approaches to change behaviour.

The term clinical psychology apparently was first used by Lightner Witmer, who in 1896 established the first psychological clinic at the University of Pennsylvania. Psychologists at that clinic, and in general over the next twenty years, worked primarily in the area of testing and educational or rehabilitative programmeming for children. It was not until World War I that clinical psychologists really began to work with adults. The United States armed forces, faced with a sudden dramatic expansion, needed some way to sort and classify recruits. Given their expertise in the area of psychometrics and test construction, psychologists were enlisted to develop classification procedures. Two group intelligence tests (Army Alpha and Beta), along with a personality test (the Woodworth Personal Data Sheet), were created to meet this need. The success of these devices led to a rapid increase in the use of testing and the development of numerous other tests over the next several years. The profession during the period was further enhanced by the development of projective tests, including the Rorschach and Thematic Apperception Test. With their special expertise in this area, clinical psychologists became increasingly identified and valued as psychodiagnosticians.

While the field was gradually growing, clinical psychology was not a recognised profession prior to World War II. Few psychologists identified themselves as clinicians, and their training had no systematised or accepted form. Furthermore, clinical psychologists were primarily limited to testing and educational work with children. Psychotherapy (primarily psychoanalysis) was considered a medical activity and (with few exceptions) was limited to physicians. Many clinical psychologists served on psychiatric teams, conducting psychological assessments to guide the treatment plan carried out by a psychiatrist.

World War II brought about a dramatic change. Many academically oriented psychologists were drafted into the armed forces and thrust into clinical roles, often to help provide therapeutic services. By the time they were discharged, many of them had become interested in clinical work; the number of clinical psychologists mushroomed. But more important were the needs of the thousands of psychological casualties of the war. Available mental health personnel resources were totally inadequate. In response, the federal government began hiring more personnel and provided funding so that more people could be trained. Not only were clinical psychologists included, but the restrictions against their practice of psychotherapy began to disappear.

However, since there was no systematic training plan for clinical psychologists at that time, the government found it difficult to identify qualified persons and the training programmes needed.

For this reason, the Veterans Administration and the U.S. Public Health Service asked the American Psychological Association (APA) to develop and publicise a training plan. In response, the APA convened a committee of leading figures, led by David Shakow. The resulting plan, referred to as the Shakow Report (APA, 1947), was published in 1947 and has served as a blueprint for the field ever since. The few training programmes in existence at the time quickly adopted the plan in order to qualify for federal, funding, as well as because of its inherent good sense. In 1949 a national conference on training in Boulder, Colorado, reaffirmed the Shakow recommendations, which then became known as the *Boulder Model* (Raimy, 1950). This model, which underscores the scientist-professional concept, is still the basic approach for training clinical psychologists.

In the thirty years since the Boulder Conference, the number of clinical psychologists has grown dramatically. Their numbers, their occupational roles, and their influence in society as well as in their job settings have increased geometrically. This growth is greatest in the United States. While clinical psychology exists in other countries, it is primarily an American profession. First, the U.S. government has the money to underwrite the cost of training by providing fellowships and traineeships to students. Both the Veterans Administration and the Public Health Service have continued their funding since the end of World War II.

This support has promoted the development of new graduate training programmes, as well as permitting graduate study for many students who could not otherwise afford it. Second, national, state, and local governments are major employers of clinical psychologists. Third, the country as a whole demands and supports social services, not the least of which is mental health care. While many clinical psychologists are in private practice or work in the private sector (e.g., industry), the majority owe their training and employment to the public.

The Boulder Model

As stated above, the Boulder Conference adopted the Shakow Report almost completely. That report provided certain general principles which were to guide the nature of training, as well as specific recommendations for actual programmes. First, the clinical psychologist was to be trained as a psychologist, sharing a common core of knowledge with other psychologists. The training programme was to be as rigorous as that of the traditional doctorate. This recommendation has placed an added burden on clinical students, who must learn clinical skills as well as the various academic and research skills mastered by their nonclinical colleagues. Also, the clinical psychologist was to earn a doctoral degree; bachelors and masters level training were presumed to be inadequate.

The Shakow Report emphasised that clinical psychologists should *not* be trained as technicians, who would only be capable of performing a limited number of tasks (e.g., giving intelligence tests). Rather, they were to be trained as scientist-professionals, capable of conducting research as well as being sophisticated consumers of the research literature. This dual role was considered especially important since the field was just beginning to develop. Little was known about the nature or causes of psychopathology and the effectiveness of available treatment techniques was uncertain. Thus, the report recommended a training strategy which would both advance the state of knowledge and allow clinical psychologists to continually update their skills as the field developed.

One implication of this recommendation was that courses should focus on theory and principles rather than only teach specific technical skills. The clinician would then have a solid basis on which to generate and integrate new ideas. Second, students should take courses in research methods (e.g., statistics) and conduct at least one independent research project (i.e., the dissertation). In practice, most programmes require students to conduct a master's thesis, which is a small-scale research project, as well as a dissertation. Third, students should be imbued with a sense of scientific skepticism. Rather than accepting ideas and procedures on faith, they should have a questioning attitude, asking "why" and "how" and looking for evidence.

The training programme must also develop clinical skills. It was recommended that clinical, academic, and research activities be integrated throughout the programme. The hope was that these potentially contrasting activities would complement one another, rather than being discrete or incompatible. Clinical training would take three forms. First, research activities and courses would refer to clinical material and issues. Essentially the entire programme was to be relevant to clinical training. Second, students would participate in clinical practicum from their first year. For beginning students this might entail interviewing and testing, observing advanced students, and participating in clinic conferences. Later, students would learn to perform psychotherapeutic interventions and conduct extensive assessment procedures. Many graduate programmes operate their own mental health clinics in order to provide practicum training. Faculty members supervise and serve as role models. Other programmes rely on community agencies to provide training opportunities. The third form of clinical training is the *internship.* This is a concentrated period of clinical work, wither for one year full time or two successive years half time, generally in the third or fourth year of graduate school. The student spends the year immersed in clinical work in the field (e.g., at a psychiatric hospital), often geographically removed from the university. Practicum training is viewed as preparation for the internship, during which clinical skills are refined and the student encounters more seriously disturbed persons.

Two other recommendations in the Shakow Report also warrant comment. The training programme was to encourage intensive "self-evaluation." Students were expected to become aware of their own motives values, anxieties, and biases so that these factors would not interfere with clinical work or appraisal of the literature. One way to do this is through intensive, one-on-one therapy supervision, in which the student's clinical activity is carefully examined and discussed. In this manner, the student might be made aware of a consistent blind spot, anger, anxiety, or other problem. Another way for the student to gain self-knowledge is through personal psychotherapy. Some programmes encourage all students to undergo therapy, but in most cases this is left to the student's discretion. It was also recommended that the programme foster a sense of social responsibility. The clinical psychologist was expected to have a commitment to society, as well as to him or herself and any particular client. This is consistent with the APA guidelines for the profession.

THE SCHOLAR-PROFESSIONAL MODEL

The Boulder Conference model for training has promoted the tremendous growth of clinical psychology. Its value is reflected in the increased number and success of programmes based on the model. Most such programmes have thirty to fifty student applicants for each opening. The job market for clinical psychologists remains solid, in contrast to the decreasing demand for nonclinical psychologists and many other professionals. The blend of research and clinical training is unique among the mental health professions and gives clinical psychologists a special identity and repertoire of skills. Nevertheless, the scientist-professional aspect of the model has recently come under increasing fire, and its utility has been severely challenged.

The basic criticism is that training students as scientists *and* professionals may be desirable in theory but is impossible in practice. Several factors have led to this conclusion. Most people who wish to become clinical psychologists have primarily applied interests. They want to become *clinicians;* their attitudes toward research activities and statistics often range from disinterest to hostility, and they attend research classes quite unwillingly. Conversely, graduate programmes are controlled and conducted by academic (i.e., research oriented) faculty members. They are neither skilled clinicians (since they do not do much clinical work) nor committed clinical supervisors. Finally, it is argued that there is simply not enough time to train people to be competent scientists *and* competent clinicians.

Too often, the graduates of Boulder Model programmes are mediocre in both spheres rather than experts in either or both. Several noted figures in the field have advocated separate training for students interested in professional as opposed to research careers. The 1973 Vail conference on training reached the same conclusion (Korman, 1974). In addition to the arguments presented above, it was felt that clinical knowledge and techniques are now so well grounded that the major justification for the Boulder Model is no longer valid. While further research and the training of scientists were certainly to be encouraged, the training of practitioners was now seen as justifiable and necessary.

Gordon Derner (1975, 1976) has used the term *scholar-professional* to describe the new model for training. This term stresses that clinical practitioners should not be technicians, but should receive rigorous training which emphasises a scholarly, creative, and sophisticated approach to the clinical enterprise.

In a clinical psychology programme that strives or excellence in preparation for clinical practice, the core of substantive courses and seminars will offer depth in scholarship but clearly relevance will serve as a crucial criteria [sic] for inclusion of such course or seminar. The programme will be marked by extensive and intensive clinical practice from the first year under qualified clinical practitioners and the programme will have available and encourage students to have a personal therapy experience. The scholarship will be encouraged through continuing reference to the literature of the field and the culminating scholarly production, the dissertation will be relevant to the person's career goal of clinical service.

Several strategies have been proposed for scholar-professional programmes. Derner advocates the Doctor of Philosophy (Ph.D.) as the professional degree, regarding it as the pinnacle of academic achievement. Others (cf. Peterson, 1968) have suggested that the professional status and competence of clinical psychologists would best be represented by a new degree: the Doctor of Psychology, or Psy.D. According to this view, the Ph.D. is a research degree which does not differentiate degree holders by discipline (i.e., physicists, sociologists, psychologists, and others all earn the Ph.D.). In contrast, the Psy.D. is unique to psychology and would be viewed publicly as comparable to the degree of Doctor of Medicine (M.D.) or Doctor of Dental Surgery (D.D.S,). Also, the requirements for the degree would be less restricted. Today, opinion on this issue is clearly divided; which degree will ultimately prevail is uncertain.

Another basic problem is, what is the best setting for professional training? Boulder Model programmes are usually found in university psychology departments. Many (most?) advocates of professional training argue that such programmes need a less restrictive setting. Two different strategies have been offered. One suggests that the programmes remain within university settings but function as separate schools, like schools of law, medicine, and dentistry. This would allow for close ties with academic psychology departments, including joint course offerings and an interactive faculty. The other model calls for independent professional schools which function autonomously. The California School of Professional Psychology, which has several branch campuses throughout the state, is a prime example of this approach. In addition to the Ph.D., it offers several lower-level degrees for psychological aides and technicians. The independent school lacks the prestige and support provided by a major university, but it has greater freedom to develop its own programmes.

Boulder Versus Vail

How will future clinical psychologists be trained? Professional programmes are now well established, and more will probably be developed in the future. While the number of independent schools may increase, the university-based programmes seem to have more promise because of their greater prestige, the availability of other resources (e.g., academic psychology faculty), and the university's economic base. However, it seems unlikely that professional training programmes will become the norm. Unlike the Boulder Report, the Vail Report has not been widely accepted by the field. Most traditional programmes still prosper, and the Boulder Model is still widely accepted. Furthermore, graduates of these programmes are still highly regarded by the public and other mental health disciplines.

Our feeling is that the Boulder Model still represents the most reasonable way to train clinical psychologists. As Leitenberg (1974) notes, the scientist-professional approach is not designed to train laboratory researchers and practicing psychoanalysts. It is most suited for training applied researchers—people who can do clinical work, evaluate it, and develop empirically based clinical procedures or programmes. Effective therapeutic techniques cannot be developed solely in the laboratory, without clinical sophistication and clinical trials. The researcher must know what depressives or phobics are like and what it means to work with them in order to devise reasonable interventions. Conversely, we do not know enough to justify the uniform adoption of today's technology. Every clinical technique used today is under continuing evaluation. We also believe that doctoral-level training is unnecessary for most clinical techniques. Technicians can be trained to conduct assessments and treatments. The doctoral-level professional can thus train and supervise, develop programmes, and evaluate programmes and procedures. Boulder Model clinical psychologists are those best qualified to conduct such critical applied research. High-quality professional programmes may be appropriate for those who have no desire or ability for research. However, we believe they cannot totally substitute for Boulder-type programmes.

Advanced Training

Education and training for any profession is a lifelong process. The lawyer must keep abreast of new statutes and court decisions, the physician must be aware of new medications and procedures, and the clinical psychologist must be familiar with research findings and new developments in the field. Various steps are involved. For one thing, professionals must continually read journals or significant new books throughout their career. Failure to keep up with the literature results in quick outdating of knowledge and potential incompetence. Another practice is attendance at regional or national meetings of professional associations, such as the APA, the Association for Advancement of Behaviour. Therapy, and the Eastern, Southeastern, Midwestern, and Western Psychological Associations. These organisations each hold national conventions with various training opportunities: symposia, workshops, seminars, demonstrations, and others. For example an expert on a new therapeutic technique may lead a workshop and demonstrate its application.

The clinical psychologist may wish to learn a new skill or develop a new area of specialisation which requires extensive training. For example, interns often develop new interests and sometimes cannot receive enough training in the new area during the internship year. For this reason, some psychologists pursue one or two years of *postdoctoral training.* The "post-doc," as it is called, is typically a full-time programme which pays a stipend or salary. The training may be offered by a skilled researcher or clinician or by an agency. For example, the person who seeks training to conduct behaviour therapy or work with learning-disabled children spends a year at an agency specialising in that area. Most clinical psychologists do not take post-docs. Most of those who do, take them immediately after their internship year, before they have begun their careers.

CLINICAL PSYCHOLOGY, LEGISLATION AND POLITICS

Over the thirty-five years since World War II, clinical psychologists have realised that certification, licensing, and other forms of accreditation (all of which bring about official recognition) have been necessary not only to uphold the standards of the profession but also to maintain and enhance its status in a sometimes hostile atmosphere. To do this, psychologists have had to influence legislation at the state and federal levels.

To do so, official lobbies have been formed and funded by members of the APA. Notable among these is the Association for the Advancement of Psychology (AAP), which has been very active and effective. For example, at the time of this writing some twenty-eight states and the District of Columbia provide reimbursement of certified or licensed psychologists by third-party payers (this is known as freedom-of-choice legislation). As noted by Fiester (1978), "Psychology has made considerable progress over the past several years toward the goal of attaining professional parity with psychiatry". Such parity was granted by federal law in the 1973 Rehabilitation Act, the 1973 Health Maintenance Organisation Development Act, and the 1970 regulations concerned with the Civilian Health and Medical Programme of the Armed Services (CHAMPUS). In 1978 the State of California supported an act to permit hospital staff rights to psychologists. In 1975 a list of 6,877 psychologists who met specific criteria was published in the National Register of Health Providers in Psychology (Council for the National Register of Health Service Providers in Psychology, 1975). This council was organised in anticipation of a future National Health Insurance plan so as to ensure the inclusion of psychology in its reimbursement policies. This list is updated yearly. Currently more than 11,000 psychologists are listed.

All these legislative actions have increased the prestige of clinical psychology—as reflected in the increasing activities of clinical psychologists. Equally important, many of these laws allow clinical psychologists to be officially paid for their services. Thus, clinical psychologists are gaining greater equality in status when competing with other professionals for clients and patients.

The first law regulating the practice of psychology was passed in Connecticut in 1945. Since then, all fifty states and the District of Columbia have enacted laws that provide either certification or licensure. In addition, in Canada the following seven provinces have certification laws: Alberta, British Columbia, Manitoba, New Brunswick, Ontario, Quebec, and Saskatchewan.

In general, a certification law states who may use the title "psychologist." By contrast, a licensing law defines not only the use of the title but, more specifically, the range of activities performed. These laws restrict the untrained and the "quacks" from offering services to the public. As stated in a 1978 APA news release, "Licensing laws ordinarily exempt from regulation members of recognised professions employing psychological skills, techniques, or knowledge provided those professionals do not hold themselves forth to the public as 'psychologist' or a variation of the term implying training or expertise in psychology." Thus, the licensing law is stronger and supersedes the certification act. Some states that originally enacted certification laws, such as Connecticut, now have passed licensing laws.

Regulations vary from one state to the next. Generally, however, state examining boards require a doctoral degree in psychology or a field primarily psychological in nature (e.g., educational psychology, counselling), an approved internship, and one or two years of postdoctoral supervised field practice. Written and/or oral examinations are mandatory in most states. These are standardised tests prepared by the American Association of State Psychology Boards (AASPB) in conjunction with the Professional Examination Service. Many states offer reciprocity when an individual licensed in one state moves to another. However, some states may required a second written or oral examination.

A higher, and quite prestigious, form of accreditation is the Diplomate, awarded by the American Board of Professional Psychology (ABPP), formerly known as the ABEPP (American Board of Examiners in Professional Psychology). This is an independent incorporated group formed in 1947, with a board of trustees selected by the APA.

Diplomates have been awarded by ABPP in clinical, counselling, industrial, and school psychology. Most of the Diplomates are clinical psychologists.

Over the years, the requirements for the ABPP have changed. Initially, both a written and an oral examination were necessary; now the written examination has been dropped. The oral examination may focus on the applicant's theoretical bent (e.g., psychoanalytic, behavioural). To qualify for an examination, the applicant, in addition to paying a rather high application fee, should be a member of the APA or Canadian Psychological Association, and should have a Ph.D from an APA-approved school and five years of relevant postdoctoral experience.

The clinical applicant is asked to submit samples of his or her work, and during the oral examination may be observed (without knowing it) interacting with a client. Basically, the examination covers four areas: (1) assessment, (2) treatment, (3) ethical and professional issues, and (4) application of theoretical principles and research findings to clinical practice.

The real value of the ABPP has long been argued. Many highly qualified and eminent clinical psychologists have refused to subject themselves to yet another evaluation. Others, concerned with legislation and reimbursement policies, think that holding the ABPP will lead to preferred status in the future. Indeed, many state boards of examiners will waive certification or licensing examinations for those who hold the ABPP. Also, in some settings the ABPP may command a higher salary.

CLINICAL EFFECTIVENESS

Research

Moss, LeVaque, and Hammond (2004) observed that "Biofeedback and neurofeed back seem to offer the kind of evidence-based practice that the health care establishment is demanding." "From the beginning biofeedback developed as a research-based approach emerging directly from laboratory research on psychophysiology and behaviour therapy, The ties of biofeedback/ neurofeed back to the biomedical paradigm and to research are stronger than is the case for many other behavioural interventions". The Association for Applied Psychophysiology and Biofeedback (AAPB) and the International Society for Neurofeed back and Research (ISNR) have collaborated in validating and rating treatment protocols to address questions about the clinical efficacy of biofeedback and neurofeed back applications, like ADHD and headache. In 2001, Donald Moss, then president of the Association for Applied Psychophysiology and Biofeedback, and Jay Gunkelman, president of the International Society for Neurofeed back and Research, appointed a task force to establish standards for the efficacy of biofeedback and neurofeed back.

The Task Force document was published in 2002, and a series of white papers followed, reviewing the efficacy of a series of disorders. The white papers established the efficacy of biofeedback for functional anorectal disorders, attention deficit disorder, facial pain and temporomandibular disorder, hypertension, urinary incontinence, Raynaud's phenomenon, substance abuse, and headache.

A broader review was published and later updated, applying the same efficacy standards to the entire range of medical and psychological disorders. The 2008 edition reviewed the efficacy of biofeedback for over 40 clinical disorders, ranging from alcoholism/substance abuse to vulvar vestibulitis. The ratings for each disorder depend on the nature of research studies available on each disorder, ranging from anecdotal reports to double blind studies with a control group. Thus, a lower rating may reflect the lack of research rather than the ineffectiveness of biofeedback for the problem.

Efficacy

Yucha and Montgomery's (2008) ratings are listed for the five levels of efficacy recommended by a joint Task Force and adopted by the Boards of Directors of the Association for Applied Psychophysiology (AAPB) and the International Society for Neuronal Regulation (ISNR). From weakest to strongest, these levels include: not empirically supported, possibly efficacious, probably efficacious, efficacious, and efficacious and specific.

Level 1: Not empirically supported. This designation includes applications supported by anecdotal reports and/or case studies in non-peer reviewed venues. Yucha and Montgomery (2008) assigned eating disorders, immune function, spinal cord injury, and syncope to this category.

Level 2: Possibly efficacious. This designation requires at least one study of sufficient statistical power with well identified outcome measures but lacking randomized assignment to a control condition internal to the study. Yucha and Montgomery (2008) assigned asthma, autism, Bell palsy, cerebral palsy, COPD, coronary artery disease, cystic fibrosis, depression, erectile dysfunction, fibromyalgia, hand dystonia, irritable bowel syndrome, PTSD, repetitive strain injury, respiratory failure, stroke, tinnitus, and urinary incontinence in children to this category.

Level 3: Probably efficacious. This designation requires multiple observational studies, clinical studies, wait list controlled studies, and within subject and intrasubject replication studies that demonstrate efficacy. Yucha and Montgomery (2008) assigned alcoholism and substance abuse, arthritis, diabetes mellitus, fecal disorders in children, fecal incontinence in adults, insomnia, pediatric headache, traumatic brain injury, urinary incontinence in males, and vulvar vestibulitis to this category.

Level 4: Efficacious. This designation requires the satisfaction of six criteria:

(a) In a comparison with a no-treatment control group, alternative treatment group, or sham (placebo) control utilizing randomized assignment, the investigational treatment is shown to be statistically significantly superior to the control condition or the investigational treatment is equivalent to a treatment of established efficacy in a study with sufficient power to detect moderate differences.

(b) The studies have been conducted with a population treated for a specific problem, for whom inclusion criteria are delineated in a reliable, operationally defined manner.

(c) The study used valid and clearly specified outcome measures related to the problem being treated.

(d) The data are subjected to appropriate data analysis.

(e) The diagnostic and treatment variables and procedures are clearly defined in a manner that permits replication of the study by independent researchers.

(f) The superiority or equivalence of the investigational treatment has been shown in at least two independent research settings.

Yucha and Montgomery (2008) assigned anxiety, chronic pain, epilepsy, constipation (adult), headache (adult), hypertension, motion sickness, Raynaud's disease, and temporomandibular disorder to this category.

Level 5: Efficacious and specific. The investigational treatment must be shown to be statistically superior to credible sham therapy, pill, or alternative bona fide treatment in at least two independent research settings. Yucha and Montgomery (2008) assigned urinary incontinence (females) to this category.

Criticisms

In a health care environment that emphasizes cost containment and evidence-based practice, biofeedback and neurofeed back professionals continue to address skepticism in the medical community about the cost-effectiveness and efficacy of their treatments. Critics question how these treatments compare with conventional behavioural and medical interventions on efficacy and cost.

The publication of white papers and rigorous evaluation of biofeedback interventions can address these legitimate questions and educate medical professionals, third-party payers, and the public about the value of these services. Biofeedback should gain greater acceptance if researchers can demonstrate that it complements traditional treatments (like physical therapy), achieves comparable or superior efficacy, is more cost effective, and enjoys a better side effect profile.

Organizations

The Association for Applied Psychophysiology and Biofeedback (AAPB) is a non-profit scientific and professional society for biofeedback and neurofeed back. The International Society for Neurofeed back and Research (ISNR) is a non-profit scientific and professional society for neurofeed back. The Biofeedback Foundation of Europe (BFE) sponsors international education, training, and research activities in biofeedback and neurofeed back.

Certification

The Biofeedback Certification International Alliance (formerly the Biofeedback Certification Institute of America) is a non-profit organization that is a member of the Institute for Credentialing Excellence (ICE). BCIA certifies individuals who meet education and training standards in biofeedback and neurofeed back and progressively recertifies those who satisfy continuing education requirements.

BCIA certification has been endorsed by the Mayo Clinic, the Association for Applied Psychophysiology and Biofeedback (AAPB), the International Society for Neurofeed back and Research (ISNR), and the Washington State Legislature.

The BCIA didactic education requirement includes a 48-hour course from a regionally-accredited academic institution or a BCIA-approved training programme that covers the complete General Biofeedback Blueprint of Knowledge and study of human anatomy and physiology. The General Biofeedback Blueprint of Knowledge areas include: I. Orientation to Biofeedback, II. Stress, Coping, and Illness, III. Psychophysiological Recording, IV. Surface Electro-myographic (SEMG) Applications, V. Autonomic Nervous System (ANS) Applications, VI. Electro-encephalographic (EEG) Applications, VII. Adjunctive Interventions, and VIII. Professional Conduct.

Applicants may demonstrate their knowledge of human anatomy and physiology by completing a course in human anatomy, human physiology, or human biology provided by a regionally-accredited academic institution or a BCIA-approved training programme or by successfully completing an Anatomy and Physiology exam covering the organization of the human body and its systems.

Applicants must also document practical skills training that includes 20 contact hours supervised by a BCIA-approved mentor designed to them teach how to apply clinical biofeedback skills through self-regulation training, 50 patient/client sessions, and case conference presentations.

Distance learning allows applicants to complete didactic course work over the internet.

Distance monitoring trains candidates from their residence or office. They must recertify every 4 years, complete 55 hours of continuing education during each review period or complete the written exam, and attest that their license/credential (or their supervisor's license/credential) has not been suspended, investigated, or revoked.

Pelvic Muscle Dysfunction

Pelvic Muscle Dysfunction Biofeedback (PMDB) encompasses "elimination disorders and chronic pelvic pain syndromes." The BCIA didactic education requirement includes a 28-hour course from a regionally-accredited academic institution or a BCIA-approved training programme that covers the complete Pelvic Muscle Dysfunction Biofeedback Blueprint of Knowledge and study of human anatomy and physiology. The Pelvic Muscle Dysfunction Biofeedback areas include: I. Applied Psychophysiology and Biofeedback, II. Pelvic Floor Anatomy, Assessment, and Clinical Procedures, III. Clinical Disorders: Bladder Dysfunction, IV. Clinical Disorders: Bowel Dysfunction, and V. Chronic Pelvic Pain Syndromes.

Currently, only licensed health care providers may apply for this certification. Applicants must also document practical skills training that includes a 4-hour practicum/personal training session and 12 contact hours spent with a BCIA-approved mentor designed to them teach how to apply clinical biofeedback skills through 30 patient/client sessions and case conference presentations. They must recertify every 3 years, complete 36 hours of continuing education or complete the written exam, and attest that their license/credential has not been suspended, investigated or revoked.

COMPARISON WITH OTHER MENTAL HEALTH PROFESSIONS

Psychiatry

Although clinical psychologists and psychiatrists can be said to share a same fundamental aim—the alleviation of mental distress—their training, outlook, and methodologies are often quite different. Perhaps the most significant difference is that psychiatrists are licenced physicians. As such, psychiatrists often use the medical model to assess psychological problems (i.e., those they treat are seen as patients with an illness) and rely on psychotropic medications as the chief method of addressing the illness—although many also employ psychotherapy as well. Psychiatrists and medical psychologists (who are clinical psychologists that are also trained to prescribe) are able to conduct physical examinations, order and interpret laboratory tests and EEGs, and may order brain imaging studies such as CT or CAT, MRI, and PET scanning.

Clinical psychologists generally do not prescribe medication, although there is a growing movement for psychologists to have limited prescribing privileges. These medical privileges require additional training and education. To date, medical psychologists may prescribe psychotropic medications in Guam, New Mexico, and Louisiana and some military psychologist.

Counseling Psychology

Counseling psychologists study and use many of the same interventions and tools as clinical psychologists, including psychotherapy and assessment. Traditionally, counseling psychologists help people with what might be considered normal or moderate psychological problems—such as the feelings of anxiety or sadness resulting from major life changes or events. Many counseling psychologists also receive specialized training in career assessment, group therapy, and relationship counseling, although some counseling psychologists also work with the more serious problems that clinical psychologists are trained for, such as dementia or psychosis.

There are fewer counseling psychology graduate programmes than those for clinical psychology and they are more often housed in departments of education rather than psychology. The two professions can be found working in all the same settings but counseling psychologists are more frequently employed in university counseling centers compared to hospitals and private practice for clinical psychologists. There is considerable overlap between the two fields and distinctions between them continue to fade.

School Psychology

School psychologists are primarily concerned with the academic, social, and emotional well-being of children and adolescents within a scholastic environment. In the U.K., they are known as "educational psychologists". Like clinical (and counseling) psychologists, school psychologists with doctoral degrees are eligible for licensure as health service psychologists, and many work in private practice. Unlike clinical psychologists, they receive much more training in education, child development and behavior, and the psychology of learning. Common degrees include the Educational Specialist Degree (Ed.S.), Doctor of Philosophy (Ph.D.), and Doctor of Education (Ed.D.).

Traditional job roles for school psychologists employed in school settings have focused mainly on assessment of students to determine their eligibility for special education services in schools, and on consultation with teachers and other school professionals to design and carry out interventions on behalf of students. Other major roles also include offering individual and group therapy with children and their families, designing prevention programmes (e.g. for reducing dropout), evaluating school programmes, and working with teachers and administrators to help maximize teaching efficacy, both in the classroom and systemically.

Clinical Social Work

Social workers provide a variety of services, generally concerned with social problems, their causes, and their solutions. With specific training, clinical social workers may also provide psychological counseling (in the U.S. and Canada), in addition to more traditional social work. The Masters in Social Work in the U.S. is a two-year, sixty credit programme that includes at least a one year practicum (two years for clinicians).

Occupational Therapy

Occupational therapy—often abbreviated OT—is the "use of productive or creative activity in the treatment or rehabilitation of physically, cognitively, or emotionally disabled people." Most commonly, occupational therapists work with people with disabilities to enable them to maximize their skills and abilities. Occupational therapy practitioners are skilled professionals whose education includes the study of human growth and development with specific emphasis on the physical, emotional, psychological, sociocultural, cognitive and environmental components of illness and injury.

SPECIALTIES OF CLINICAL PSYCHOLOGISTS

Clinical psychologists who focus on treating mental health specialize in evaluating patients and providing psychotherapy and prescribing medication. There are a wide variety of therapeutic techniques and perspectives that guide practitioners, although most fall into the major categories of Psychodynamic, Cognitive Behavioural, Existential-Humanistic, and Systems Therapy (e.g. family or couples therapy).

In addition to therapy, clinical psychologists are also trained to administer and interpret psychological personality tests such as theMMPI and the Rorschach inkblot test, and various standardized tests of intelligence, memory, and neuropsychological functioning. Common areas of specialization include: specific disorders (e.g. trauma or depression), neuropsychological disorders, child and adolescent, family and relationship counselling. Internationally, psychologists are generally not granted prescription privileges. In the US, prescriptive rights have been granted to appropriately trained psychologists only in the states of New Mexico and Louisiana, with some limited prescriptive rights in Indiana and the US territory of Guam.

Educational Requirements for Clinical Psychologists

Clinical psychologists, having completed an undergraduate degree usually in psychology or other social science, generally undergo specialist postgraduate training lasting at least two years (e.g. Australia), three years (e.g. UK), or four to six years depending how much research activity is included in the course (e.g. US). In countries where the course is of shorter duration, there may be an informal requirement for applicants to have undertaken prior work experience supervised by a clinical psychologist, and a proportion of applicants may also undertake a separate PhD research degree. Today, in the U.S., about half of licensed psychologists are trained in the Scientist-Practitioner Model of Clinical Psychology (PhD)—a model that emphasizes both research and clinical practice and is usually housed in universities. The other half are being trained within a Practitioner-Scholar Model of Clinical Psychology (PsyD), which focuses on practice (similar to professional degrees for medicine and law). A third training model called the Clinical Scientist Model emphasizes training in clinical psychology research. Outside of coursework, graduates of both programmes generally are required to have had 2 to 3 years of supervised clinical experience, a certain amount of personal psychotherapy, and the completion of a dissertation (PhD programmes usually require original quantitative empirical research, whereas the PsyD equivalent of dissertation research often consists of literature review and qualitative research, theoretical scholarship, programme evaluation or development, critical literature analysis, or clinical application and analysis).

Counselling Psychologist or Psychotherapist

Counselling generally involves helping people with what might be considered "normal" or "moderate" psychological problems, such as the feelings of anxiety or sadness resulting from major life changes or events. As such, counselling psychologists often help people adjust to or cope with their environment or major events, although many also work with more serious problems as well. One may practice as a counselling psychologist with a PhD or EdD, and as a counselling psychotherapist with a Masters degree. Compared with clinical psychology, there are fewer counselling psychology graduate programmes (which are commonly housed in departments of education), counsellors tend to conduct more vocational assessment and less projective or objective assessment, and they are more likely to work in public service or university clinics (rather than hospitals or private practice). Despite these differences, there is considerable overlap between the two fields and distinctions between them continue to fade.

Behaviour Analyst

Behaviour analysts are licensed in five states to provide services for clients with substance abuse, developmental disabilities, and mental illness. This profession draws on the evidence base of applied behaviour analysis, behaviour therapy, and the philosophy of behaviorism. Behaviour analysts have at least a master's degree in behaviour analysis or in a mental health related discipline as well as at least five core courses in applied behaviour analysis. Many behaviour analysts have a doctorate. Most programmes have a formalized internship programme and several programmes are offered online. Most practitioners have passed the examination offered by the behaviour analysis certification board or the examination in clinical behaviour therapy by the World Association for Behaviour Analysis . The model licensing act for behaviour analysts can be found at the Association for Behaviour Analysis International's website.

Certified Mental Health Professional

The Certified Mental Health Professional (CMHP) certification is designed to measure an individual's competency in performing the following job tasks. The job tasks are not presented in any particular order of importance.

1. Maintain confidentiality of records relating to clients' treatment.
2. Encourage clients to express their feelings, discuss what is happening in their lives, and help them to develop insight into themselves and their relationships.
3. Guide clients in the development of skills and strategies for dealing with their problems.
4. Prepare and maintain all required treatment records and reports.
5. Counsel clients and patients, individually and in group sessions, to assist in overcoming dependencies, adjusting to life, and making changes.
6. Collect information about clients through interviews, observations, and tests.
7. Act as the client's advocate in order to coordinate required services or to resolve emergency problems in crisis situations.
8. Develop and implement treatment plans based on clinical experience and knowledge.
9. Collaborate with other staff members to perform clinical assessments and develop treatment plans.
10. Evaluate client's physical or mental condition based on review of client information.

School Psychologist

School psychologists' primary concern is with the academic, social, and emotional well-being of children within a scholastic environment. Unlike clinical psychologists, they receive much more training in education, child development and behaviour, and the psychology of learning, often graduating with a post-Masters Educational Specialist Degree (EdS), EdD or Doctor of Philosophy (Ph D) degree. Besides offering individual and group therapy with children and their families, school psychologists also evaluate school programmes, provide cognitive assessment, help design prevention programmes (e.g. reducing drops outs), and work with teachers and administrators to help maximize teaching efficacy, both in the classroom and systemically.

Social Worker

Social workers in the area of mental health may assess, treat, develop treatment plans, provide case management and/or rights advocacy to individuals with mental health problems. They can work independently or within clinics/service agencies, usually in collaboration with other health care professionals. In the US, they are often referred to as clinical social workers; each state specifies the responsibilities and limitations of this profession. State licensing boards and national certification boards require clinical social workers to have a masters or doctoral degree (MSW or DSW/PhD) from a university. The doctorate in social work requires submission of a major original contribution to the field in order to be awarded the degree.

In the UK there is a now a standardized three-year undergraduate social work degree, or two-year postgraduate Masters for those who already have an undergraduate social sciences degree and relevant work experience. These courses include mandatory supervised work experience in social work, which may include mental health services. Successful completion allows an individual to register and work as a qualified social worker. There are various additional optional courses for gaining qualifications specific to mental health, for example training in psychotherapy or, in England and Wales, for the role of Approved Mental Health Professional (two years' training for a legal role in the assessment and detention of eligible mentally disordered people under the Mental Health Act (1983) as amended in 2007).

In general, it is the social model rather than, or in addition to, the dominant medical model, that is the underlying rationale for mental health social work. This may include a focus on social causation, labelling, critical theory and social constructivism. Many argue social workers need to work with medical and health colleagues to provide an effective service but they also need to be at the forefront of processes that include and empower services users.

PSYCHIATRIC AND MENTAL HEALTH NURSE

Psychiatric Nurses or Mental Health Nurse Practitioners work with people with a large variety of mental health problems, often at the time of highest distress, and usually within hospital settings. These professionals work in primary care facilities, outpatient mental health clinics, as well as in hospitals and community health centres. MHNPs evaluate and provide care for patients who have anything from psychiatric disorders, medical mental conditions, to substance abuse problems. They are licensed to provide emergency psychiatric services, assess the psychosocial and physical state of their patients, create treatment plans, and continually manage their care. They may also serve as consultants or as educators for families and staff; however, the MHNP has a greater focus on psychiatric diagnosis, including the differential diagnosis of medical disorders with psychiatric symptoms and on medication treatment for psychiatric disorders.

Educational Requirements for Psychiatric and Mental Health Nurses

Psychiatric and mental health nurses receive specialist education to work in this area. In some countries it is required that a full generalnurse training be completed prior to specializing as a psychiatric nurse. In other countries, such as the U.K., an individual completes a specific nurse training course that determines their area of work. As with other areas of nursing, it is becoming usual for psychiatric nurses to be educated to degree level and beyond. In order to become a nurse practitioner in the U.S., at least six years of college education must be obtained. After earning the Bachelor's degree (usually in nursing, although there are Masters Entry Level Nursing graduate programmes intended for individuals with a Bachelors degree outside of nursing) the test for licensure as a registered nurse (the NCLEX-RN) must be passed. Next, the candidate must complete a state-approved Masters Degree advanced nursing education programme which includes at least 600 clinical hours. Several schools are now also offering further education and awarding a DNP (Doctorate of Nurse Practice).

Individuals who choose a Masters Entry Level pathway will spend an extra year at the start of the programme taking classes necessary to pass the NCLEX-RN. Some schools will issue a BSN, others will issue a certificate. The student then continues with the normal MSN programme.

6

Developmental Psychology in Human Beings

Developmental psychology, also known as Human Development, is the scientific study of progressive psychological changes that occur in human beings as they age. Originally concerned with infants and children, and later other periods of great change such as adolescence and aging, it now encompasses the entire life span.

This field examines change across a broad range of topics including motor skills and other psycho-physiological processes, problem solving abilities, conceptual understanding, acquisition of language, moral understanding, and identity formation.

Developmental psychologists investigate key questions, such as whether children are qualitatively different from adults or simply lack the experience that adults draw upon. Other issues that they deal with is the question of whether development occurs through the gradual accumulation of knowledge or through shifts from one stage of thinking to another; or if children are born with innate knowledge or figure things out through experience; and whether development is driven by the social context or by something inside each child.

Developmental psychology informs several applied fields, including: educational psychology, child psychopathology and developmental forensics. Developmental psychology complements several other basic research fields in psychology including social psychology, cognitive psychology, cognitive development, and comparative psychology.

HISTORY OF DEVELOPMENTAL PSYCHOLOGY

The modern form of developmental psychology has its roots in the rich psychological tradition represented by Heraclitus, Aristotle and Descartes. William Shakespeare had his melancholy character Jacques (in As You Like It) articulate the seven ages of man: these included three stages of childhood and four of adulthood. In the mid-eighteenth century Jean Jacques Rousseau described three stages of childhood: infans (infancy), puer (childhood) and adolescence in Emile: Or, On Education. Rousseau's ideas were taken up strongly by educators at the time.

In the late nineteenth century, psychologists familiar with the evolutionary theory of Darwin began seeking an evolutionary description of psychological development; prominent here was G. Stanley Hall, who attempted to correlate ages of childhood with previous ages of mankind.

A more scientific approach was initiated by James Mark Baldwin, who wrote essays on topics that included Imitation: A Chapter in the Natural History of Consciousness and Mental Development in the Child and the Race: Methods and Processes.

In 1905, Sigmund Freud articulated five psychosexual stages. Later, Rudolf Steiner articulated stages of psychological development throughout human life. The first three of these stages, which correspond closely with Piaget's later-described stages of childhood, were first presented in Steiner's 1911 essay The Education of the Child; his descriptions have been taken up by educators (in the Waldorf Schools) and by psychologists. By the early to mid-twentieth century, the work of Vygotsky and Piaget, had established a strong empirical tradition in the field.

The Role of Mothers: Traditionally mothers (and women generally) were emphasized to the exclusion of other caregivers. This has begun to change, with the emphasis now placed on a primary caregiver (regardless of gender or biological relation), as well as all persons directly or indirectly influencing the child (the family system). However, studies are showing that the role of the mother/father are more significant than first thought as we moved into the concept of primary caregiver. For example, the traditional father had little to do with an infant directly, but his method of interacting with the mother (supportive, abusive, neglectful) had a great deal of impact on the infant indirectly.

STAGES OF DEVELOPMENT

Prenatal: The prenatal development of human beings is viewed in three separate stages:

1. Germinal (conception through week 2)
2. Embryonic (weeks 3 through 8)
3. Fetal (week 9 through birth)

These stages are not the same as the trimesters of a woman's pregnancy.

The germinal stage least resembles a grown human. It begins when a sperm penetrates an egg in the act of conception (normally the result of sexual intercourse between a man and a woman). At this point a zygote is formed. Through the process of mitosis the cells divide and double.

The embryonic stage occurs once the zygote has firmly implanted itself into the uterine wall. It is in this stage that the vital organs are formed, and while the external body is still extremely dissimilar from an adult human, some features such as eyes and arms, and eventually ears and feet become recognizable. The fetal period is when the brain most substantially forms, becoming more and more complex over the last few months.

During pregnancy the risk to the developing child from drugs and other teratogens, spousal abuse and other stress on the mother, nutrition and the age of the mother are quite acute. Three methods of determining fetal defects and health include the ultrasound, amniocentesis, and chorionic villus sampling.

Ultrasound uses sound waves and a computer monitor, and is non-invasive, thus minimizing potential harm to fetus and mother. Unfortunately its ability to determine potential defect is also far less comprehensive than more risky methods. Chorionic villus sampling is a form of prenatal diagnosis to determine genetic abnormalities in the fetus. It entails getting a sample of the chorionic villus (placental tissue) and testing it. It is generally carried out only on pregnant women over the age of 35 and those who have a higher risk of Down syndrome and other chromosomal conditions.

The advantage of CVS is that it can be carried out at 10-12 weeks of pregnancy, earlier than amniocentesis (which is carried out at 15-18 weeks). However, it is more risky than amniocentesis, with a 1 in 100 to 200 risk that it will cause a miscarriage.

Amniocentesis is another medical procedure used for prenatal diagnosis, in which a small amount of amniotic fluid is extracted from the amnion around a developing fetus. It is usually offered when there may be an increased risk for genetic conditions (i.e. Down syndrome, sickle-cell disease, cystic fibrosis, etc.) in the pregnancy. Amniocentesis done in the second trimester is often said to have a risk of fetal death between about 1 in 400 and 1 in 200. Often, genetic counseling is done before amniocentesis, or other types of genetic testing, is offered.

Although difficult, some methods of treating fetal disorders have been developed, both surgical and drug based. Genetic testing prior to pregnancy is also increasingly available.

Infancy: From birth until the child begins to speak, they are referred to as an infant. Developmental psychologists vary widely in their assessment of the infant's psychology, and the influence the outside world has upon it, but certain aspects are relatively clear. While no agreement has yet been reached regarding the level of stimulation an infant requires, we are well aware that a normal level of stimulation is very important, and that a lack of stimulation and affection can result in retardation and a host of other developmental and social disorders.

Some feel that classical music, particularly Mozart is good for an infant's mind. While some tentative research has shown it to be helpful to older children, no conclusive evidence is available involving infants.

The majority of an infant's time is spent in sleep. At first this sleep is evenly spread throughout the day and night, but after a couple of months they generally become diurnal. Infants can be seen to have 6 states, grouped into pairs:

- quiet sleep and active sleep (dreaming, when REM occurs)
- quiet waking, and active waking
- fussing and crying

Infants respond to stimuli differently when in these different states. Habituation is frequently used in testing psychological phenomenon. Both infants and adults look less and less as a result of consistent exposure to a particular stimulus. The amount of time spent looking to a presented alternate stimulus (after habituation to the initial stimulus) is indicative of the strength of the remembered percept of the previous stimulus, or dishabituation. Habituation is used to discover the resolution of perceptual systems, for example, by habituating a subject to one stimulus, and then observing responses to similar ones, one can detect the smallest degree of difference that is detectable by the subject. Infants have a wide variety of reflexes, some of which are permanent (blinking, gagging), and others transient in nature. Some with obvious purposes, some are clearly vestigial and some do not have obvious purposes. Primitive reflexes reappear in adults under certain conditions. Namely, neurological conditions like dementia, traumatic lesions, etc. A partial list of infantile reflexes includes:

- Moro reflex or startle reflex:
    1. Startle
    2. spreading out the arms (abduction)
    3. unspreading the arms (adduction)
    4. Crying (usually)
- Tonic neck reflex or fencer's reflex
- Rooting reflex, sucking reflex, suckling reflex: can be initiated by scratching the infant's cheek; the reaction is pursing of the lips for sucking.
- Stepping reflex, step-up reflex: can be initiated if you support the infant upright from its armpits below a given surface so the baby lifts its foot and steps up on the surface (like climbing a stair).

- Grasp reflex: can be initiated by scratching the infant's palm.
- Parachute reflex the infant is suspended by the trunk and suddenly lowered as if falling for an instant. The child spontaneously throws out the arms as a protective mechanism. The parachute reflex appears before the onset of walking.
- Plantar reflex or Babinski reflex a finger is stroked firmly down the outer edge of the baby's sole; the toes spread and extend out.

Infants have particularly poor vision, and are legally blind. They are capable of sight, however blurry. This improves over time, based on experience. Infants less than 2 months old are also thought to be colour blind. Hearing is well-developed prior to birth, however, and a preference for the mother's heartbeat is well established. Infants are fairly good at detecting the direction from which a sound comes, and by 18 months their hearing ability is approximately equal to that of adults. Smell and taste are present, with infants having been shown to prefer the smell and taste of a banana, while rejecting the taste of shrimp. There is good evidence for infants preferring the smell of their mother to that of others.

Infants have a fully developed sense of touch at birth, and the myth believed by some doctors even today that infants feel no pain is inaccurate. Doctors are slowly becoming aware of the need for pain prevention for newborns.

Piaget felt that there were several sensorimotor stages within his broader Theory of cognitive development.

- The first sub-stage occurs from birth to six weeks and is associated primarily with the development of reflexes. Three primary reflexes are described by Piaget: sucking of objects in the mouth, following moving or interesting objects with the eyes, and closing of the hand when an object makes contact with the palm (palmar grasp). Over these first six weeks of life, these reflexes begin to become voluntary actions; for example, the palmar reflex becomes intentional grasping. (Gruber and Vaneche, 1977).
- The second sub-stage occurs from six weeks to four months and is associated primarily with the development of habits. Primary circular reactions or repeating of an action involving only ones own body begin. An example of this type of reaction would involve something like an infant repeating the motion of passing their hand before their face. Also at this phase, passive reactions, caused by classical or operant conditioning, can begin (Gruber et al., 1977).
- The third sub-stage occurs from four to nine months and is associated primarily with the development of coordination between vision and

prehension. Three new abilities occur at this stage: intentional grasping for a desired object, secondary circular reactions, and differentiations between ends and means. At this stage, infants will intentionally grasp the air in the direction of a desired object, often to the amusement of friends and family. Secondary circular reactions, or the repetition of an action involving an external object occur begin; for example, moving a switch to turn on a light repeatedly. The differentiation between means also occurs. This is perhaps one of the most important stages of a child's growth as it signifies the dawn of logic (Gruber et al., 1977). Towards the late part of this sub-stage infants begin to have a sense of object permanence, passing the A-not-B error test.

- The fourth sub-stage occurs from nine to twelve months and is associated primarily with the development of logic and the coordination between means and ends. This is an extremely important stage of development, holding what Piaget calls the "first proper intelligence." Also, this stage marks the beginning of goal orientation, the deliberate planning of steps to meet an objective (Gruber et al. 1977).
- The fifth sub-stage occurs from twelve to eighteen months and is associated primarily with the discovery of new means to meet goals. Piaget describes the child at this juncture as the "young scientist," conducting pseudo-experiments to discover new methods of meeting challenges (Gruber et al. 1977).
- The sixth sub-stage is associated primarily with the beginnings of insight, or true creativity. This marks the passage into the preoperational stage.

When studying infants, the habituation methodology is an example of a method often used to assess their performance. This method allows researchers to obtain information about what types of stimuli an infant is able to discriminate. In this paradigm, infants are habituated to a particular stimulus and are then tested using different stimuli to evaluate discrimination. The critical measure in habituation is the infants' level of interest. Typically, infants prefer stimuli that are novel relative to those they have encountered previously. Several methods are used to measure infants' preference. These include the high-amplitude sucking procedure, in which infants suck on a pacifier more or less depending on their level of interest, the conditioned foot-kick procedure, in which infants move their legs to indicate preference, and the head-turn preference procedure, in which the infant's level of interest is measured by the amount of time spent looking in a particular direction. A key feature of all these methods is that, in each situation, the infant controls the stimuli being presented. This gives researchers a means of measuring discrimination. If an infant is able to discriminate between the habituated stimulus and a novel stimulus, they will show a preference for the novel stimulus. If, however, the infant cannot discriminate between the two stimuli, they will not show a preference for one over the other.

Object permanence is an important stage of cognitive development for infants. Numerous tests regarding it have been done, usually involving a toy, and a crude barrier which is placed in front of the toy, and then removed, repeatedly. In sensorimotor stages 1 and 2, the infant is completely unable to comprehend object permanence. Jean Piaget conducted experiments with infants which led him to conclude that this awareness was typically achieved at eight to nine months of age. Infants before this age are too young to understand object permanence, which explains why infants at this age do not cry when their mothers are gone. "Out of sight, out of mind." A lack of Object Permanence can lead to A-not-B errors, where children reach for a thing at a place where it should not be.

Toddler: Intelligence is demonstrated through the use of symbols, language use matures, and memory and imagination are developed. Thinking is done in a nonlogical, nonreversible manner. Egocentric thinking predominates.

Socially, toddlers are little people attempting to become independent. They walk, talk, use the toilet, and get food for themselves. Self-control begins to develop. If taking the initiative to explore, experiment, risk mistakes in trying new things, and test their limits is encouraged by the caretaker(s) the child will become autonomous, self-reliant, and confident. If the caretaker is overprotective or disapproving of independent actions, the toddler may begin to doubt their abilities and feel ashamed for the desire for independence. The child's autonomic development will be inhibited, be less prepared to successfully deal with the world in the future.

Early Childhood: When children go to preschool, they broaden their social horizons and become more engaged with those around them. Impulses are channeled into fantasies, which leaves the task of the caretaker to balance eagerness for pursuing adventure, creativity and self expression with the development of responsibility. If caretakers are properly encouraging while being consistently disciplinary, children are more likely to develop positive self-esteem while becoming more responsible, and will follow through on assigned activities. If not allowed to decide which activities to perform, children may begin to feel guilt upon contemplating taking initiative. This negative association with independence will lead them to let others make decisions in place of them.

Childhood: In this stage intelligence is demonstrated through logical and systematic manipulation of symbols related to concrete objects. Operational thinking develops, which means actions are reversible, and egocentric thought diminishes.

Children go through the transition from the world at home to that of school and peers. Children learn to make things, use tools, and acquire the skills to be a worker and a potential provider. Children can now receive feedback from outsiders about their accomplishments. If children can discover pleasure in intellectual stimulation, being productive, seeking success, they will develop a sense of competence. If they are not successful or cannot discover pleasure in the process, they may develop a sense of inferiority and feelings of inadequacy that may haunt them throughout life. This is when children think of them selves as industrious or as inferior.

Adolescence: Adolescence is the period of life between the onset of puberty and the full commitment to an adult social role, such as worker, parent, and/or citizen. It is the period known for the formation of personal and social identity and the discovery of moral purpose. Intelligence is demonstrated through the logical use of symbols related to abstract concepts and formal reasoning. A return to egocentric thought often occurs early in the period. Only 35% develop the capacity to reason formally during adolescence or adulthood.

The adolescent asks "Who am I? Who do I want to be?" Like toddlers, adolescents must explore, test limits, become autonomous, and commit to an identity, or sense of self. Different roles, behaviours and ideologies must be tried out to select an identity. Role confusion, inability to choose vocation, sexual orientation and one's role in life can result from a failure to achieve a sense of identity.

Early Adulthood: The person must learn how to form intimate relationships, both in friendship and love. The development of this skill relies on the resolution of other stages. It may be hard to establish intimacy if you haven't developed trust or a sense of identity. If this skill is not learned the alternative is alienation, isolation, a fear of commitment and the inability to depend on others.

Middle Age: Middle adulthood generally refers to the period between ages 35 to 60. During this period, the middle-aged experience a conflict between generativity and stagnation. They may either feel a sense of contributing to the next generation and their community or a sense of purposelessness.

Physically, the middle-aged experience a decline in muscular strength, reaction time, sensory keenness, and cardiac output. Also, women experience menopause and a sharp drop in the hormone estrogen. Men do not have an equivalent to menopause, but they do experience a decline in sperm count and speed of ejaculation and erection. Most men and women remain capable of sexual satisfaction after middle age.

Old Age: This stage generally refers to those over 60 years. During old age, people experience a conflict between integrity vs. despair. When reflecting on their life, they either feel a sense of accomplishment or failure.

Physically, older people experience a decline in muscular strength, reaction time, stamina, hearing, distance perception, and the sense of smell. They also are more susceptible to severe diseases such as cancer and pneumonia due to a weakened immune system. Mental disintegration may also occur, leading to Dementia or Alzheimer's Disease. However, partially due to a lifetime's accumulation of antibodies, the elderly are less likely to suffer from common diseases such as the cold or flu Whether or not intellectual powers increase or decrease with age remains controversial. Longitudinal studies have suggested that intellect declines, while cross-sectional studies suggest that intellect is stable. It is generally believed that crystallized intelligence increases up to old age, while fluid intelligence decreases with age.

NATURE OF HUMAN BEINGS

Human beings begin life as simple organic units and develop into personalities with complex spiritual qualities.

From a helpless beginning they grow into spiritual dynamos, capable of mastery of themselves and of their social environment. The process is largely one of *intersocial stimulation* and*response,* and the product is human personalities with their attitudes and values of life. According to this analysis social psychology studies intersocial stimulation; and response, social attitudes, values, and personalities.

It begins with individual human beings and original human nature and traces their growth through intersocial stimulation into persons with socialized attitudes. Out of intersocial stimulation personal nature slowly and fitfully evolves. That it has a physical basis, akin to that of animal nature, no one can well disprove. It is in part a neuro-muscular system, vastly complex and not very well understood; it is also psychical and social. It is at once a product and a cause, a resultant and a generator. When Dr. William Healy refers to the individual "as the product of conditions and forces which have been actively forming him from the earliest moment of unicellular life," he is emphasizing a part of the truth, the product phase to the exclusion of the ascendancy phase. Dr. Healy's experiences with delinquents and persons who are "victims of circumstance" have led him perhaps to overlook somewhat the inventor, the leader, or even normal persons who modify or change material and spiritual environments. Social psychology deals primarily with normal persons as both products and initiators in the intersocial stimulation process.

ORIGINAL HUMAN NATURE

Human nature originates in the psycho-physical patterns that develop in the unicellular stage of human life. Environment, however, begins to operate significantly in prenatal life. An undernourished, anaemic, or chronically fatigued condition of the mother during the pre-natal months undoubtedly has serious effects upon the physical nature and psychical quality of the offspring. A mother suffering from malnutrition cannot give the unborn child a physical constitution that will ordinarily develop into a sturdy physique. Alcoholism on the part of the mother is believed to have serious effects on offspring, for the circulation of alcoholic poisons through the mother's system naturally reaches the unborn babe. Toxins from venereal disease also circulate through the blood and may permanently distort the unborn child's mental and psychical development. A sudden, violent neural shock to the mother, such as the unexpected death of a loved one, or the experiencing of great fear, an automobile accident, or other disaster, may cause disturbing results.

At birth, the environmental contacts are greatly multiplied. The physical changes are extraordinary and the processes of bodily activity are numerous and varied. The earliest years are devoted to making physical and psychical co-ordinations, but therewith the psycho-social development proceeds apace. The child is born into dynamic social environments with their countless stimuli; the result is the modification and development of the original human nature traits. Communication, suggestion, imitation, and other processes operate, and personality takes definite form. Before tracing further the development of personality by means of intersocial stimulation processes, let us examine the inherited equipment. In other words, what is original human nature?

At the beginning of life the human organism is endowed with tropistic and reflex characteristics as are the lower animal forms. It has mechanisms for responding to environmental stimuli in peculiar ways. Some of the mechanisms produce reflex and simple responses, while others are far more complex, being the bases of impulsive, habitual, and attentive activities. These mechanisms consist of a structural equipment, which in the case of many ordinary human reactions, includes sense organs, affector neurones, synapses, higher neurone centres, muscles, and glands; or receptors, conductors, and effectors. The activities of these factors fall into established types with a corresponding mechanistic nature. A specific stimulus creates vibrations in the sense organ, which are transmitted along the afferent neural system to the central neural system whence an impulse is sent out over efferent neurones to muscles or glands or both, and if to the latter then with emotional accompaniments. Every time the given stimulus operates it tends to discharge the whole system of stimuli and responses in the same way, and an organized habit may result.

Every person inherits certain ready-made coÿrdinations, such as those represented by the beating of the heart, respiration, digestion, as well as other neuro-muscular mechanisms, more complicated in type, such as the so-called "instincts" with expressions that are partly innate and partly habitual. Simple and complex impulses alike are inherited ways of meeting common problems and conditions of life. Their origins are obscure but there can be no doubt about their transmission biologically from parent to offspring. Whenever the organism receives a certain stimulus, a neuro-muscular mechanism for meeting a given type of situation is set off automatically. These standardized types of response energize the whole individual. An impulse is not a specific phase of personality, but the whole personality expressing itself in a specific way. These organized impulsive types of activity are pre-determined ways of meeting recurring situations. They serve the individual well until he faces a new problem and needs a new type of response.

Intersocial stimulation implies receptors or organs for receiving stimuli and conducting them into the neural system where responses are inaugurated. The development of receptors in the human organism makes possible seeing, hearing, smelling, touching, tasting, and the discrimination of cold, heat, pain, and kinesthetic stimuli. Then, there are inherited organic stimuli, as evidenced by the fact that when the individual organism experiences hunger-stimuli it grows restless and seeks food; when it becomes tired, it falls asleep; or when it is repeatedly irritated by perplexing stimuli, it grows nervous and perhaps develops insomnia, or otherwise suffers a loss in efficiency.

Moreover there are internal stimuli popularly known as motives, intentions, aspirations. A motive is explained by Woodworth in objective terms. It originates in a stimulus that has not promptly achieved its goal, and which thus persists in organic activity. The internal neuromuscular mechanisms may be set off by stimuli from the receptors and thus constitute the technique of motive. The discharge of one neural mechanism, for example, of a receptor, may act as an internal stimulus to discharge another internal neural mechanism, and thus internal activities may multiply and even be organized into standard types of reaction or response. In writing this treatise, for example, I find that upon interruption it is best to make a notation in pencil of the next idea which is to be developed, or that otherwise after an interim the "next idea" which seemed so pertinent, at the time the interruption occurred may not be recalled at all or only with difficulty. In other words, as I write, one thought leads to another, and so on. There seems to be a neural process, whereby the discharge of one thought-mechanism acts as a stimulus to create or at least to release another thought-mechanism. In addition to stimuli, receptors, simple neural mechanisms, there is the central neural system and the sympathetic neural system. The former refers to the brain and the spinal cord; through one or both of these every nerve stimulus must pass before reaching its motor completion. Here are located the centres of what are called consciousness and sub-consciousness. The latter, the sympathetic neural system, carries motor currents as distinguished from sensory currents, to the internal organs of the body and the glands.

The neural discharges of the central neural system go out to the effectors, namely, the striped muscles which produce the visible evidences of bodily motion and activity. Then there are the unstriped muscles by which the sympathetic neural system regulates the actions of the internal organs, and also the glands which function in digestion, secretion, and excretion. There are duct glands, such as the salivary glands, the digestive glands of the stomach, the pancreas, the liver, the kidneys, and excretory skin glands. There are also the ductless or endocrine glands which in recent years have received special attention, because of their relation to the emotional tone of the human organism. The three leading endocrine glands are the thyroid, the suprarenal, and the pituitary. The striped muscles, the unstriped or smooth muscles, and the duct and ductless glands therefore constitute the effector system.

Impulses to activity are the most common traits of human nature. In the main they are not highly developed at first, but are aroused by many different kinds of stimuli. As a person's experiences multiply they become organized into definite habits and attitudes. There are also inherited impulses which are specialized although largely potential at the time of a child's birth. They are best known as *aptitudes,* being *general,* as the aptitude for speech which is inherited by all, and also being *specific,* as the aptitude for music, for mathematics, or for languages, which are possessed in varying degrees by some individuals, but scarcely at all by many. Native impulses, unorganized and organized alike, may result in promoting the welfare (1) of the individual organism, or (2) of social groups. In the vast majority of instances these ends are not sought consciously, even by human beings. The chick which hears the warning cluck and runs to the mother hen does not stop to inform itself that it must hasten to cover for self-preservation. The warning cry was the stimulus which released the chick's innate fleeing mechanism, and energized the whole chick to run to cover. Chicks that do not respond to warning calls soon lose their lives; those that respond promptly will probably be saved, and become the progenitors of a line of chicks which are characterized by this type of instinctive behaviour.

The prevalence of large families a century ago in the United States, or today among the poorer classes, does not mean at all that the parents in question were or are motivated by definite plans to build up the race numerically. Most self-sacrificing, altruistic deeds are performed without thought of benefitting the race, for example, the countless acts of maternal self-sacrifice in behalf of children. It is most fortunate, in fact, that socialized conduct can thus become standardized, habitual, and sub-attentive.

The assertion that inherited tendencies are the essential springs or motive forces of feeling, thought, and action, whether individual or collective, has probably been overstressed by William McDougall. The role played by habituation has clearly been neglected. Furthermore, McDougall has isolated individual "instincts" too definitely.

An "instinct" is perhaps more of a result than a cause—a result in which the purely inherited element is largely submerged in habit. The term, "instinct," has developed a cluster of meanings which imply too much, and hence it is necessary to use instead the idea of innate potential impulses. These are the core of original human nature and the elements from which personality develops. They determine the possible effects of social interstimulation; when they become organized into habitual reactions they are scarcely recognizable. Human interstimulation plays continually upon original human nature, modifying it beyond recognition and organizing it into social patterns or institutions. It is the *modification* of original human nature by social stimulation that transforms it into the personality traits that we know.

Although the beaver needs no practice in order to cut down a tree and the first nest of a robin is as well made as the last, the human being has no such highly organized equipment. His relatively long period of immaturity, beginning with a period of helplessness when all his psychic equipment cannot keep him alive for more than a few days or hours is the organization stage of his impulses and other innate characteristics. As a result of this organization period of several years' duration, the human individual does not require the instinct equipment of higher animals. Instead, his native impulses are transformed into habits, socially and personally determined. Thus, he escapes an instinct equipment with its pre-determinism. He possesses, on the other hand, great flexibility, and limitless opportunities for personal development.)

APPROACH TO EVOLUTIONARY PSYCHOLOGY

Evolutionary psychology is a theoretical approach to psychology that attempts to explain "useful" mental and psychological traits-such as memory, perception, or language-as adaptations, i.e., as the functional products of natural selection. The purpose of this approach is to bring the functional way of thinking about biological mechanisms such as the immune system into the field of psychology, and to approach psychological mechanisms in a similar way. In short, evolutionary psychology is focused on how evolution has shaped the mind. Though applicable to any organism with a nervous system, most research in evolutionary psychology focuses on humans.

Evolutionary Psychology is, to quote Steven Pinker, "not a single theory but a large set of hypotheses" and a term which "has also come to refer to a particular way of applying evolutionary theory to the mind, with an emphasis on adaptation, gene-level selection, and modularity." Evolutionary Psychology proposes that the human brain comprises many functional mechanisms, called psychological adaptations or evolved cognitive mechanisms designed by the process of natural selection.

Examples include language acquisition modules, incest avoidance mechanisms, cheater detection mechanisms, intelligence and sex-specific mating preferences, foraging mechanisms, alliance-tracking mechanisms, agent detection mechanisms, and so on. Evolutionary psychology has roots in cognitive psychology and evolutionary biology. It also draws on behavioral ecology, artificial intelligence, genetics, ethology, anthropology, archaeology, biology, and zoology. Evolutionary psychology is closely linked to sociobiology, but there are key differences between them including the emphasis on domain-specific rather than domain-general mechanisms, the relevance of measures of current fitness, the importance of mismatch theory, and psychology rather than behaviour.

Many evolutionary psychologists, however, argue that the mind consists of both domain-specific and domain-general mechanisms, especially evolutionary developmental psychologists. Most sociobiological research is now conducted in the field of behavioral ecology.

The term evolutionary psychology was probably coined by Michael Ghiselin in his 1973 article in Science. Jerome Barkow, Leda Cosmides and John Tooby popularized the term in their highly influential 1992 book The Adapted Mind: Evolutionary Psychology and The Generation of Culture. Evolutionary psychology has been applied to the study of many fields, including economics, aggression, law, psychiatry, politics, literature, and sex.

General Evolutionary Theory

The idea that organisms are composed of a number of parts that serve different functions (i.e., living things are, in some sense, machines) goes back at least to Aristotle. This idea is the foundation of modern medicine and biology. William Paley, drawing upon the work of many others, argued that organisms are machines designed to function in particular environments.

Paley believed that this evidence of 'design' was evidence for a designer-God. Charles Darwin appears to have been impressed with Paley's argument that organisms are designed for particular environments. The theory of natural selection, created by Charles Darwin and Alfred Russel Wallace, provided a scientific account of the origins of functional design in the natural world that did not invoke a supernatural designer.

Evolutionary psychology is ultimately rooted in the basic theoretical principles of evolutionary theory. It is sometimes seen not simply as a sub-discipline of psychology but as a way in which evolutionary theory can be used as a meta-theoretical framework within which to examine the entire field of psychology.

Natural selection, a key component of evolutionary theory, involves three main ingredients:

- Variation refers to a state in which there exists a variety of genetically determined traits within a population.
- Heritability refers to genetically determined traits which vary in their expression within a population (hair color, intelligence, height, anxiety-level, etc.)
- Selection refers to those heritable traits that remain in, and spread through, a population because those traits increased the reproduction of the organism.

Many traits that are selected for can actually hinder survival of the organism while increasing its reproductive opportunities. Consider the classic example of the peacock's tail. It is metabolically costly, cumbersome, and essentially a "predator magnet." What the peacock's tail does do is attract mates. Thus, the type of selective process that is involved here is what Darwin called sexual selection." Sexual selection can be divided into two types:

- Intersexual selection, which refers to the traits that one sex generally prefers in the other sex, (e.g. the peacock's tail).
- Intrasexual competition, which refers to the competition among members of the same sex for mating access to the opposite sex, (e.g. two stags locking antlers).

Darwin and Wallace proposed that natural and sexual selection, and not a supernatural designer, explain why organisms comprise a number of functional mechanisms that often exhibit surprisingly complex evidence of design. This theory has two important implications for the nature of these mechanisms, including the mechanisms of the brain. First, all evolved mechanisms must serve some function that ultimately increased the reproduction of the organism. Second, the design of each mechanism will be best understood in relation to the environment in which it evolved.

Inclusive fitness theory, which was proposed by William D. Hamilton in 1964 as a revision to evolutionary theory, is basically a combination of natural selection, sexual selection, and kin selection.

It refers to the sum of an individual's own reproductive success plus the effects the individual's actions have on the reproductive success of their genetic relatives. General evolutionary theory, in its modern form, is essentially inclusive fitness theory.

Inclusive fitness theory resolved the issue of how "altruism" evolved. The dominant, pre-Hamiltonian view was that altruism evolved via group selection: the notion that altruism evolved for the benefit of the group.

The problem with this was that if one organism in a group incurred any fitness costs on itself for the benefit of others in the group, (i.e. acted "altruistically"), then that organism would reduce its own ability to survive and/or reproduce, therefore reducing its chances of passing on its altruistic traits. Furthermore, the organism that benefited from that altruistic act and only acted on behalf of its own fitness would increase its own chance of survival and/or reproduction, thus increasing its chances of passing on its "selfish" traits. Inclusive fitness resolved "the problem of altruism" by demonstrating that altruism can evolve via kin selection as expressed in Hamilton's rule:

$$\text{cost} < \text{relatedness} \times \text{benefit}$$

In other words, altruism can evolve as long as the fitness cost of the altruistic act on the part of the actor is less than the degree of genetic relatedness of the recipient times the fitness benefit to that recipient. This perspective reflects what is referred to as the gene-centered view of evolution and demonstrates that group selection is a very weak selective force. However, in recent years group selection has been making a comeback, (albeit a controversial one), as multilevel selection, which posits that evolution can act on many levels of functional organization, (including the "group" level), and not just the "gene" level.

Middle-level Evolutionary Theories

Middle-level evolutionary theories are theories that encompass broad domains of functioning. They are compatible with general evolutionary theory but not derived from it. Furthermore, they are applicable across species. During the early 1970's, three very important middle-level evolutionary theories were contributed by Robert Trivers:

- The theory of reciprocal altruism explains how altruism can arise amongst non-kin, as long as there is a sufficient probability of the recipient of the altruistic act reciprocating at a later date. The possibility was also noted by Trivers, later coined 'indirect altruism' by Richard Alexander, that reciprocation could be provided by third parties, raising the issue of social reputation.

- Parental investment theory refers to the different levels of investment in offspring on the part of each sex. For example, females in any species are defined as the sex with the larger gamete. In humans, females produce approximately one large, metabolically costly egg per month, as opposed to the millions of relatively tiny and metabolically cheap sperm that are produced each day by males. Females are fertile for only a few days each month, while males are fertile every day of the month. Females also have a nine month gestation period, followed by a few years of lactation. Males' obligatory biological investment can be achieved with one copulatory act. Consequently, human females have a significantly higher obligatory investment in offspring than males do. (In some species, the opposite is true.) Because of this difference in parental investment between males and females, the sexes face different adaptive problems in the domains of mating and parenting. Therefore, it is predicted that the higher investing sex will be more selective in mating, and the lesser investing sex will be more competitive for access to mates. Thus, differences in behaviour between sexes is predicted to exist not because of maleness or femaleness per se, but because of different levels of parental investment.
- The theory of parent-offspring conflict rests on the fact that even though a parent and his/her offspring are 50% genetically related, they are also 50% genetically different. All things being equal, a parent would want to allocate their resources equally amongst their offspring, while each offspring may want a little more for themselves. Furthermore, an offspring may want a little more resources from the parent than the parent is willing to give. In essence, parent-offspring conflict refers to a conflict of adaptive interests between parent and offspring.

However, if all things are not equal, a parent may engage in discriminative investment towards one sex or the other, depending on the parent's condition. Recall that females are the heavier parental investors in our species. Because of that, females have a better chance of reproducing at least once in comparison to males. Thus, according to the Trivers-Willard hypothesis, parents in good condition are predicted to favor investment in sons, and parents in poor condition are predicted to favor investment in daughters.

Evolutionary Process of Psychology

All biological traits are products of the evolutionary process. Adaptationist methods, including evolutionary psychology, attempt to distinguish between adaptations and traits produced as by-products of adaptation.

- Adaptations are specially designed, species-typical traits that, (in terms of fitness costs), are "cost-efficient" and function to solve problems related to one's inclusive fitness. An example would be the Giant Panda's so-called 'thumb'.

- Evolutionary by-products are traits that were not specially designed for an adaptive function, although they may also be species-typical and may also confer benefits on the organism. A "spandrel" is a term coined by S.J.Gould and R.Lewontin (1979a) for traits which confer no adaptive advantage to an organism, but are 'carried along' by an adaptive trait. Their example being the lengthening of a bone in the hind limb of the Giant Panda, as a result of the lengthening of the corresponding bone in the forelimb. The bone in the forelimb has adapted to perform a function similar to that of an opposable thumb. The change in the hind limb, arguably, confers no adaptive advantage, whereas the change in the forelimb certainly does. The important implication of this idea for Evolutionary Psychology being, that therefore not every trait can be accounted for in terms of adaptive advantage. For instance, Gould puts forward the hypothesis that language itself in humans came about as a spandrel: "Natural selection made the human brain big, but most of our mental properties and potentials may be spandrels-that is, nonadaptive side consequences of building a device with such structural complexity" (S.J.Gould. The Pleasures of Pluralism, p.11) But of course, once a trait confers an adaptive advantage, as arguably most of our "mental properties and potentials" do, it is no longer a spandrel, and thus opens the debate concerning the importance of the concept of spandrels.

Natural selection is not the only evolutionary process that can change gene frequencies and produce novel traits. Genetic drift, or noise, refers to random effects resulting from chance variation in the genes, environment, or development. An example would be dry earwax in humans. Unlike natural selection, genetic drift does not produce complex, functionally designed adaptations.

Evolutionary psychology is based on the belief that, just like hearts, lungs, livers, kidneys, and immune systems, cognition has functional structure that has a genetic basis, and therefore has evolved by natural selection.

Like other organs and tissues, this functional structure should be universally shared amongst a species, and should solve important problems of survival and reproduction. Evolutionary psychologists seek to understand psychological mechanisms by understanding the survival and reproductive functions they might have served over the course of evolutionary history. Evolutionary psychologists subdivide the concept of psychological mechanisms into two general categories:

- Domain-specific mechanisms, which deal with recurrent adaptive problems over the course of human evolutionary history
- Domain-general mechanisms, which deal with evolutionary novelty.

The Environment of Evolutionary Adaptedness

The term environment of evolutionary adaptedness, often abbreviated EEA, was coined by John Bowlby as part of attachment theory. It refers to the environment to which a particular evolved mechanism is adapted. More specifically, the EEA is defined as the set of historically recurring selection pressures that formed a given adaptation, as well as those aspects of the environment that were necessary for the proper development and functioning of the adaptation. In the environment in which ducks evolved, for example, attachment of ducklings to their mother had great survival value for the ducklings. Because the first moving being that a duckling was likely to see was its mother, a psychological mechanism that evolved to form an attachment to the first moving being would therefore properly function to form an attachment to the mother. In novel environments, however, the mechanism can malfunction by forming an attachment to a dog or human instead. The genus Homo, which includes modern humans, appeared between 1.5 and 2.5 million years ago, a time that roughly coincides with the start of the Pleistocene 1.8 million years ago. Because the Pleistocene ended a mere 12,000 years ago, most human adaptations either newly evolved during the Pleistocene, or were maintained by stabilizing selection during the Pleistocene. Evolutionary psychology therefore proposes that the majority of human psychological mechanisms are adapted to reproductive problems frequently encountered in Pleistocene environments. In broad terms, these problems include those of growth, development, differentiation, maintenance, mating, parenting, and social relationships. To properly understand human mating psychology, for example, it is essential to recognize that in the EEA (as now) women got pregnant and men did not.

If humans are mostly adapted to Pleistocene environments, then some psychological mechanisms should occasionally exhibit "mismatches" to the modern environment, similar to the attachment patterns of ducks. One example is the fact that although about 30,000 people are killed with guns in the US annually (CDC pdf), whereas spiders and snakes kill only a handful, people nonetheless learn to fear spiders and snakes about as easily as they do a pointed gun, and more easily than an unpointed gun, rabbits or flowers (Öhman and Mineka 2001). A potential explanation is that spiders and snakes were a threat to human ancestors throughout the Pleistocene, whereas guns, rabbits and flowers were not. There is thus a mismatch between our evolved fear learning psychology and the modern environment. In sum, evolutionary psychology argues that to properly understand the functions of the brain one must understand the properties of the environment in which the brain evolved.

Controversies

Animal behavior studies have long recognized the role of evolution; the application of evolutionary theory to human psychology, however, is controversial. There are many families of criticism of the idea.

Some critics of evolutionary psychology claim that because little is known about the Pleistocene, the evolutionary context in which humans developed (including population size, structure, lifestyle, eating habits, habitat, and more), there is little basis on which evolutionary psychology may operate. Most EP research is thus confined to certainties about the past, such as pregnancies only occurring in women, and that humans lived in groups.

Many evolutionary psychologists argue that this criticism is based on a misunderstanding. Evolutionary psychologists argue that they use knowledge of the environment of evolutionary adaptedness to generate hypotheses regarding possible psychological adaptations, and subsequently, these hypotheses can be tested and evaluated against the empirical evidence in just the same way that any other hypothesis generated from any other theoretical perspective can be assessed.

Furthermore, evolutionary psychologists posit that there are many environmental features that we can be sure played a part in our species' evolutionary history. They argue that our hunter-gatherer ancestors most certainly dealt with predators and prey, food acquisition and sharing, mate choice, child rearing, interpersonal aggression, interpersonal assistance, diseases and a host of other fairly predictable challenges that constituted significant selection pressures.

There also exists debate within evolutionary psychology about the nature of the EEA. Many evolutionary psychologists contend that many aspects of the EEA were not as consistent as other evolutionary psychologists would argue. This argument is used to support the notion that the mind consists of not only domain-specific psychological mechanisms but of domain-general ones as well, that deal with environmental novelty.

Critics claim that many valid hypotheses, including contradictory ones, can be drawn from the same evolutionary principles. Evolutionary psychology can predict many, or even all, behaviours for a given situation, including contradictory ones. Therefore many human behaviours will always fit some hypotheses. The central paradigm of evolutionary psychology is impossible to prove, and the predicting power of evolutionary psychology is doubtful. For example, kin selection predicts that humans will be altruistic toward relatives in proportion to their relatedness, while reciprocal altruism predicts that we will be altruistic toward people from whom we can expect altruism in the future (not strangers). However, altruism towards a complete stranger fits the handicap principle. Thus altruism toward every class of person fits some well-known hypothesis. This doesn't seem to give us any way to predict how a human will act in a given situation.

Evolutionary psychologists respond that their discipline is not primarily concerned with explaining the behavior of specific individuals, but rather broad categories of human behaviors across societies and cultures. It is the search for species-wide trends in behavior that distinguishes evolutionary psychology from cultural or social explanations. Thus hypotheses will attempt to explain contradictory human behavior because human behavior is often contradictory.

Critics claim that many of the propositions of evolutionary psychology are not falsifiable. It is not possible to conduct definitive experiments on humans on an evolutionary timescale. This criticism in particular is common and often refers to evolutionary psychological theories as just-so stories. The methods that evolutionary psychologists actually use for testing include comparing different species, comparing males and females, comparing individuals within a species and comparing the same individuals in different contexts. Their sources of data for testing evolutionary hypotheses include archeological records, data from hunter-gatherer societies, observations, self-reports, life-history data and public records, and human products. Source: Evolutionary Psychology: The New Science of the Mind by David Buss.

Some studies have been criticized for their tendency to attribute to evolutionary processes elements of human cognition that may be attributable to social processes (e.g. preference for particular physical features in mates).

Evolutionary psychologists respond that many traits have been shown to be universal in humans and that social processes are related to evolutionary processes. They argue that statements such as "biology vs. environment" and "genes vs. culture" amount to false dichotomies. Evolutionary psychologists justify this claim by arguing that behavior results from an organism interacting with its environment. Psychological mechanisms, they argue, are created by genes, (which, in turn, were selected for by the evolutionary process), and those mechanisms help the organism negotiate its environment. Furthermore, they assert that many aspects of the environment, (e.g. culture and social institutions), are rested upon those mechanisms. In short, evolutionary psychologists argue that there is a bidirectional influence between things like "biology and environment" and "cognition and social processes."

Evolutionary Psychology is grounded on the theory that fundamentally our psychology is based on biology, the composition of our brains. This is a form of reductionism, a research philosophy according to which the nature of complex things can be understood in terms of simpler or more fundamental things (i.e. reduced). Importantly, reductionism as applied to consciousness and the brain, comes in various forms, some of which may be more philosophically problematic for Evolutionary Psychology than others. It is a long-standing matter of debate in Philosophy of Mind as to whether Mental States are identical with physical Brain States, or what sort of relation could be said to hold between the two.

However, it can be argued that Evolutionary Psychology is not committed to any particular answer to this question, being potentially compatible with Supervenience, Interactionism, Epiphenomenalism and both Token and Type physicalism, for example. Nevertheless, some people remain sceptical about any form of reduction from psychology to biology, and question its validity as an approach.

Why then, is the accusation of reductionism commonly used as a criticism of Evolutionary Psychology, and not say, as a criticism of Neuropsychopharmacology? (A discipline in which an implicit premise as regards psychology is that all states of mind, including both normal and drug-induced altered states, and diseases involving mental or cognitive dysfunction, have a neuro-chemical basis at the fundamental level.)

The reason is that Evolutionary Psychology is a controversial field in itself, and to quote Richard Dawkins: "'reductionism', like sin, is one of those things only mentioned by people who are against it." The Blind Watchmaker, 1986 p.13. Here Dawkins makes a distinction between "direct" and "hierarchical" reductionism: organisms can be described in terms of DNA, DNA in terms of atoms, atoms in terms of sub-atomic particles etc.; but knowledge of sub-atomic particles will not directly explain animal or human behavior, nevertheless, one can make adequate explanations and predictions at a higher levels.

That human psychology may be determined by our biology, which is shaped by our evolutionary past, is an important idea for those involved in Ethics. The implications are as broad and varied as the field of Ethics itself however, but generally, it is thought that Evolutionary Psychology describes factors which limit our free will, in that it can be seen to imply that we behave in ways in which we are 'naturally inclined'. Evolutionary Psychology is not in itself of course a theory of Ethics, it merely states what is, not what ought to be, but this idea of 'natural inclination' is a recurring theme in Ethics, arising not just out of Evolutionary Psychology, but almost all of the Social Sciences.

To quote J. Mizzoni from his article Ruse's Darwinian Ethics and Moral Realism: "There are some moral philosophers (e.g., Thomas Nagel) who believe that evolutionary considerations are irrelevant to a full understanding of the foundations of ethics. Other moral philosophers (e.g., J.L. Mackie) tell quite a different story. They hold that the admission of the evolutionary origins of human beings compels us to concede that there are no foundations for ethics." As we can see, the matter is subject to debate, some believing that evolutionary considerations are correct and necessary, others that they are incorrect and a form of the naturalistic fallacy, and others indeed that they are morally harmful whether correct or not. This idea of the supposed moral harm done by bringing together the Social Sciences and Ethics is arguably where the greatest controversy lies.

Some commentators, like philosopher David Buller, agree with the general argument that the human mind has evolved over time but disagree with the specific claims evolutionary psychologists make. Buller has argued, among other things, that the so-called Cinderella Effect, the argument that there are gender differences with respect to sexual jealousy, and the contention that the mind consists of thousands of modules, are unsupported by the available empirical evidence.

An alternative to the "mental module" view of how human minds evolved is offered by cognitive psychologist Merlin Donald. He argues that over evolutionary time the mind has gained adaptive advantage from a general problem solver. Donald articulates this view in his book "A Mind So Rare: The Evolution of Human Consciousness".

Another criticism regarding empirical evidence is a perceived lack of cross-cultural proofs. Many empirical studies come from a single culture. In these cases it is unknown if discoveries hold across all cultures.

THEORIES OF HUMAN INTELLIGENCE

A popular theory of intelligence is based on psychometric testing, i.e. intelligence quotient (IQ) tests; however, some researchers' dissatisfaction with traditional IQ tests prompted their developing alternative theories of intelligence suggesting that intelligence results from independent capabilities that uniquely contribute to human intellectual performance.

Psychometric Approach

Despite the variety of concepts of intelligence, the approach to understanding intelligence with the most supporters and published research over the longest period of time is based on psychometric testing. Such intelligence quotient (IQ) tests include the Stanford-Binet, Raven's Progressive Matrices, the Wechsler Adult Intelligence Scale and the Kaufman Assessment Battery for Children.

Charles Spearman is generally credited with defining general intelligence, which he reported in his 1904 *American Journal of Psychology* article titled "'General Intelligence,' Objectively Determined and Measured." Based on the results of a series of studies collected in Hampshire, England, Spearman concluded that there was a common function (or group of functions) across intellectual activities including what he called intelligence (i.e., school rank, which Spearman thought of as "present efficiency" in school courses; the difference between school rank and age, which was conceptualized as "native capacity;" teacher ratings; and peer ratings provided by the two oldest students, which was termed "common sense") and sensory discriminations (i.e., discrimination of pitch, brightness, and weight). This common function became known as "g" or general intelligence.

To objectively determine and measure general intelligence, Spearman invented the first technique of factor analysis (the method of Tetrad Differences) as a mathematical proof of the Two-Factor Theory. The factor analytic results indicated that every variable measured a common function to varying degrees, which led Spearman to develop the somewhat misleadingly named Two-Factor Theory of Intelligence. The Two-Factor Theory of Intelligence holds that every test can be divided into a "g" factor and an "s" factor. The g-factor measures the "general" factor or common function among ability tests. The s-factor measures the "specific" factor unique to a particular ability test. Spearman's g-factor account for positive correlations among any cognitive ability tests. However, the necessary condition for g-factor to exist is routinely violated in correlation matrices of cognitive tests, according to the work by Peter Schönemann and others..

L.L. Thurstone extended and generalized Spearman's method of factor analysis into what is called the Centroid method and which became the basis for modern factor analysis. Thurstone demonstrated that Spearman's one common factor method (Spearman's method yielded only a single factor) was a special case of his multiple factor analysis. Thurstone's research led him to propose a model of intelligence that included seven orthogonal (unrelated) factors (i.e., verbal comprehension, word fluency, number facility, spatial visualization, associative memory, perceptual speed and reasoning) referred to as the Primary Mental Abilities. In a critical review of the adult testing literature, Raymond B. Cattell found that a considerable percentage of intelligence tests that purported to measure adult intellectual functioning had all of the trappings of using college students in their development.

To account for differences between children/adolescents and adults, which past theory did not address, Cattell proposed two types of cognitive abilities in a revision of Spearman's concept of general intelligence. Gluid intelligence (Gf) was hypothesized as the ability to discriminate and perceive relations (e.g., analogical and syllogistic reasoning), and crystallized intelligence (Gc) was hypothesized as the ability to discriminate relations that had been established originally through Gf, but no longer required the identification of the relation (commonly assessed using information or vocabulary tests). In addition, fluid intelligence was hypothesized to increase until adolescence and then to slowly decline, and crystallized intelligence increases gradually and stays relatively stable across most of adulthood until it declines in late adulthood.

With his student John L. Horn, Cattell indicated that Gf and Gc were only two among several factors manifest in intelligence tests scores under the umbrella of what became known as Gf/Gc Theory. General visualization (Gv; visual acuity, depth perception), general fluency (F, facility in recalling words), general speediness (Gs; performance on speeded, simple tasks) were among several cognitive ability factors added to Gf/Gc Theory.

J.P. Guilford sought to more fully explore the scope of the adult intellect by providing the concept of intelligence with a strong, comprehensive theoretical backing. The Structure-of-Intellect model (SI model) was designed as a cross classification system with intersections in the model providing the basis for abilities similar to Mendeleev's periodic table in chemistry.

The three-dimensional cube—shaped model includes five content categories (the way in which information is presented on a test; visual, auditory, symbolic, semantic, and behavioural), six operation categories (what is done on a test; evaluation, convergent production, divergent production, memory retention, memory recording, and cognition), and six product categories (the form in which information is processed on a test; units, classes, relations, systems, transformations, and implications). The intersection of three categories provides a frame of reference for generating one or more new hypothetical factors of intelligence.

John B. Carroll re-analysed 461 datasets in the single most comprehensive study of cognitive abilities. This analysis led him to propose the Three Stratum Theory, which is a hierarchical model of intellectual functioning.

The strata represent three different levels of generality over the domain of cognitive abilities. At the bottom is the first stratum, which is represented by narrow abilities that are highly specialized (e.g., induction, spelling ability). The second stratum is represented by broad abilities that include moderate specializations in various domains.

Carroll identified eight second-stratum factors: fluid intelligence, crystallized intelligence, general memory and learning, broad visual perception, broad auditory perception, broad retrieval ability, broad cognitive speediness, and processing speed (reaction time decision speed). Carroll has noted the similarity of his second stratum abilities and the Gf/Gc factors, although the Three-Stratum Theory does not incorporate the developmental trajectories associated with Gf/Gc Theory. Carroll accepted Spearman's concept of general intelligence, for the most part, as a representation of the uppermost third stratum.

More recently, an amalgamation of the Gf-Gc theory of Cattell and Horn with Carroll's Three-Stratum theory has led to the Cattell-Horn-Carroll (CHC) Theory of cognitive abilities. CHC researchers have produced numerous studies that have influenced diagnostic issues and test development.

Intelligence tests are widely used in educational, business, and military settings due to their efficacy in predicting behaviour. *g* is highly correlated with many important social outcomes—individuals with low IQs are more likely to be divorced, have a child out of marriage, be incarcerated, and need long-term welfare support, while individuals with high IQs are associated with more years of education, higher status jobs and higher income. Intelligence is significantly correlated with successful training and performance outcomes, and *g* is the single best predictor of successful job performance.

Controversies

IQ tests were originally designed to identify mentally "defective" children. The inventors of the IQ did not necessarily believe they were measuring fixed intelligence. Despite this, critics argue that intelligence tests have been used to support nativistic theories which view intelligence as a qualitative object with a relatively fixed quantity.

Critics of the psychometrics point out that intelligence is often more complex and broader in conception than what is measured by IQ tests. Furthermore, skeptics argue that even though tests of mental abilities are correlated, people still have unique strengths and weaknesses in specific areas. Consequently they argue that psychometric theorists over-emphasize *g*, despite the fact that *g* was defined so as to encompass all inter-correlated capabilities and skills.

Researchers in the field of human intelligence have encountered a considerable amount of public concern and criticism—much more than scientists in other areas normally receive.

A number of critics have challenged the relevance of psychometric intelligence in the context of everyday life. There have also been controversies over genetic factors in intelligence, particularly questions regarding the relationship between race and intelligence and sex and intelligence.

Another controversy in the field is how to interpret the increases in test scores that have occurred over time, the so-called Flynn effect. Stephen Jay Gould was one of the most vocal critics of intelligence testing. In his book *The Mismeasure of Man* Gould argued that intelligence could not be quantified to a single numerical entity. He also challenged the hereditarian viewpoint on intelligence. Many of Gould's criticisms were aimed at Arthur Jensen, who responded that his work had been misrepresented. Gould also investigated the methods of 19th-century craniometry. Jensen stated that drawing conclusions from early intelligence research is like condemning the auto industry by criticizing the performance of the Model T.

PSYCHOLOGICAL THEORY OF DEVELOPMENT

Many theoretical perspectives attempt to explain development, among the most prominent are: Jean Piaget's Stage Theory, Lev Vygotsky's Social Contextualism (and its heir, the Ecological Systems Theory of Urie Bronfenbrenner), and especially the information processing framework employed by cognitive psychology. Historical theories continue to provide a basis for additional research, among them are Erik Erikson's eight stages of psychosocial development and John B. Watson's and B. F. Skinner's Behaviorism. Many other theories are prominent for their contributions to particular aspects of development. For example, Attachment theory describes kinds of interpersonal relationships and Lawrence Kohlberg describes stages in moral reasoning.

Ecological Systems Theory: Generally regarded as one of the world's leading scholars in the field of developmental psychology, Bronfenbrenner's primary contribution was his Ecological Systems Theory, in which he delineated four types of nested systems, with bi-directional influences within and between systems.

1. *Microsystem:* Immediate environments (family, school, peer group, neighborhood, and childcare environments)
2. *Mesosystem:* A system comprised of connections between immediate environments (i.e., a child's home and school)
3. *Exosystem:* External environmental settings which only indirectly affect development (such as parent's workplace)
4. *Macrosystem:* The larger cultural context (Eastern vs. Western culture, national economy, political culture, subculture)

Each system contains factors that can powerfully shape development, as can the interaction of factors across systems.

The major statement of this theory, The Ecology of Human Development (1979) had widespread influence on the way psychologists and others approached the study of human beings and their environments.

It has been said that before Bronfenbrenner, child psychologists studied the child, sociologists examined the family, anthropologists the society, economists the economic framework of the times and political scientists the structure. As a result of Bronfenbrenner's groundbreaking work in "human ecology," a field that he created, these environments-from the family to economic and political structures-were viewed as part of the life course from childhood to adulthood.

Role of Experience: A significant question in developmental psychology is the relation between innateness and environmental influence in regard to any particular aspect of development. This is often referred to as "nature versus nurture" or nativism versus empiricism. A nativist account of development would argue that the processes in question are innate, that is, they are specified by the organism's genes. An empiricist perspective would argue that those processes are acquired in interaction with the environment. Today developmental psychologists rarely take such extreme positions with regard to most aspects of development; rather they investigate, among many other things, the relationship between innate and environmental influences. One of the ways in which this relationship has been explored in recent years is through the emerging field of evolutionary developmental psychology. One area where this innateness debate has been prominently portrayed is in research on language acquisition. A major question in this area is whether or not certain properties of human language are specified genetically or can be acquired through learning. The nativist position argues that the input from language is too impoverished for infants and children to acquire the structure of language. Linguist Noam Chomsky asserts that, evidenced by the lack of sufficient information in the language input, there is a universal grammar that applies to all human languages and is pre-specified. This has led to the idea that there is a special cognitive module suited for learning language, often called the language acquisition device. The empiricist position on the issue of language acquisition suggests that the language input does provide the necessary information required for learning the structure of language and that infants acquire language through a process of statistical learning. From this perspective, language can be acquired via general learning methods that also apply to other aspects of development, such as perceptual learning. There is a great deal of evidence for components of both the nativist and empiricist position, and this is a hotly debated research topic in developmental psychology.

On the other hand, Chomsky's critique of a specific empiricist position on this issue, radical behaviorist Burrhus Frederic Skinner's Verbal Behaviour written in 1957, is widely considered among developmental psychologists to have sparked the decline in influence of behaviorism and signaled the beginning of the cognitive revolution in psychology.

Mechanisms of Development: Developmental psychology is concerned not only with describing the characteristics of psychological change over time, but also seeks to explain the principles and internal workings underlying these changes. Understanding these factors is aided by the use of models. Developmental models are often computational, but they do not necessarily need to be. A model must simply account for the means by which a process takes place. This is sometimes done in reference to changes in the brain that may correspond to changes in behaviour over the course of the development. Computational accounts of development often use either symbolic, connectionist (neural network), or dynamical systems models to explain the mechanisms of development.

FEELING REACTIONS

Feeling is the nominalization of the verb *to feel*. The word was first used in the English language to describe the physical sensation of touch through either experience or perception. The word is also used to describe experiences, other than the physical sensation of touch, such as "a feeling of warmth".

In psychology, the word is usually reserved for the conscious subjective experience of emotion. Phenomenology and heterophenomenology are philosophical approaches that provide some basis for knowledge of feelings. Many schools of psychotherapy depend on the therapist achieving some kind of understanding of the client's feelings, for which methodologies exist. Some theories of interpersonal relationships also have a role for shared feelings or understanding of another person's feelings.

Perception of the physical world does not necessarily result in a universal reaction among receivers, but varies depending on one's tendency to handle the situation, how the situation relates to the receiver's past experiences, and any number of other factors. Feelings are also known as a state of consciousness, such as that resulting from emotions, sentiments or desires.

Human nature possesses *a tonal quality,* somewhat after the fashion perhaps of a musical instrument, only far more complex and significant. If all goes well the human organism experiences a pleasant tone or feeling. If the environment impinges harshly upon the organism, then a disagreeable tone is experienced. An unbroken continuance of favourable or unfavourable circumstances may cease to bring out the organic tonal quality. If the environment has few new stimuli and arouses no new responses then the human organism lapses into a chronic state of disagreeableness, or ennui. If the environmental factors repeatedly defeat the organism at every turn then an essentially unpleasant organic tone becomes chronic and is accompanied by cynicism and fatalism. If circumstances present new problems from time to time the organism is likely to be stimulated to its highest efficiency.

The tones of psychic nature are as old as psychic nature itself. They appear almost simultaneously with the causal stimuli. They are the first or advance responses of the organism to specific stimuli. A type of stimuli which as a rule has been favourable in the past to the organism or to the race or to both produces an agreeable tone in the organism. If some one were to suggest to me a visit to the dentist's chair, I should experience an unpleasant tone, providing my previous experiences have been exceedingly painful.

The stimulus releases an habitual reaction that has been built up on the basis of painful dental experiences, and I experience disagreeable feelings again. On the other hand if some one were to suggest to me a beefsteak fry in the Rockies, I should experience a highly agreeable psychic tone, providing I have enjoyed several such occasions.

This tonal character of one's nature seems to give a quicker-than-thought evaluation to a proposed activity upon the basis of past experience. It was this which Plato undoubtedly had in mind when he said that there are two counsellors in one's bosom, one is pleasure and the other is pain. A pleasurable feeling is the beginning of a whole response of the organism and indicates that in the history of the organism or the species, the act which the given stimulus is calling forth has been helpful. The pleasurable tone is a blind guide, implying but not necessarily proving the present value of a proposed response. The fact that a certain type of responses has been helpful or harmful in the past indicates that in all probability this type will continue to be helpful or harmful. If, however, conditions have changed, the tonal voice may prove a misleader. Before he responds to his tonal or feeling guidance, it is necessary, therefore, for a person to notice whether or not the main factors in a given social situation have changed.

People are alike in their tonal responses because they have had about the same fundamental experiences of gain and loss. In the history of the human species, certain ways of doing have proved favourable to race development; and others, unfavourable. Advantage is accompanied by agreeable tones or feelings, and disadvantage by a disagreeable tonal quality, ranging from a sense of complete loss (sorrow) to one of complete energization (angry determination). Upholders of race prejudice and race pride should observe that all races irrespective of colour are characterized under similar circumstances by the same psychic tones or feelings. Social traditions have developed variations, but after all, the white, yellow, and black races alike experience joy, sorrow, and anger when responding to the respective types of stimuli.

The feeling or tonal qualities developed earlier than thinking in the species. The feelings have longer roots than ideas. They are more definitely a part of the inner core of personality. They have helped to make personality, long before thinking reached its full development, either in the individual or in the race. It is difficult to argue down the feelings.

Again, feeling is not on the plane of thinking. It is not in the same class of phenomena. Thinking is superior in quality to feeling in that it can describe and analyse feeling, but it is inferior in that it can rarely overcome feeling.

If one has been taught throughout the earlier years of life that thirteen is an unlucky number, it is with difficulty in later years that one can throw off the feeling response that thirteen had better be avoided. Years of thinking to the contrary do not always succeed in overcoming feeling. An idea which is thrown against the feelings by way of argument does not meet them on their plane. It would seem that the best way to cope with the feelings is to stimulate counter feelings.

Emotional Reactions

Our desire to be free of emotional suffering and pain is real and authentic. However, when we express our desire for change with an attitude laced with judgment, rejection, disdain, or frustration, it now becomes another emotional reaction. We are now having emotional reactions about our emotional reactions. Another type of inherited response is the emotional. An emotion, may be considered a *complex of feeling responses.* It is usually accompanied by marked activity of the glandular system and hence is related to the autonomic neural system as well as to the central neural system. It may be accompanied not only by muscular responses but also by special activity of both the duct and the ductless glands, that is, in the case of anger, for example, there may be not only clenched fists, but also perspiration, and marked activity by the adrenals. An emotion is a complete organic disturbance.

It arises when the organized inherited impulses or the habitual responses are blocked. Whenever an obstacle appears in the path of a human tendency a disturbance occurs, accompanied by affective manifestations. In a way, an emotion is a heightened affective phase of a mental crisis. Whenever a conflict in the central neural system takes place, an emotional disturbance occurs; when no conflict exists, ennui is likely to ensue.

Emotions and ennui are the opposite feeling poles of personality. It may also be said that ennui is the dead centre between the extremes represented by the joyful and the sorrowful feeling responses. *Angry emotion* accompanies the conflict stages of a crisis when an individual is struggling against obstacles. The function of anger is apparently that of energizing the individual so that he may overcome obstructions in the path of his tendencies. Anger is clearly a combatant emotion, but it becomes transformed into joyful or sorrowful responses when the given conflict begins to eventuate into gain or loss for the individual as judged by the individual.

A joyful response full of animation and expressions of surplus energy marks the more or less sudden realization of some important personal desire. *A sorrowful* response indicates the individual's realization of defeat, at least temporary, in some of his aims; while remorse, forlornness, pessimism, fatalism are permanent expressions of defeated desires. The joyful tone of the human organism accompanies a general expansion of the individual's powers—his heart beats faster, circulation and respiration increase, and the organism is actually larger; while a sorrowful tone accompanies a general organic shrinking. Joyfulness is accompanied by a reckless organic offensive type of attitude; while sorrowfulness is paralleled by a retiring defencelessness.

Fear is an emotional response, which occurs whenever the individual realizes that his life, his possessions, or his loved ones are in great danger. Fear is an emotional response of a defensive nature and is closely associated with the desire for security. Fear may easily be acquired and developed into a standard set of habitual responses. That which is peculiarly strange naturally causes the individual to shrink away or to assume a defensive attitude. As concentrations of feeling tones, the emotions often run to extremes and are expressed in wild, blind discharges of energy or possibly in a more or less complete paralysis of organic activity. For example, anger results in concentrated but irrational outbursts of activity or it may completely block all motor activity; while sorrow usually tends to produce only impotence.

One of the most elemental of emotional responses, basic to joy, sorrow, and even anger, is *sympathy*. As the term implies, sympathy means "feeling with," and it may be regarded as a generic social tone of all higher organic life. An example of the expression of an elemental form of sympathetic emotion is the immediate and appropriate response of the brood of chickens to the warning cry of the mother hen. As a result of sympathetic emotion, the vigorous crying of a baby is followed often by the simultaneous wailing on the part of all nearby infants, even when they apparently cannot have the slightest conception of the cause of the crying of the first child. For the same reason a scream of terror on the part of an adult evokes a similar pang on the part of bystanders, although the latter do not know the cause of the scream. By virtue of sympathetic emotion, anger provokes anger. If the parent or teacher spoken to angrily is able only by a great effort to keep angry feelings from arising, how much less is a child able to control angry response when spoken to in an angry tone. The wise parent, or teacher speaks authoritatively, but not angrily.

The characteristic of "feeling with" others varies in degree with individuals and circumstances. In an extreme form it often decreases personal efficiency. It is unfortunate, for example, for a surgeon to be over-sympathetic. At the other extreme a want of sympathy permits one's egoistic, selfish impulses to run riot. Sympathy enables the individual to understand the experiences, attitudes, and behaviour of other people. While its generic nature contributes to self-sacrifice and unselfish living, it may be used by the shrewd in highly selfish ways. Through sympathy one can learn to understand other people, and then by playing upon their sympathy, gain their confidence and take advantage of them. Courtship is often characterized by this abuse of sympathy, and many hasty and unwise marriages are to be explained in this way. Politicians often acquire an unsavory reputation by overmuch appeal to the sympathy of people.

When an important issue is to be settled, the party which is successful in enlisting the sympathies of the public possesses a great advantage. The sympathies often lead to erratic behaviour. Inasmuch as they, like the feelings, are not always in accord with the cognitive phases of mental life, they may be expressed in strange, irrational, and at times in unreliable ways. Sympathy does not always connote dependable conduct. Perhaps the most conspicuous social characteristic of sympathy is its tendency to go out to the under dog in a conflict. It is also commonly allied with the old, the tried, and the true. It is a gigantic stabilizing force, but oftentimes it adds too much stability. Occasionally it is so closely attached to outworn habits and customs that it constitutes a stumbling block to progress. Nevertheless every new reform measure tries to win the permanent sympathy of the people. In fact, it must win these, if it is to achieve real success. Sympathetic feelings "always follow activities, and if the new activities can be established long enough feeling is sure in time to give them sanction. In this way new social values may be established and social attitudes changed and improved.

Sentiments

Sentimentality originally indicated the reliance on feelings as a guide to truth, but current usage defines it as an appeal to shallow, uncomplicated emotions at the expense of reason. Sentimentalism in philosophy is a view in meta-ethics according to which morality is somehow grounded in moral sentiments or emotions. Sentimentalism in literature is both a device used to induce a tender emotional response disproportionate to the situation at hand, (and thus to substitute heightened and generally uncritical feeling for normal ethical and intellectual judgments), and a heightened reader response willing to invest previously prepared emotions to respond disproportionately to a literary situation.

Emotions tend to become organized in relation to personal values, and may then be referred to as *sentiments.* For example, there is the sentiment of *admiration,* or a certain extension of one's personality towards another person who manifests fine qualities of behaviour. It always involves admirer and admired; it implies the expression of a measure of curiosity and wonder, or self-abasement, and also of being responsive to the person for whom admiration is experienced. A leader who is genuinely, successful must gain the permanent admiration of other persons. Admiration plus fear constitutes awe; and awe with the sense of indebtedness leads to reverence—the highest religious sentiment. Closely allied to admiration is *respect.* It involves more judgment and less emotion, and hence is more permanent than admiration. Respect is perhaps the most rationalized sentiment. Self respect means that one has given thought to his behaviour and has justified it in the light of social standards. Without self respect it is almost impossible for one to maintain the respect of other persons, for by suggestion one's attitudes towards one's self influence the attitudes of others. Respect for another person means that one has analysed the activities of the other person and approved them. The available evidence seems to show that McDougall may be mistaken in assuming that we always respect those who respect themselves and that our respect for other persons is always a sympathetic reflection of their self respect. It is usually true that others must respect themselves before we will truly respect them, but if the social standards of others are below our own or if their dependableness falls short of our own ideal of dependableness, respect for them fails to develop.

There is a mild sentiment which arises out of sympathy for other persons but which does not result in positive sacrifice for others; this sentiment is commonly known as*pity.* The person who pities usually feels that he is definitely separated by some barrier from the one who is pitied. Pity may be regarded as a differentiated form of sympathy which is held in check by a feeling of superiority, of inability to render aid, or of the impractability of giving aid. Pity rarely instigates activity but it may stay ruthless or vengeful action. When a person finds himself depreciated or when he falls below the standards which others expect of him, his normal reaction *is shame. To* protect himself from such an experience, he is apt to submit unflinchingly to severe discipline. The group or the leaders in the group will often capitalize a person's aversion to shame in order to secure his otherwise unattainable support of either a worthy or unworthy cause.

When native impulses are closely organized and egoism has become standardized, an exaggerated sense of self-feeling easily becomes stimulated into the emotion of*jealousy.* Wherever invidious comparisons are made in one's own field of activity, jealousy easily flares up. The suitor is "jealous" of all rivals, because somebody whom he is willing to die for is in danger of being won by other persons. The egoistic parent is sensitive regarding the success of the companions of his children, for he does not want *his* children to be outshone. He is especially jealous of those persons whom his children listen to more than to him, for thereby his own opinions are being flouted. The egoistic jealousy of artists, dbutantes, prima donnas, and others, "painters of the limelight and wooers of public favour," comes from their having hinged their lives on applause. When that applause is transferred, their lives are flattened out entirely, except as jealousy blazes up. As a rule jealousy narrows personality, lowers one's social standing, and cuts down one's usefulness. In the long run one is justified in being "jealous" only for his character, for the character of other persons and of social institutions.

A more aggressive but often subtler type of sentiment than jealousy is *revenge.* It arises when a person feels that he or someone in whom he is interested has been grievously injured and when the alleged offender does not make what is considered adequate amends. It is fitful, flaring high and dying down quickly, or it may smolder for years and break out in unexpected ways. It demands at least "an eye for an eye," and because of its emotional nature it is likely to overrun its goal and to exact a double portion of atonement. Furthermore it invites retribution, arousing furious emotional reactions on the part of the persons against whom it is directed. Thus when the vindictive attempt to secure justice, they use methods which prolong the justice-securing processes indefinitely and inflict serious injustices.

Revenge easily becomes generalized, and organized into group reactions which assume socially deep-seated and long term proportions, as in the case of blood feuds. The development of courts of justice has met the general need which is served by vengeance; and consequently the overt and group-organized expressions of the sentiment are losing their original function, although still persisting tenaciously. Vengeance blazes up as in the case' of lynchings; it also holds a concealed place in many lives as evidenced in class and race prejudices.

Sentiments, diametrically opposed, are *hate* and *love.* Hate is an organization of emotional energy against a person or a group believed to be hostile. It differs from revenge and jealousy in containing less pure feeling, and in being more rationally organized. It is also more openly expressed; it does not cover itself up, except for conventional reasons. It stages open warfare and declares publicly its reasons. It is a long-lived, ingrained sentiment that functions unfortunately in behalf of narrow loyalties as distinguished from larger ideals. It hinders the progress of both its subject and its object. It is an ominous element in race prejudice. Its constructive value appears when it is directed not against people as such, but against evil behaviour of any person and any group.

Love is a conserving, stabilizing, and yet tumultous sentiment of unmeasured power. In its more primitive, elemental nature it may be made up largely of sex impulses, and consequently it may easily lead to license. A higher form is romantic love, which prompts one to great undertakings and sacrifices in behalf of the one who is loved. The primitive nature of romantic love is demonstrated by its fickleness. It may lead, however, to conjugal love which possesses remarkable qualities of endurance.

The strength of conjugal love develops out of the fact that husbands and wives have common experience of great joys and sorrows. It is particularly in the suffering together of husband and wife that fitful romantic love becomes transformed into strong, deep, and abiding conjugal love. Maternal love is the keenest, deepest, and most concentrated form of the love of one person for another.

The love of a mother for her child is the most enduring; it persists despite continued gross neglect and even of utterly despicable conduct on the part of the son or daughter. Paternal love is far less intense and permanent than maternal; it is more akin to fraternal love. Filial love is often strongly expressed in childhood and adolescence; it may then subside but be revived in the later years of life and assume its earlier strength, gladdening parental hearts.

Consanguineal love ranges from the close attachment that is characteristic of fraternal love, to the affective elements in the brotherhood-of-man principle. It frequently takes on idealistic forms, and easily extends beyond blood relationships, producing the highest bonds of friendship, as of him "who sticketh closer than a brother." Consanguineal love leads to the most dependable types of loyalty. In it lies the energizing power for socializing the world.

Desire

Desire is a sense of longing for a person or object or hoping for an outcome. Desire is the fire that sets action aflame. The same sense is expressed by emotions such as "craving" or "hankering". When a person desires something or someone, their sense of longing is excited by the enjoyment or the thought of the item or person, and they want to take actions to obtain their goal. The motivational aspect of desire has long been noted by philosophers; Hobbes (1588–1679) asserted that human desire is the fundamental motivation of all human action. In Buddhism, for an individual to effect his or her liberation, the flow of sense-desire must be cut completely; however, while training, he or she must work with motivational processes based on skilfully applied desire. The Buddha stated, according to the early Buddhist scriptures, that monks should "generate desire" for the sake of fostering skilful qualities and abandoning unskilful ones.

While desires are often classified as emotions by laypersons, psychologists often describe desires as different from emotions; psychologists tend to argue that desires arise from bodily structures, such as the stomach's need for food, whereas emotions arise from a person's mental state.

Marketing and advertising companies have used psychological research on how desire is stimulated to find more effective ways to induce consumers to buy a given product or service. While some advertising attempts to give buyers a sense of lack or wanting, other types of advertising create desire associating the product with desirable attributes, either by showing a celebrity or model with the product.

The theme of desire is at the core of the romance novel, which often create drama by showing cases where human desire is impeded by social conventions, class, or cultural barriers. As well, it is used in other literary genres, such as gothic novels such as *Dracula* by Bram Stoker, in which desire is mingled with fear and dread. Poets ranging from Homer to Toni Morrison have dealt with the themes of desire in their work. Just as desire is central to the written fiction genre of romance, it is the central theme of melodrama films, which use plots that appeal to the heightened emotions of the audience by showing "crises of human emotion, failed romance or friendship", in which desire is thwarted or unrequited.

Repeated inability to respond to moderate environmental stimuli creates in time a somewhat turbulent state known as *desire.* If the organism is unable after repeated attempts to secure the object of desire, then a chronic unpleasant tone results. Desire, declared Lester F. Ward, is painful. He asserted that the sensation must be a disagreeable one because the organism struggles to end it. The reasoning is hardly complete. Many of the objects of desire involve an expansion of the organism in definitely sought directions. The desire for wealth if once gratified maintains itself, not because it is painful but rather because wealth gives a person increased control over things and people. This control results in an expansion *of* the person's sense of the "me" and particularly of the "mine." It secures him an increased degree of attention from and perhaps admiration of other persons. Desire itself may contain a painful element, because the individual is temporarily unable to respond the way he has been stimulated to do. The agreeable psychic tone which results from the gratification of desire more than offsets a temporarily painful element. It is this aroused but temporarily unsatisfied condition of psychic nature, or desire, that Ward believed to be the dynamic force in individual life and hence in social life. To point simply to an unsatisfied state of the psychic organism as the dynamic social agent is to overlook the factors conditioning desire. Desire is a complex of affective and cognitive mechanisms resulting from the interplay of environmental stimuli and innate tendencies. It is in part an habitual seeking after objects, which thereby become values that give the organism a pleasant reaction tone but do not entirely satisfy it, and thus act as stimuli for further search after the desired objects or values.

All the natural impulses, the feelings, emotions, sentiments may become organized into what W. I. Thomas calls "wishes;" he classifies four : (1) the desire for new experience, (2) the desire for security, (3) the desire for recognition, (4) and the desire for response. The last mentioned should perhaps be put first, for it appears to be basic to all the others. The simpler forms of life, even the most elementary, are characterized by response to stimuli but cannot be said to have desires, with attention fixed on remote objectives. We therefore may refer to the fourth mentioned desire as a basic mechanism of organic life. In a higher form it appears as a desire for social response. The desire for recognition definitely reflects the stimuli which come from social life; it expands into the desire for power. The desire for security is evidently elemental and primary; it is made up largely of the self-preservation impulses. The desire for new experience leads out into the desire to do, to achieve. Thomas' fourfold classification seems to be primarily individualistic. There may be also a fundamental desire to aid, to help. Its objective is not primarily the individual's satisfaction, but rather the growth and satisfaction that others experience. This ultimately becomes an ethical attitude.

Repressed Feelings and Emotions

When a neuro-muscular mechanism is stimulated the natural tendency is for the neural process to run its course and issue in some form of motor activity. This process being largely physiological and psychological takes place in accordance with the nature of the environmental stimulus and not necessarily in harmony with socially derived standards of conduct. The child cries for candy when it would be bad for him; he wishes to stay up beyond his regular bedtime, but regularity in sleeping hours is decreed; he wants a bicycle when in the judgment of his parents the dangers of bicycle riding are great, and the request is denied: in these illustrative instances, which might be multiplied without end, environmental factors have served as stimuli to perform actions that better adult judgment cannot permit. The ordinary adult reply to the child is "don't", and the stimulated activity in the child is repressed before reaching its fruition. This released but "blocked" energy wells up and acts as a drive to emotional mechanisms, and thus may be expressed in harmful ways. Sometimes an individual after suffering bitter disappointment threatens to take his own life. Crying often serves as a means of discharge of energy that is blocked by some objective "don't" to a desire that is in process of being fulfilled. Occasionally when a desire mechanism has been thwarted, the individual is "too angry" to express himself or to secure emotional satisfaction. In cases such as these repression may do great and lasting harm. The released but undischarged energy is held up in "mid-air" as it were, producing a fundamental disturbance of the whole organism. It is to complexes of this type that psychotherapy has offered considerable aid. It is important that the resentment which commonly follows repression be dissipated quickly and not be allowed to assume chronic forms, such as a permanently "balked disposition."

A boy or girl who possesses a high degree of energy naturally responds to countless environmental stimuli to activity, and his parents find themselves unwittingly "sitting on the lid." Through ignorance or sheer lack of ingenuity, they fail to keep the boy's energies engaged in constructive enterprises, and sooner or later find him guilty of destructive mischief. In rural life, there are wholesome opportunities for expressions of energy in field and farmyard, but in the city, these opportunities are cut off, one by one.

Vacant lots disappear, and the streets become increasingly dangerous playgrounds until city ordinance forbids all play upon them. Houses encroach on all available yard space until dark hallways and alleyways alone are left as spaces in which the normal energies of youth may be released, but in these remaining places of rendezvous the stimuli are too often of a vicious and evil nature.

Cities, through their encroachment upon the playgrounds of youth act as crass repressive agents, meanwhile letting loose influences, which prey upon the repressed energies of untrained human nature. It is well to remember that psychic energy cannot be abolished. "If it is neither exploded nor converted, it is turned inwards, to lead a surreptitious, subterranean life."

The Puritanic attitude, being repressive with reference to childhood, often produced a rooted hatred of the Sabbath, of church, or of other religious institutions or practices.

Repression does not destroy, but causes a "welling up" of psychical energy which too frequently takes the form of sullenness, hatred, or even recalcitrancy. In its worthy aims of discipline, Puritanism neglected to study the psychology of repressed desires. Many church bodies have likewise neglected the psychology of repression and sublimation in their emphases upon the "Thou shalt pots" of religious discipline as related particularly to the play impulses of young people.

The "only" child has received a considerable amount of attention on the part of the Freudians and other psychoanalysists. The repression is that of the gregarious impulses and is produced indirectly by an absence of proper environmental stimuli of the gregarious and playful types, The "only" child has a normal social nature but possessing limited opportunities for expression of his social traits in the company of other children, his energies are not released. They well up until they force themselves over the void into non-social or anti-social directions. They may turn into organized moroseness, selfishness, sexual self-abuse, or other unfortunate channels. Such a child may receive a surplus of attention from parents, and hence develop a chronic expectation of receiving attention.

A child with a large endowment of energy may react to repression by "contrariness." He often makes requests which cannot be granted; his environment as he sees it impinges upon him at nearly every turn. Being continually repressed, his energies express themselves in beliefs that the world is against him, that all is wrong. Sometimes these beliefs may lead to murder or suicide. Most phenomena of the last mentioned type have been preceded by long periods of repression of certain dominant desires, although occasionally life is taken as a result of an abrupt repression, as in the case of the jilted lover, or the jealous spouse.

Repression often leads to a super-development of imagination. Balked impulses may seek satisfaction in religious imagery. In fact one of the chief constructive phases of religious beliefs is that they are often sublimated opportunities for broken hopes and defeated ambitions. Of course the imagery results of repression may easily take harmful trends as well as helpful ones. Then there is wise repression, *i.e., rational discipline.* Without repression, the developing child succumbs to pernicious stimuli, and anti-personal as well as anti-social habits result.

Youth cannot have the discretion of age, and thus many tendencies are repressed by parent or by society. This process is basic to *self control,* without which there can be no dependable conduct. But where repression is resorted to, the disciplinarian normally will provide for adequate sublimation. This need may often be met by a simple explanation of the dangers in the given stimulus, but if the stimuli are strong and insistent, then an alternative activity, future or present, will need to be provided.

Discipline is essential to both personal and social progress, but it cannot be achieved without obliging the individual to run the gauntlet of the psychical dangers incident to repression. As a youth cannot well safeguard himself from these evils, the major responsibility rests on his elders, or those who have his training in charge. Since these persons may be unversed in the psychology of repression, they perpetrate all kinds of blunders upon relatively helpless children.

The importance of disseminating the available knowledge concerning the nature of repression and sublimation is seen in the cases of lenient parents who, dismayed by the effects of repression in their children, find themselves baffled. Oftentimes they have neglected to provide sublimated opportunities until repression produces such a storm of angry opposition, based on untoward habits, that they lose all control over their children.

Undue repression of the feelings and emotions has led to warped personalities, insanity, and social radicalism. Psychiatry offers valuable data for social psychology when it reveals case after case in which the impingement of social conditions or personal insult and injustice has upset an individual's feeling and emotional nature and thrown it into a distorted condition. The life histories of revolutionists in various countries would doubtless reveal that their revolutionary attitude arose out of feelings distorted by genuine or imagined injustice. Affective human nature is evidently the most delicately adjusted and at the same time the most dynamic of all the factors involved in intersocial stimulation. It operates now subtly, now rashly, now without control, but always significantly in the formation of all social attitudes and values, while being at the same time the colourful dynamo of personal achievement and social progress.

THEORY OF THE ORIGINAL HUMAN NATURE

The Theory of the Original Human Nature is a study concerning the image of what the original human being, but for the human fall, would have been like. Because of the human fall, human beings have lost their original condition. They have lost not only their original selves, but also their original world. As, a result, up to the present time they have been endeavouring, sometimes even unconsciously, to restore the original human self and the original world.

This means that, throughout their entire lives, human beings harbour the idea of becoming better selves and the hope of living in a better world. Yet, human history has continued, even until today, without the ideal being realized. Fish swim freely in the water; birds fly in the sky as they please.

But what would happen if they were taken out of their natural environment? If fish were taken out of the water and thrown on land, they would stiffer tremendous pain. They would desire to go back to the water, their natural habitat. Similarly, if a bird is caught and put in a cage, it feels restrained and longs to go back to the open sky.

In the same way, people ardently desire the realization of the ideal, and at the same time feel disappointed in the world as it actually is. This means that human beings have lost their original selves and the ideal world.

Since that ideal, even until today, could not be realized many have lived in constant disappointment, under dire hardships and difficulties; but having no other choice, they could not but live in this world as it is. Some people, however, have never ceased to pursue the original human way of life, especially religious people and philosophers.

They seriously grappled with the question, "What is the human being?" and looked for ways to recover the original way of life. Buddha, for example, spent six years of his life in strict monasticism and asceticism, engaging in deep meditation. As a result, he came to realize that human beings originally possessed Buddhahood, but through ignorance came to be bound by worldly desires and fell into suffering. Buddha taught that the way to recover one's original nature is through a life of spiritual discipline. Jesus, likewise, inquired deeply into the problems of human life while travelling through many places, until he started his public ministry at the age of thirty. Consequently, he preached that human beings are sinners and have a satanic blood lineage resulting from the human fall, and that everyone must be born again by believing in the Son of God, that is, in Jesus himself

Socrates said, that the true way of human life is to love true knowledge. In Plato, the supreme ideal of human life is to recognize the idea of the Good. For Aristotle, reason is what makes a person human, and he said that virtue is best realized in the communal life of the polis (city-state) and that the human being is a social animal (or polis-animal). Greek philosophers, broadly speaking, held the view that reason is the essence of human nature, and that if a person's reason is allowed to operate fully, that person will become an ideal being.

In the Middle Ages, Christian theology reigned over philosophy, and the Christian view of human nature was that human beings are sinful beings and can be saved only by God's grace. In this view, reason was regarded as ineffective. In the modern period, however, currents of philosophy that believed in human reason again came to appear.

Descartes considered human beings to be rational beings, but he believed that people incur error or become confused because they do not know how to make proper use of reason. Therefore, Descartes discussed the method of how to use reason properly.

Kant claimed that human beings are personal beings that obey the voice of moral obligation ordered by practical reason, and that human beings are personal beings that obey the voice of moral obligation ordered by practical reason, and that human beings should live according to reason, without succumbing to temptations or desires. Hegel, too, regarded human beings as rational beings.

Reason was something that would self-actualize in the world. Freedom, the essence of reason, was to be realized along with the development of history. According to Hegel's theory, human beings and the world should have become rational beings with the establishment of the modern state (*i.e.*, the national state). In reality, however, people have remained deprived of their human nature just as they always had, and the world has continued as irrational as it had been before.

Kierkegaard opposed extreme types of rationalism such as the one offered by Hegel. Kierkegaard did not agree that humankind would become increasingly rational as the world progresses, as Hegel had claimed. In actual society, lie said, human beings are nothing but average people, whose true nature has been lost. Accordingly, only when a person carves out life independently as an individual, apart from the general public, can that person's true human nature be regained. Thus, the conceptual framework for dealing with people in actual society, who have lost their original nature, and for seeking to restore human nature independently, was subsequently developed as the thought of Existentialism.

Feuerbach, in opposition to Hegel's rationalism, regarded the human being as a sensuous being. According to Feuerbach, human beings alienated from themselves their essence as a species, objectified it, and came to revere it as a god. Therein lay the loss of human nature, lie thought. Thus, Feuerbach asserted that human beings must recover their original human nature, and that this can only be done through denying religion. Departing from Hegel's idea of actualizing freedom, Karl Marx called for the true liberation of human beings. In the society of Marx's time, the lives of laborers were indeed miserable. They were forced to endure long hours of labour, and were given wages that barely could sustain their lives.

Diseases and crime were rampant among labourers, who were deprived of their human nature. In contrast, the capitalists were living in great affluence gained from their merciless exploitation and oppression of labourers. But in Marx's view, the capitalist themselves were deprived of their own original human nature.

Determined to liberate humankind, Marx first started with Feuerbach's humanism as a way to restore human nature; later, however, he came to realize that human beings were not only species beings, but also beings engaged in productive activity—and this led him to the view that the essence of humankind is the freedom of labour in capitalist society, labourers were deprived of all the products of their labour, and they laboured not by their own will, but by the will of the capitalists. Therein, precisely, lay the labourers' loss of human nature-according to Marx.

From that, Marx concluded that in order to liberate the working class, what must be done is to overthrow capitalist society, where labourers are exploited. When such liberation occurred, the capitalists themselves would regain their own human nature, Marx thought.

Furthermore, based on the materialist view, Marx concluded that human consciousness is determined by the relations of production, which are the basis of society, and that the economic system must be changed by force. Nevertheless, the Communist nations, in which revolutions took place in accordance with Marx's theory, have become dictatorial societies where freedom is suppressed and human nature is violated and neglected.

Those are societies in which people have increasingly been losing their original nature. This implies that Marx was mistaken both in his grasp of the cause of human alienation and in his method for solving the problem of human alienation. Human alienation, however, is not a problem of Communist society alone. In capitalist society as well, individualism and materialism are rampant, and a self-centred way of thinking-whereby people think they are permitted to do anything they want-has become pervasive. As a result, in capitalist society, too, human nature is quickly being lost.

In this way, numerous religious people and philosophers have developed their own views of human nature, devoting great effort to the recovery of the original human nature; yet they have been unsuccessful in actually liberating humankind. The difficult problem for everyone has always been how to determine what the human being is. The Reverend Sun Myung Moon has trod his entire life course trying to provide fundamental solutions to such unresolved questions in human history. He has proclaimed that, originally, every human being is a child of God, even though, having lost their original nature, people have become miserable.

Human beings were created in the image of God, but due to the fall of the first human ancestors, they have become separated from God. They can restore their original nature, however, by living in accordance with God's word, thus coming to receive God's love. The problems of the human fall and the way to restore the original human nature will not be discussed (these topics are entrusted to Divine Principle); our focus will be on describing the original human nature itself.

HEALTH PSYCHOLOGY

Health psychology is a relatively new field which is evolving and developing as one of the main areas of applied psychology. Although its early beginnings can be traced to the kindred field of clinical psychology, four different approaches to health psychology have been defined: clinical, public health, community and critical health psychology (Marks, Murray et al., 2005).

Many researchers believe that physical health may be influenced by psychology through a variety of direct and indirect means. There is some evidence that certain negative mental states (such as depression and anxiety) can directly affect physical immunity through production of stress hormones, such as the catecholamines and glucocorticoids.

Although this research is widely debated, there is also some indication that negative psychological states may lead to faster disease progression in certain diseases (such as HIV and heart disease) through these direct biological mechanisms. Negative emotional states may also indirectly affect disease processes through their influence on health behaviors. For example, depression has been related to many risk factors for poor health including overeating, smoking, physical inactivity, and poor medication compliance.

Health psychology is the "...use of psychological principles to promote health and to prevent illness" ; it is also part of clinical treatment for established illness. This approach considers the biological, cognitive, behavioral, emotional, social, psychosomatic and environmental factors as they relate to health, illness and health care at the level of individuals. This approach has adopted what it calls the biopsychosocial model.

- Clinical health psychology (ClHP) adopts a definition reflecting the fact that the field was originally a branch of clinical psychology; it is also a major contributor to the field of behavioral medicine within psychiatry. Clinical practice includes the techniques of education, behavioral change, and psychotherapy; with additional training, a clinical health psychologist can become a medical psychologist in certain countries and, consequently, prescribe medication.
- Organizational health psychology (OHP) is the use of health psychology knowledge and techniques as applied to health and illness in the workplace, at the individual and group levels.
- Public health psychology (PHP) tries to determine causation between psychological factors and health for the population as a whole, and present this information to educators, policy makers, and health care practitioners for the promotion of better public health. It gives prominence to population-level health outcomes and interventions. It is allied to other disciplines in the fields of global and public health including epidemiology, nutrition, genetics and statistics. Interventions are determined and "targeted" using population health statistics which evaluate health needs of various population groups as perceived by health authorities and policy makers. These interventions are "top-down" and tend to have varying levels of effectiveness across diverse population groups.
- Community health psychology (CoHP) approach tries to understand what is happening at a local level. Interventions are generated collaboratively with coalitions of stakeholders and are aimed to facilitate community empowerment to improve the physical and/or mental health of local people outside of any formal involvement of the health care system.
- Critical health psychology (CrHP) is concerned with the distribution of power and the impact of power differentials on health experience and behaviour, health care systems and health policy. It prioritises social justice and the universal right to health of peoples of all races, genders, ages, and socioeconomic positions. A major concern is health inequalities. The CrHPist is an agent of change, not simply an analyst or cataloguer. The field was developed through the foundation of the Journal of Health Psychology and the International Society of Critical Health Psychology.

Health psychology is both a theoretical and applied field. Many different methods are employed including questionnaires, interviews, controlled studies, and actions designed to bring about change using "action research". Health psychologists conduct health interviews with clients that aim to construct a more holistic picture of each person's health, one that includes their genes, religious beliefs, social supports, living conditions, emotional state, and beliefs of health, etc. They use this information to work alongside a person's physicians and therapists to develop a treatment tailored for individual needs or to develop greater empowerment among the community's members so that the community is able to strengthen and sustain its own quality of life.

Objectives of Health Psychology

Understand behavioral Factors

Health psychologists seek to identify the behaviors and experiences that promote health, lead to illness, influence the effectiveness of health care, and recommend improvements to health policy in their light. There are many examples of this. Smoking, diet, and regular exercise all contribute to the formation of disease.

There are some minor associations between illness and individual characteristics such as personality. For example, it is claimed that individuals with thrill seeking personalities are more likely to drive fast, making them more likely to injure themselves in car accidents.

And also that people distrustful of physicians will not get regular checkups. However there are contextual factors in the form of political, economic, cultural, community, social and lifestyle factors that have a more major influence on the health of particular individulas, although they will not generally recognise these.

Factors that lead to the behaviors that cause illness are of interest because they help psychologists to predict who is most susceptible to illness and why. There are many contributing factors that help determine our behaviors, and all of the dimensions of the biopsychosocial model can be applied to understand these interconnectons. Biologically, physical addiction plays an important role in smoking cessation. As does the psychological dependency on tobacco brought about largely by seductive advertising and other forms of tobacco promotion. Psychologically, people with high stress jobs are more likely to develop cardiovascular disease. Socially, people with low incomes have less access to health resources and screening processes. They also are exposed to greater environmental toxigens, lower levels of education, poorer housing, less healthy foods, higher smoking prevalence, and many other toxic socially determined living conditions.

Health psychologists also aim to change health behaviors for the dual purpose of helping people stay healthy and helping patients adhere to disease treatment regimens. Cognitive behavioral therapy and behavior modification are techniques often used for this purpose.

Prevent Illness

Psychologists work towards promoting health through behavioral change, as mentioned above, but they prevent illness in other ways as well. Practitioners emphasize education as a large part of illness prevention, as many people do not recognize the risk to illness present in their lives. Or they are unable to implement the knowledge that they have owing to the pressures of their everyday existence.

A common example of this is anti-smoking campaigns. Those least able to afford tobacco products consume them the most. It is a method for controlling emotional states, the daily experiences of stress that characterise the lives of deprived and vulnerable people. Health psychologists also aim at educating health professionals like physicians and nurses in communicating with patients in a way that highlights the psychosocial barriers to understanding, memorising and implementing effective strategies for reducing risk factors and making behaviour changes and that will help them to develop appropriate means for communicating information relevant to diagnosis, treatment and prognosis .

Explore the Effects of Disease

There is much to know about how disease affects our mental well being. When illness or accidents befall a person, their entire life is affected. A psychologically healthy individual who gets severely injured, say, now has many different practical issues to contend with that will in turn affect their psychological wellbeing.

Who will take care of them while they recover? If they can't work, how will they pay for bills or care for dependents? If this person sees themselves as being self-reliant, how do they handle this new identity? What if they cannot pursue their usual hobbies and interests?

All of these possibilities can affect a person's relationships, self-esteem, stress level, happiness and belief system. Many of these issues are economic and social in nature rather than psychological but they have a direct impact on psychological wellbeing.

This important field of study considers how those with terminal illnesses can lead a better life. When there is little hope of recovery, health psychology therapists can improve the quality of life of the patient by helping them recover their mental well-being.

Critical Analysis of Health Policy

Critical health psychologists are exploring how health policy can impact on inequities, inequalities and social injustice. This expands the scope of health psychology beyond the level of individual health to an examination of the social and economic determinants of health experience both within and between regions and nations. The individualism of mainstream health psychology has been critiqued and deconstructed by critical health psychologists and newer qualitative methods and frameworks for investigating health experience and behaviour are advocated (Marks, Murray et al., 2005).

Improving Doctor-patient Communication

Health psychologists attempt to aid the process of communication between doctors and patients during medical consultations. There are many problems in this process, particularly the use of jargon by doctors (using long, complex, usually medicine-specific words often not understood by the patient). Researchers such as Boyle and McKinlay have investigated this process and discovered not only that patient understanding is low (40% of women on a maternity ward understood 13 medical terms that they were given), but that even doctors do not expect their patients to understand their jargon!

One main area of research on this topic involves 'doctor centred' or 'patient centred' consultations. Doctor centred consultations are generally directive, with the patient answering questions and taking little part in decision-making. Although this style is preferred by elderly people and others, many people dislike the sense of hierarchy or ignorance that it inspires. They prefer the patient centred consultations, which focus on the patient's needs, involve the doctor listening to the patient completely before making a decision, and involving the patient in the process of choosing treatment and finding a diagnosis.

Adherence to Medical Advice

Getting people to obey medical advice and adhere to their treatment regimens is a difficult task for health psychologists. Mostly, people forget to take their pills or find their side effects too difficult to cope with (rational non-adherence), but failing to take prescribed medication costs the Health Service millions of pounds per year, as well as wasting millions of usable, viable medicines that could otherwise be used to help other people. Estimated adherence rates are very hard to measure due to the issues raised by the various techniques available. Sarafino estimates adherence to be very low, however, he judges adherence to be following every part of the treatment programme, whereas Taylor encourages the tailoring of the programme to one's personal routine.

Ways of Measuring Adherence

- Counting the number of pills in the medicine bottle-although this has problems with privacy and seems patronising or showing lack of trust in patients
- Using self report measures-although participants may fail to return the self report or lie about their adherence
- Asking doctor or health worker-although this presents problems on doctor-patient confidentiality
- Using 'Trackcap' bottles, which measure the number of times the bottle is opened-however, this either raises problems of informed consent or, if informed consent is gained, demand characteristics.

Bibliography

Assagioli, R. : *Psychosynthesis*, Hobbs, Dorman, New York, 1965.
Beach, F.A.: *Patters of Sexual Behaviour.* New York: Harper, 1951.
Beloff, J.: *Psychological Sciences. A Review of Modern Psychology.* London: Crosby Lockwood Staples, 1973.
Boring, E.G.: *A History of experimental psychology.* Englewood Cliffs, NJ: Prentice-Hall, 1950.
Braithwaite, R.B.: *Scientific Explanation.* Cambridge: Cambridge University Press, 1953.
Breuer, G.: *Sociobiology and the Human Dimension.* Cambridge: Cambridge University Press, 1982.
Buss, A. H., & Plomin, R. *A temperament theory of personality development.* New York: John Wiley & Sons, 1975.
Dobzhansky, T.: *Studies in the Philosophy of Biology.* Berkeley: University of California Press, 1974.
Ellis, A. :*Humanistic Psychology, The Rational-emotive Approach,* Julian Press, New York, 1973.
Ferracuti, F.: *The Subculture of Violence. Towards an Integrated Theory of Criminology.* London: Tavistock Publications, 1967.
Flavell, J. H. *Cognitive Development. Engle*wood Cliffs, N.J.: Prentice-Hall, 1977.
Frankl, V. : *Man's Search for Meaning,* Pocket Books, New York, 1984.
Fromm, E. : *The Art of Loving,* New York, Harper & Row, New York, 1989.
Georgi, A. : Psychology as a Human Science, Harper & Row, New York, 1970.
Goitein, L. : *The Importance of the Book of Job for Analytic Thought*, American Imago, 1954.
Holland, N. : *The Dynamics of Literary Response*, New York, Oxford University Press, 1968.
Hull, C.L.: *Principles of Behaviour.* New York: Appleton-Century, 1943.
Hurt, K. F. : *The Quest of the Psychological Jesus*, Unitarian Universalist Christian, 1982.
James. W. *The Principles of Psychology.* New York: Henry Holt & Co., 1896.
Jones, D. M.: *Models of Man.* Leicester: The British Psychological Society, 1980.
Kelly, C. A.: *Clinical Psychology and Personality.* New York: Wiley, 1969.
Kunkel, F. : *Creation Continues, A Psychological Interpretation of the Gospel of Matthew,* New York, Paulist, 1987.
Michaels, J.J.: *Handbook of Psychiatry.* Mew York: basic Books, 1959.
Miller, N.E.: *Personality and Psychotherapy. An analysis in terms of learning, thinking, and culture.* New York: McGraw-Hill, 1950.

Mischel, W.: *Personality and assessment.* New York: John Wiley & Sons, 1968.

Mukta Singhvi and Abhimanyu Sharma: *Fundamentals of Clinical Psychology,* Ritu Publications, Delhi, 2010.

Neisser, U.: *Cognitive Osychology.* New York: Appleton-Century-Crafts, 1967.

Plomin, R. *A temperament theory of personality development.* New York: John Wiley & Sons, 1975.

Pratt, C.C.: *The Logic of Modern Psychology.* New York: MacMillan, 1948.

Pribram, K. H.: *Plans and the Structure of Behaviour.* London: Holt, Rinehart and Winston, 1960.

Reich, W. : *Character Analysis,* Orgone Institute Press, New York, 1949.

Rogers, C. R. : *Client-centered Therapy,* Houghton Mifflin, Boston, 1951.

Ross, S. A.: *Hyperactivity: Research, theory and action.* New York: John Wiley & Sons, 1976.

Sam Vaknin: *Clinical Psychology,* Sublime, Delhi, 2005.

Sartre, J.-P. : *Being and Nothingness,* Philosophical Library, New York, 1956.

Sharma, Arti : *Global Encyclopaedia of Clinical Psychology,* Global Vision Pub, Delhi, 2008.

Sonika Sharma: *Introduction to Clinical Psychology,* RBSA Publishers, Delhi, 2010.

Wheelis, A. : *The Quest for Identity,* W. W. Norton, New York, 1958.

Index

❑❑❑